W9-CNP-417

The New Architecture of the International Monetary System

edited by

Paolo Savona
LUISS Guido Carli University
and
Guido Carli Association, Rome

Reprinted from
Open Economies Review
Volume 11, Supplement 1, August 2000

KLUWER ACADEMIC PUBLISHERS
Boston / Dordrecht / London

Distributors for North, Central and South America:
Kluwer Academic Publishers
101 Philip Drive
Assinippi Park
Norwell, Massachusetts 02061 USA
Telephone (781) 871-6600
Fax (781) 871-6528
E-Mail <kluwer@wkap.com>

Distributors for all other countries:
Kluwer Academic Publishers Group
Distribution Centre
Post Office Box 322
3300 AH Dordrecht, THE NETHERLANDS
Telephone 31 78 6392 392
Fax 31 78 6546 474
E-Mail <services@wkap.nl>

 Electronic Services <http://www.wkap.nl>

Library of Congress Cataloging-in-Publication Data

The new architecture of the international monetary system / edited by Paolo Savona.
    p. cm.
    Paper presented at conferences held in Florence, Italy in June 19, 1998 and Oct.15, 1999
    Includes bibliographical references.
    ISBN 0-7923-7854-7
    1. International finance–Congresses. 2. Banking law–Congresses. I. Savona, Paolo,
    1936-

    HG203.N49 2000
    332.4'5–dc21

                          00-036831

Printed on acid-free paper.

Printed in the United States of America

OPEN ECONOMIES REVIEW

Contents   Volume 11   Supplemental Issue   August 2000
The New Architecture of the International Monetary System
Edited by Paolo Savona

Part II: Legal Aspects

This supplemental issue has been made possible by the financial support of the Cesifin Foundation and of the Guido Carli Association.

The conference was held in Florence on October 15, 1999, at Palazzo degli Incontri, headquarter of the Cesifin Foundation.

Open economies review 11:S1 1 (2000)

Editor's Preface

PAOLO SAVONA
LUISS Guido Carli University and Guido Carli Association, Rome, Italy

The 1998 and 1999 conferences held in Florence on reforming the international monetary system were dedicated to the memory of Guido Carli. Carli was a respected and authoritative participant in all the major events involving the international monetary system—from the Bretton Woods agreement to the Maastricht Treaty. At various moments in his illustrious career he served as director of the European Union of Payments, executive director of the International Monetary Fund, governor of the Bank of Italy, and treasury minister in the government that brought Italy into the European Monetary Union.

The two conferences were sponsored by the Fondazione della Cassa di Risparmio di Firenze (CESIFIN) and organized by the Guido Carli Association in collaboration with the Aspen Institute Italia and, in 1999, by the Permanent Advisory Committee on Euro and Dollar (PACE&D) as well. The secretary of PACE&D, Professor George Sutija, played an important role in the organization of the 1999 conference. Both conferences examined the problems created by the unsatisfactory functioning of the international monetary system, a topic that always influenced Guido Carli's work and that remains relevant today.

In preparation for the first conference on June 15, 1998, a team of experts drawn from the principal industrialized countries did a good deal of research with a twofold aim. The first was an examination of how the international monetary system functions, with a special focus on the role that the euro would and should have. The other aim was to prepare suggestions on how to resolve the great problems, financial ones above all, that affect the development of the entire world. One of the characteristics of these Carli conferences has been the attention paid to the juridical problems arising from European and international integration and from the new architecture of the international monetary system.

The 1999 conference focused on the efforts taking place in many different institutions to construct what has been termed the new international financial architecture (IFA).

Acknowledgments

The ideas and conclusions expressed in each article in this volume are solely those of the authors and not the institutions or the individuals that are members of the Association.

Open economies review **11:S1** 3–14 (2000)
© 2000 *Kluwer Academic Publishers. Printed in The Netherlands.*

Summary of Findings of the Guido Carli Association's Second International Conference

PAOLO SAVONA
LUISS Guido Carli University and Guido Carli Association, Rome, Italy

The work done to build a new architecture of the international monetary system (IMS) is described effectively by Fabrizio Saccomanni in one of the papers written for the conference and included in this volume. Saccomanni represented the Bank of Italy in the various venues where this issue was discussed and in this context personified the fine traditions established by Italy in both scholarship and monetary diplomacy.[1] The paper by Maxwell C. Watson describes the operational results obtained thus far in this area, dealing particularly with the aspects that involve the International Monetary Fund (IMF). The concluding remarks by Antonio Casas-Gonzáles, president of the Central Bank of Venezuela, complete the picture with an agenda of actions that might prevent complications. The work of these three scholars represents one of the most precise and well-reasoned syntheses of an issue now being examined by officials in the world's major industrialized countries.

The studies published here offer a significant panorama of the changes taking place in how the reform of the international monetary system is viewed. The regulatory capacity of government authorities suffered an eclipse following the wide acceptance of the philosophy of the superiority of market discipline, but this theme made a reappearance in the agenda of the Group of Seven (G-7) countries (Canada, France, Germany, Italy, Japan, the United Kingdom, and the United States) following a series of crises in currencies, in banking systems, and in the finances of various countries. These crises were increasingly severe and widespread, leading to worries that the global market could be vulnerable to systemic contamination. Unlike what happened during the Great Crash of 1929 to 1931, the recent events did not lead to talk about market failure but rather to an awareness that the policies of public intervention were being badly administered. The awareness grew out of the need for a new international financial architecture (IFA) characterized by better integration among the rules of the game, public institutions, and market forces.

The participants in the second conference concentrated their attention on the following issues:

- Dissatisfaction with the functioning of flexible exchange rates and the possible corrections of the existing mechanism;

- Changes in the political climate toward the approach to be taken regarding problems rising from international monetary instability;
- The monetary nature of derivatives and the implications for the policy of targeting; and
- Juridical aspects of the new architecture of the international financial system.

Participants at the conference, in analyzing the relationship between flexible exchange rates and the free circulation of capital in the world, reached a unanimous opinion that flexible exchange rates were not functioning in a satisfactory way with respect to what the theory promised. Robert Z. Aliber and Dominick Salvatore strongly emphasize that flexible rates have created an hysteresis in foreign trade net commercial balances, leading to imbalances that are more severe than those recorded during the regime of fixed exchange rates, due to the hesitation by government authorities to alter the parities. Watson observes, for example, that "it is puzzling that instability [in exchange rates] has not diminished at a time of low inflation and interest rates in advanced economies." These scholars conclude that the regime of flexible rates—even if it has not been fully experimented as yet due to the presence of various regimes and exchange-rate policies in the world—is governed by capital flows and not by the flow of goods. And since financial flows, particularly short-term ones, are highly unstable, a vicious cycle develops whereby the practical results of flexible rates diverge from the ones that should theoretically occur.

Paolo Savona, Aurelio Maccario, and Chiara Oldani do not deny that instability is born when capital is moved but argue that its extent and the way in which it can spread is due more to the derivatives' market than to official markets. It would be a mistake, therefore, for governmental authorities to concentrate their attention and their interventions on the capital markets. These three economists also concur, principally but not exclusively, with the analysis offered by Jeffrey R. Shafer, whereby the freedom of the movement of capital does carry risks for the stability of currencies and stock markets but also offers numerous advantages in terms of the efficient allocation of resources in the world. It would therefore be wrong to "throw sand into the gears," as Tobin put it, to limit freedom of movement in some respect, or, even worse, to adopt policies of target zones, reference zones, or soft zones in exchanges. Such a system would be destined to failure, without meeting the problem (and resolving it) of bringing under control the international money supply as it has logically been redefined in this era of financial innovation, the Internet, and information technology.

The repeated outbreaks of currency, banking, and financial crises have led to a shift in political attitudes toward a reform of the international monetary system from the concept of "first putting your own house in order" to one of "putting the global market in order as well." The conference participants, however, felt that actions taken so far have been inadequate and have not really faced up to the problem. Saccomanni observes that "the reform of the international financial architecture ... has been a necessary step in the effort to contain international financial instability but has not been sufficient to bring about a comprehensive reform of the international monetary system. *The latter remains an unfulfilled dream"* (emphasis added). Going to the heart of the problem Watson adds that "the new architecture may begin at home, in domestic reforms, but it cannot end there."

If one accepts the growing awareness that putting one's own house in order is no longer enough—in a time when global operators are ever more powerful and equipped with rapid and sophisticated information technology and with instruments (such as derivatives) that allow them to act swiftly and at low cost—one must also admit that a corresponding awareness has not developed around the fact that sources of monetary creation now exist at the international level (derivatives, in fact) that are under the control of market operators and that leap across even the most rigid national monetary controls. Every attempt to keep one's house in order, therefore, is upset by the operational freedom and the inventiveness of the international markets.

There is a growing consensus that the development of the global market makes it necessary to increase international cooperation to find an effective substitute for the indispensable figure of an international central banker. As of now the "seven bigs" of the G-7 do not intend to ordain the International Monetary Fund to fulfill this function, resulting in markets that are left with the power to set the rules of the international financial game. This decentralization is part and parcel of the dominant political philosophy that the private sector can arrive at more effective decisions than the public one, even in setting monetary policies. The current thinking could also be motivated by a fear that if central banks were put to the test of taking over those decision-making powers and proved ineffective, then it would undermine confidence in the central banks—a confidence they still possess despite repeated crises.

The highest price for this situation was paid by the IMF, which was compelled by the "great powers" to experiment with ways of alleviating those crises. It has been transformed from an organization that was established to supervise the orderly functioning of exchanges, according to the philosophy accepted at Bretton Woods, into an agency that dispenses credit. Crisis after crisis nailed down the change in the IMF's primary role, without, however, creating an institutional replacement to restore control over the creation of money and therefore make the system function effectively. The IMF's interventions were criticized by practically everyone at the conference, with the Fund receiving only a modest degree of support. Aliber noted that the credit flow instituted by the IMF was indirectly effective, serving as a tool to make countries willing to accept constraints on or modifications of their economic policies—in particular regarding their foreign-exchange regimes, which are usually at the heart of the crisis. Without losing contact with the reality of the markets, Alexander K. Swoboda instead stresses the central function of the IMF and the need to "give the Fund a more independent voice ... to reconcile the globalization of markets with the fragmentation of policies and politics made at the national level."

From the work of the two Carli conferences it becomes obvious that neither the current literature nor government authorities present as yet any clear picture of the endogenous nature of the creation of international money within the malfunctioning of the IMS. Peter M. Oppenheimer points out that a great deal of attention was devoted to this subject in the eighteenth and nineteenth centuries, leading to the creation of two opposing schools of thought: the banking school, which argued for the free market of deposits and credits (and therefore of money), and the monetary school, which called for the control of the quantity of money by public authorities. In the twentieth century the need to control the quantity of money, to create a central bank, and to make it politically independent won the argument, but the banking school, escorted to the door by national economic systems, year by year built a new fortress within the global market, greatly aided by the existence of offshore centers and the "blackmail" these represented for the national systems. In order not to lose a significant share of international banking business to the offshore centers, the industrialized countries found themselves obliged to allow the free exchange of any kind of "capital," giving the markets a *de facto* freedom to create money, while they barricaded themselves behind the rationale that the only thing they could do was "to put their own house in order"—which soon became the only thing that had to be done.

The result of this state of affairs is the one described by Saccomanni: we've gone from a "government-led international monetary system" (G-IMS) to a "market-led international monetary system" (M-IMS) in which the markets and not the authorities provide for mechanisms for international money creation and exchange-rate determination. According to the definition proposed by Saccomanni, a "M-IMS is a system based on the freedom of capital mobility, in which exchange rates, as well as the creation and distribution of international liquidity, are determined by market forces." In other words, money is once again endogenous, as it was before the rise to power of the ideas of the monetary school and the restatement of those ideas by the Chicago school.

The thesis of the monetary nature of derivative instruments as an important component of the endogenicity of monetary creation was tested econometrically by Savona and Maccario, and their results were presented at the first conference. This test was perfected by the same authors in collaboration with Oldani and presented with new arguments and empirical logic during this year's conference. The three authors concentrated their attention particularly on the relationship between monetary creation as it is known traditionally and the way in which derivative markets function. Their conclusion is that interest rates react to the demand for derivatives according to the relationship set forth in the liquidity preference schedule first identified by Keynes and afterward in the common patrimony of different schools of economic thought. Derivatives are therefore an excellent substitute for money in speculative activities.

The authorities should therefore pay attention to the problem of integrating the monetary targets that are normally used (M2 or M3) with derivative instruments or, alternatively, make extensive use (as is happening without the reason being explained) of monetary policies oriented to interest rates. In this latter case, the authorities tacitly accept the negative consequences that, according to economic theory, affect the stability of real growth.[2]

Given the impossibility of supervision by an international monetary government, a greater coordination between national policies is needed. Casas-Gonzáles stresses two points: (1) "a new financial architecture that works efficiently must be built on the basis of active participation by all countries" and (2) "a central element of international financial reform is related to the need to provide sufficient and timely liquidity during crises associated with massive capital outflows." It has been noted, however, that the biggest obstacle is the refusal by the United States to accept foreign influence over its policies and also the inability of many other countries to accept a reduction in their national monetary sovereignty. One can only hope that the European Union (EU), having reached a relative standardization of policies among its member states, will accept as one of its responsibilities the search for internal and external monetary and financial stability, which will contribute to the creation of a greater degree of cooperation among the world's economic leaders (the United States, the European Union, and Japan) to stabilize the functioning of the IMS. Salvatore believes that two factors limit the effect of European Monetary Union (EMU). The first is the unresolved problem of how to handle asymmetric shocks; and the other is the relationship between the ins and outs—whether these are the founding members that have chosen to remain outside EMU (the United Kingdom, Denmark, and Norway), the one that has not yet qualified (Greece), or the numerous countries that would like to be admitted (such as the postcommunist countries of Central Europe). Oppenheimer believes, instead, that a central bank like the one established by the Maastricht Treaty (in which the monetary functions are separate from the ones governing the stability of the banking system) cannot function properly, especially if the decision-making powers are in the hands of the European governments rather than in the hands of the central bankers who participate in the European Central Bank (ECB), and he wonders "how far this sharp separation of powers can be maintained."

At the present time, the efforts to establish a new international financial architecture fall into five baskets:

- Enhancing transparency and promoting best practices,
- Strengthening financial regulation in industrial countries,
- Strengthening macroeconomic policies and financial systems in emerging markets,
- Improving crisis prevention and management and involving the private sector, and
- Promoting social policies to protect the poor and the most vulnerable.

The breadth and the limitations of each of these five components are examined in Saccomanni's paper on the progress reached by the panoply of groups working on this subject. He observes that, for the moment, the principal site of coordination on questions of monetary and financial stability is not the IMF but the Bank for International Settlements (BIS) in Basle.

What appears evident from the papers and the discussions that followed at the conference is that the problem of the stability of exchange rates (perhaps one can even say the abandoning of the current regime officially defined as "flexible" because the status of the central currency of the system, the U.S. dollar, is so great) is not on the agenda of the authorities, of their working groups, or even of the scholarly experts. Professor Aliber points out that the political establishment now seems to have less use for contributions from academia and seems to attempt to go forward by relying on its own forces, thus depriving itself of precious support that, in the past, was the driving force behind reform in this field.

The problem of the unsatisfactory functioning of flexible exchange rates as a source of real and financial stability was studied by Aliber and by Salvatore, who traces the reasons that flexible rates were adopted after the 1960s. It was felt that they would provide a greater degree of adaptability, given the different inflation rates between one country and another; that the currency markets possessed a greater capacity to evaluate the situation than did the authorities; that they would allow a government more freedom of choice in framing its policies, and that they would reduce the need to maintain official reserves and lessen the chances that a currency crisis would erupt.

Aliber observes that, in the last analysis, everything depends on the validity of the first proposition—that is, the greater adaptability of exchange rates to achieve parity with purchasing power. But that expectation proved unfounded because of the influence exerted on operational freedom by monetary and capital movements.

The central problem facing the new international financial architecture according to Aliber, is therefore the one of intervening at the source of instability as represented by the combination of the variability of capital flows and the floating exchange-rate system. "Since uncertainty about exchange rates ... is larger when currencies are floating than when they are pegged, then the inference is that the differential between domestic and foreign returns when currencies are floating ... is larger when currencies are pegged and are pegged by more than enough to compensate for the increase in the uncertainty." In brief, uncertainty feeds on itself, and it finds in exchange rates a compensatory mechanism that creates a vicious circle of monetary and financial instability in that it is moved by, and in turn moves, monetary and financial resources between countries.

Aliber's pragmatic conclusion is that the variations in exchange rates are prevalently the result of the market's reply to the desire on the part of investors to change the composition of currencies representing the activity of their portfolios—a desire induced by the comparative movement of real growth rates, inflation, and interest rates.

The Savona-Maccario-Oldani thesis is that the characteristics of derivatives make it superfluous to move capital. In other words, by buying or selling securities and accepting the cost of those transactions, it is sufficient to "bet" on the movement of interest rates, exchange rates, or economic indexes (such as those of the stock exchanges or commodities markets) to reach the same goals at a much lower cost. Derivative contracts, in fact, cost less than the underlying ones.

Savona takes a step further, observing that derivatives act first of all on the rate of substitution between portfolio activities. They therefore play an important role in the mechanism that transmits impulses arising from monetary policies, in a more general sense from economic policies, and finally from the private operators themselves. This takes the theoretical problem back to the unresolved debate between economists on the role played by the substitutability between financial assets (and between these and real assets) in the effectiveness of policies directed at influencing savings and investments schedules and the rates of accumulation and employment (Savona, 1999, pp. 151–155). Oppenheimer believes that this is a promising line of analysis, but he also points out that an obstacle exists to making progress in this area: the scant knowledge that scholars have about how these markets really function.

A comment by Michele Fratianni underlines one aspect of Aliber's analysis, which that author was aware of even if he did not state it explicitly: the absence of a solution to the problem of financial instability. Fratianni points out that "there is little evidence that the G-3 (Germany, Japan, and the United States) has any stomach for currency management" and that "the paucity of global thinkers on reforming the international monetary system may reflect awareness that there is not a dominant solution" beyond international cooperation, above all now that the European Monetary Union has shown that it wants to adopt the line of nonparticipation in defining and governing a different international monetary system from the one followed by the United States.

Salvatore is basically in agreement with Fratianni and believes that, however you look at it, the objective of changing the rules of the IMS is not easily (and perhaps not at all) attainable. The only alternative is therefore to improve the current system (or nonsystem), which he defines as "hybrid," through the imposition on the part of the authorities of a greater degree of transparency of operations to better inform the markets. Salvatore believes that private operators should accept a higher cost due to their behavior in terms of moral hazard. In other words, they should not be bailed out. Also, emerging countries should receive greater financial assistance to help them in their development and not simply to be able to fend off an unstoppable speculative attack. This same theme is taken up by Oppenheimer, who, in more traditional language, emphasizes that three instruments should be reviewed: "last-resort lending, moral hazard, and the form and extent of prudential capital requirements."

Fratianni thinks that the origin of monetary crises does not lie with the authorities but rather with the banks that commit too many errors in evaluating credit risks. This theme is taken up at greater length in the paper written by David T. Llewellyn, who concentrates on the characteristics of the regulatory regime under which banks operate. Llewellyn believes that the external regulatory bodies, such as central banks and the agencies that supervise banking, have a decreasing influence in governing financial systems. Instead of trying to exert more control, they should create incentive programs that can convince the banks to adopt more appropriate mechanisms of internal control. Without such incentives, he adds, any hope of improving the way banks are managed by reducing their exposure to risk is doomed to failure; Casas-Gonzáles gives authoritative support to this view.

On the basis of recent experience, Llewellyn's opinion is that the regulatory regime necessary to face crises should be strengthened in all its six components: regulation, monitoring and surveillance, incentive structures, intervention, market discipline, and the rules of corporate governance.

Llewellyn's paper offers an extensive and penetrating analysis of the problem areas involved in each of the six components that make up the regulatory system and that also provide a tool for measuring its effectiveness. He indicates that he has faith in the virtues of self-regulation among market operators despite the negative results of their most recent actions, which he attributes to the operators having found themselves involved in a process of transition toward a deregulated system for which they (and the authorities) were insufficiently prepared. The regulatory regime that was in force at that time did not provide incentives either for a proper management of risk on the part of bank executives or for an increase in competition, since the authorities were fearful of weakening the stability of the system.

Shafer dissents from this approach. His point of view is that the instability of the global monetary and financial system is the result of structural factors, not transitory ones, and that this is the price that needs to be paid for benefiting from the advantages of a system of free movement of capital, which he regards as unquestionably useful. Sharing in the unanimous viewpoint of all the conference participants, he rejects as illogical any curbing of the freedom of action of market operators. He also thinks that the shift of surveillance systems, from external ones to ones within the banks and the markets, can be effective only in a very limited way and at any rate should not be tried in developing countries where the institutions are still imperfect. Shafer proposes a tradeoff between the choice of voluntary systems of control and the simplicity of rules imposed by the authorities. If those rules are easy to interpret and if they can easily be adapted to innovations generated by the markets, they function better.

Shafer's skepticism about the ability of bank managers to interpret the dynamics of markets and consequently to be able to govern themselves and to govern the international monetary system is even more striking when one considers that he is not only an expert on these problems but also a leading operator in the global market. It should be noted that even Saccomanni, Aliber, and Fratianni recall that the most forceful criticism of the *laissez-faire* philosophy adopted these days by the authorities that govern IMS—if one can speak of governing—and of the line followed in the construction of the new international financial architecture—have come precisely from operators of the calibre of George Soros, Henry Kaufman, and Paul Volcker. In the 1999 New Task Force Report promoted by the U.S. Council for Foreign Relations, these three illustrious financial experts insisted very strongly that the authorities should take an active role in curbing the speculation in currencies, for without such controls the reform of the IFA would be, like "watching *Hamlet* without the Prince."

Barry Eichengreen (1998), who made a significant contribution to the study commissioned by the Guido Carli Association on the international monetary system and presented at the first conference of 1998, notes that it took half a century for countries in Europe to arrive at the euro and concluded that it would be "fantastic to think that this process could be replicated on a global scale in a few years."

Despite the criticism directed at European Monetary Union, Watson declares that he has more faith in the ability of the system of European central banks to serve as an agency promoting international monetary coordination or at least to serve as a blueprint for a mechanism that can guarantee a greater stability in the world's financial system. Swoboda goes further, saying that "the euro is the manifestation of the erosion of the hegemony of the United States and the dollar. Although the dollar does remain the dominant currency, it is a role that is now being challenged." Pointing to the step-by-step "convergence" that led to Eurolandia (in other words, the 11 countries that are part of the EMU), Watson concentrates on the conditions that will have to be met for emerging countries or those in transition to be able to participate successfully in the process of their own integration into the European and international financial system, exploiting forms of exchange-rate stability that can also be achieved through official interventions in the market. To protect themselves from asymmetrical shocks, they will have to meet several requirements usually identified as "fiscal sustainability, the subordination of monetary policy to the anchor, sound debt management, and adequate wage-price flexibility." In other words, they need to "put their house in order."

The need for European countries to satisfy certain requirements of the European Monetary Union, in fact, has a wider validity. We can see that Italy, for example, which is already part of the euro zone and therefore has a currency that is protected from external attacks, has an economy that lacks this protection. In the event of external shocks hitting the system in an asymmetrical manner, such countries can continue to enjoy a habitat of financial stability while at the same time finding themselves dragged into a whirlpool of real instability consisting of a fall in production and in jobs.

Watson also recognizes, as Aliber and other scholars point out, that there exists a problem of financial vulnerability on the part of emerging countries or those in transition that is due to the erratic movement of capital and that this problem can be faced (as Italy did, in fact) only by entering into a regime of common defense of exchange rates accompanied by steps "to put one's house in order." Salvatore believes that the right policy is the currency board—that is, a policy of making a currency balance managed in a regime of fixed rates responsible for modulating the creation of money. He admits that this can be reasonably accomplished in the arena of EMU only by countries that wish to become part of it, on the condition that the countries forming part of Eurolandia give them precise guarantees that their currencies will be protected.

In conclusion, a corrected system is still far from being implemented. It is reasonable to accept the point of view of Saccomanni and Salvatore that we will continue to live for a long time under a hybrid international monetary system that will contain several kinds of regimes of exchange rates and banking and financial regulations and that capital will allow to be essentially free to move where it wishes. This will therefore create well being but also a chronic instability that can be partially or periodically reduced through increased transparency on the part of operators and through banking, financial, and company regulations that are more stringent than the present ones, whether self-imposed or imposed by the authorities. There remains the question of what level of competition the system of intermediaries should reasonably work under so as not to be driven to a struggle of the fittest and, therefore, to forms of moral hazard in the choice of risks. This is a point that Oppenheimer raises (as he himself affirms) as a provocation to remind everyone that money is a "unique" good that cannot be treated like any other good.

In the opinion of this author, until the creation of traditionally defined money and its substitutes is brought under the control of the authorities, the market will continue to play the role of *dominus* of the international monetary system. The quantity of money will maintain its endogenous characteristics, currency and financial crises will continue to break out, and the world will remain seated on a monetary powder keg. There is only one way to correct this situation—to coordinate national economic policies and, to turn the coin over, not to pursue policies of autonomy exploiting flexible exchange rates. Such a strategy makes sense if the belief in the global market's virtues, so widely touted, is more than just lip service, and if a real desire exists to reinforce it at the political level. In the global market, real growth and inflation respond to the logic of a closed market where monetary conditions have a significant impact. Every attempt to escape from that logic using flexible exchange rates to create the conditions for dichotomous movements away from the overall trend signifies an interruption of the benefits of the global market and the appropriation of these benefits on the part of the strongest and most able national economies.

This conclusion is apparently the same as Swoboda's, but it stresses the importance of going to the source of instability (endogenous money creation) instead of trying to control the outcome (the financial crisis). This author shares Swoboda's conclusion that "we should not have the illusion that we can build a crisis-proof system" because the historical fight between official authorities and market operators will continue in the future. We are not at the end of the monetary history; perhaps we are at the beginning.

In the session dealing with the juridical aspects of the new international financial architecture, Alberto Predieri took up the themes discussed by the economists, underlining that the projected benefits deriving from the "invisible hand" presupposed the "sovereign hand" of a government "producer of norms that will enable trade to prosper and favor the division of labor." It is therefore up to the sovereign state and not to the market to determine what shape the new IFA will have. Among the state's responsibilities, since it holds a monopoly on the creation of laws, is monetary and financial stability viewed as a fundamental support for a free system. For this reason the principle of stability was written into the German constitution and in the European treaties as well, standing in opposition to the destabilizing will of the markets. In particular, if the global market is allowed to act without a juridical structure, it will create—and here Predieri has borrowed Robert Triffin's words—"labyrinths and disorders."

Money has become an "unpredictable raw material" and the new international financial architecture must take account of this. If money also includes derivatives, we face the double consequence that derivatives render markets more efficient because they are used to cover risks, while they serve economic policies that can use derivatives to achieve a degree of acceptance by the markets that is greater than their real effectiveness. If, however, as Antonio Fazio (governor of the Bank of Italy and chair of the Guido Carli Association) maintained at the first Carli conference, we consider that the risk intermediaries run in creating derivatives is not easily quantified, then we find ourselves up against a dangerous condition: "When one no longer has an accurate perception of the risks, one enters the antechamber of a financial panic" (the quote is from Antonio Pollio Salimbeni).

Predieri observes that the juridical weakness of international agreements on monetary policy—and in other areas as well—is due to the absence of a body that governs the global market and sets rules. The current juridical usage that induces respect for the decisions taken, for example, at G-7 meetings consists of a shared agreement that single nations will assume the responsibility "of assuring that the private institutions in our countries respect these principles, standards, or codes of conduct" (quoted from point 8 of the final communiqué of the 1998 Summit).

Predieri applied a strict logical and juridical analysis to the terms of the 1998 accords in the area of global financial stability, while recognizing that "the G-7 is not an international body that produces binding legislative acts" and that the weakness of the international financial architecture, new or old as the case may be, will continue if its components are not written into law by the juridical arm of the single countries.

Sergio M. Carbone examines the problem of derivatives from a perspective that is wholly Italian, stating that they do not fit into any of our legal statues but rather fit into the rules of international law, which become a valid part of domestic law, as Predieri points out, only if they are recognized by national governments. Without this legislative recognition everything remains in the sphere of private agreements that have a contractual force if there is a mutual will-ingness to respect them but that are shorn of the possibility of appealing to the national courts to make these agreements legally enforceable. This does not mean that derivative contracts have been ignored by our civil code of law because a ruling was made that they should be assimilated in principle within the legal parameters governing every other kind of monetary obligation since they are a by-product of other obligations. Italian code, however, does not reg-ulate the many complex details that derivatives involve. There exists, therefore, a considerable blank area in the laws covering derivatives that weakens their legal certainty, at least in Italy. The only secure legal reference is the 1980 Rome Convention on the Law Applicable to Contractual Obligation, and operators must necessarily take account of it.

In her paper, Maria Chiara Malaguti agrees with Predieri's analysis of the legal agreements reached by the G-7 and emphasizes the essentially self-regulating nature of derivatives contracts. The private sector welcomes this solution, but it is also the inevitable result of the absence of public regulation. The question of what to do to avoid a crisis therefore falls back on the thesis of giving the private sector more responsibility in establishing financial stability, but this approach is practical rather than theoretical. It turns necessity into a virtue and not virtue into a necessity, as Llewellyn maintaines. As for legal validity in the absence of a specific reference in the domestic body of laws, Malaguti looks favorably on agreements reached within the WTO, feeling that these would be a primary source for domestic legislation.

During the conference, the juridical experts made a strong appeal to the economists to give due importance in their analysis to the legal uncertainties surrounding derivatives contracts and the self-regulating nature of their respect, since this aspect amounted, in effect, to a limitation (and therefore an ineffi-ciency) in the choice of economic policies and a higher degree of responsibility for private operators to establish the stability that is being sought with the new international financial architecture.

Notes

1. On this subject one can find an extensive production of documents on the part of the Bank of Italy on the occasion of its centenary in the *Collana Storica* (Historical Editions) published by Laterza (Rome/Bari, from 1993 to 1999) and in the references to scientific research in Italy (from 1582 onward) through the research of Bartolo Scaruffi, cited in Savona (1999, Technical Appendix).
2. This issue is treated at length in Savona (1999, Technical Appendix).

References

Eichengreen, B. (1998) "Exchange-Rate Stability and Financial Stability." In Michele Fratianni, Dominick Salvatore, and Paolo Savona (eds.), *Ideas for the Future of the International Mone-tary System*. Boston: Kluwer, 569–608.
Savona, Paolo (1999) *Alla Ricerca della sovranità monetaria: Breve storia della finanza straniera in Italia*. Milan: Edizioni Scheiwiller.

Open economies review **11:S1** 15–41 (2000)
© 2000 *Kluwer Academic Publishers. Printed in The Netherlands.*

Introduction: A New Architecture or New System? A Survey of International Monetary Reform in the 1990s

FABRIZIO SACCOMANNI
Banca d'Italia, Rome, Italy

Keywords: exchange-rate regime, international monetary system, international financial architecture, regulation, standards

JEL Classification Numbers: F33, F34, G18

Abstract

The international monetary system (IMS) is a macroeconomic concept that encompasses the foreign exchange-rate regulation, the capital movement system, and all "the rules of the game" for the adjustment of international payment imbalances. The international financial architecture (IFA) is, in contrast, a microeconomic concept and should not be considered synonymous with the IMS. The IFA is one element of the IMS. The current set of international monetary arrangements has been frequently called a "nonsystem." Today there are two missing pillars in the reform efforts: a framework for managing the interdependence among the macroeconomic policies of the global powers (the United States, Europe, and Japan) and the market-oriented approach to the financing of the IMF.

1. A question of semantics

The vocabulary of international monetary debates, both in official and academic fora, has been enriched since the mid-1990s by the increasingly frequent reference to the term *architecture*. Gradually, the concept of international financial architecture (IFA) developed, and it is now fiercely competing with the more traditional expression of *international monetary system* (IMS) that was officially sanctioned in the Treaty of Bretton Woods in 1944. This development is not just a phenomenon of linguistic evolution but reflects an important shift of emphasis in the field of international monetary and financial relations by the major industrial countries of the Group of Seven (G-7: Canada, France, Germany, Italy, Japan, the United Kingdom, and the United States). However, this distinction is not always immediately perceived, giving rise to misunderstandings.

It is with the aim of not increasing the confusion (or perhaps because I was a student of Professor Fritz Machlup at Princeton, who wrote memorable pages about the role of language in international monetary affairs) that I feel compelled to initiate this article by stating what I mean by using certain expressions. To me, the IMS is a macroeconomic concept that encompasses the exchange-rate regime, the regime for capital movements, the mechanism for international liquidity creation and distribution, and the "rules of the game" for the adjustment of international payment imbalances. By the IFA, in contrast, I mean the principles and practices that influence the behavior of participants in international financial markets—that is, borrowers, investors, intermediaries, and regulators. The IFA is thus a microeconomic concept and should not be considered as a synonym of IMS. In fact, the IFA is just one element, although an important one, of the IMS. I regard this semantic distinction as essential, and I argue in this article that the reform of the international financial architecture—which has been proposed by the G-7 since the outburst of the Asian crisis in 1997—has been a necessary step in the effort to contain international financial instability but has not been sufficient to bring about a comprehensive reform of the international monetary system. The latter remains an unfulfilled dream.

2. A brief survey of IMS crises and reforms

It may be useful at this point to briefly recall the main episodes of the evolution of the international monetary system from the inception of Bretton Woods system and of the related attempts to reform it.[1] This will help set the stage for the analysis of current monetary arrangements and of efforts to revise the international financial architecture. The following periods may be singled out as especially relevant:

1946 to 1971.   This is the period of the operation of the Bretton Woods system, whose main feature was the fixed exchange-rate regime. During this period, reform initiatives begin to be considered only in the 1960s and were concentrated on the objective of preserving the stability of the exchange-rate regime by bolstering the liquidity-creation function of the International Monetary Fund (IMF)—that is, through the establishment of the general arrangements to borrow (GAB) and the creation of the special drawing rights (SDR).

1971 to 1973.   The dollar convertibility into gold is suspended, and the dollar is devalued twice. Efforts are being made to rebuild a "new Bretton Woods system" based on a comprehensive reform of all elements of the IMS.

1974 to 1979.   The world economy and the exchange-rate regime are shaken by two oil crises (1974 and 1978). The IMF provides support through the "oil facilities." Failure of IMS reform plans leads to the legalization of the generalized floating of exchange rates (Jamaica Agreement of 1976). Following the Jamaica Agreement, international monetary cooperation remains formally based within the Bretton Woods institutions (IMF and the World Bank) but is increasingly conducted in smaller groupings of major industrialized countries—initially by the Group of 10 (G-10: G-7 plus Belgium, the Netherlands,

Sweden, and Switzerland), subsequently by the Group of Five (G-5: G-7 minus Canada and Italy), finally by the G-7—and becomes more sporadic and issue-oriented. The proposal to absorb the excess dollar liquidity through the establishment of a "substitution account" in the IMF is rejected. The European Monetary System (EMS) is established to restore some degree of exchange-rate stability among European currencies. It will eventually lead to the European Economic and Monetary Union (EMU).

1982 to 1984. The debt crisis of developing countries is countered with an increase in IMF financial resources (a 50 percent increase in IMF quotas and an expansion of the GAB).

1985 to 1987. The G-7 take the initiative to correct the overvaluation of the dollar (1985) and to stabilize it (1987) through coordinated exchange-market intervention. The G-7 consider the possibility of establishing a framework for broader policy coordination based on target zones for exchange rates but fail to reach agreement.

1992 to 1999. A series of exchange-rate and financial crises occurs (EMS, 1992 to 1993; Mexico, 1994; Asia, 1997 to 1998; Russia, 1998; and Brazil, 1999) against the background of deepening globalization of financial markets. The G-7 take the initiative to reform the IFA (1995).

From this brief survey it appears that the adoption of a more flexible IMS after the collapse of Bretton Woods has not reduced international monetary and financial instability as had been promised by its advocates. If anything, with the increasing pace of financial globalization, episodes of crisis have become more frequent and have tended to involve more countries at a time, as tensions have spread around through contagion. This does not imply that financial crises are solely the result of the evolution of the IMS. Charles Kindleberger (1978) has shown in a famous historical survey that financial crises, both of a domestic and international character, have occurred under any type of IMS and have been generated by what he calls "excessive credit and monetary expansion." It is thus important to analyze whether there is a connection between the IMS and the framework in which individual countries conduct their monetary and credit policies—that is, their "domestic monetary constitution." In particular, it is worthwhile to find out whether, and to what extent, the present configuration of IMS is conducive to the establishment of monetary constitutions that are prone to excessive credit expansion.

3. An assessment of the current international monetary system

The current set of international monetary arrangements has frequently been called, by economists, government officials, and central bankers, a "nonsystem," especially if confronted with the Bretton Woods system of rules and institutional arrangements.

Tommaso Padoa-Schioppa and myself (1994) have questioned the factual accuracy and the analytical relevance of this characterization in a paper written for the fiftieth anniversary of the Bretton Woods Conference of 1944. Our view was that both Bretton Woods and the present arrangements constitute a system, in the sense that they have mechanisms for international money creation and exchange-rate determination and contain codes of conduct for market participants and policy makers.[2]

The main difference, we argued, is that Bretton Woods was a "government-led international monetary system" (G-IMS), while the current arrangements are a "market-led international monetary system" (M-IMS). The distinction is more than a matter of semantics.

A G-IMS is a system in which exchange rates are determined by the monetary authorities (national and international), capital movements are restricted by government-imposed controls, and international liquidity is created by an international institution (controlled by the governments of member countries) that distributes liquidity to members with a balance of payments needed to help them maintain exchange-rate stability. Two key features of the G-IMS are especially important: it provides an anchor for economic policies and therefore dictates the domestic monetary constitution of individual members, and it is perceived by economic agents and market participants as pursuing public interests such as monetary stability, balance of payments equilibrium, and noninflationary growth.

A M-IMS is a system based on the freedom of capital mobility, in which exchange rates, as well as the creation and distribution of international liquidity, are determined by market forces. In this context each individual country is free to adopt its own domestic monetary constitution as there are no external institutional constraints on policy making. The essential question then is, How do the market forces determine exchange rates and allocate international liquidity?

In a globalized financial system, an increasingly large share of the world's savings is entrusted to professional portfolio managers who are able to allocate funds across the full spectrum of available market instruments. The number of such global market players is relatively high, but they tend to operate on the basis of a common set of principles and on the same information about social, political, and economic developments. They have therefore a determinant influence on the behavior of other market participants.

The set of principles governing the activity of global market players is heavily influenced by the objectives of maximizing the return on the portfolio while minimizing risk. These objectives cannot be achieved simultaneously because maximizing the return implies increasing the risk and minimizing the risk implies reducing the return. Global market players are therefore obliged to reassess continuously the combination of risk and return to exploit new opportunities of increasing returns or to run away from suddenly materialized risks. To this end they have to constantly monitor all possible developments (economic, social, and political) that may affect the value of the invested assets or their risk. In this sense they are literally speculators: they try to anticipate future developments. In the process of evaluation, global players follow a rather conservative market-oriented approach. For example, in judging the policy stance of a country, they tend to reward stability-oriented monetary and fiscal policies and to penalize deficit spending or otherwise unsustainable demand management measures. Measures to liberalize capital movements or exchange controls are appreciated, while capital restrictions are negatively rated. Privatization is good, nationalization is bad, and so on.

In their search for high returns, global players normally invest in countries that are in the process of becoming creditworthy but are not quite such as yet. The evaluation of the country's convergence toward full creditworthiness is thus a crucial element in the investment decision, and, to this end, global players are constantly looking for indicators or proxies of convergence. Among the broad range of indicators that are regularly monitored, political-institutional factors have been increasingly important in the international allocation of funds.

In sum, in a M-IMS, market mechanisms for the determination of exchange rates and the allocation of international liquidity operate on the basis of decisions taken primarily in pursuit of private interests such as increasing profits or protecting the value of investments. However, because of the prevailing conservative approach that guides global players, under the M-IMS broader public interests, price stability, fiscal rectitude, and balance-of-payments equilibrium are also indirectly pursued as under the G-IMS.

Although both the G-IMS and M-IMS may ultimately be considered equivalent inasmuch as they pursue the same fundamental objectives, they differ significantly in the aspect that is crucial for the analysis of financial crises—namely, the degree of control over credit and monetary expansion. From this point of view, there is no doubt that in a M-IMS the degree of monetary control is potentially less stringent than in a G-IMS. Any country considered "creditworthy" by the markets would be likely to register large inflows of capital, fueling in turn a monetary and credit expansion. The fact that such credit can be quickly curtailed in the event of developments negatively affecting the country's creditworthiness does not eliminate the risk of excessive credit expansion; it only makes more painful to deal with its consequences once credit is curtailed. As Governor Fazio (1998) of the Banca d'Italia stated in the previous Conference of the Associazione Guido Carli: "The risks of instability are enormous. The possibility of financing imbalances may cause their correction to be put off. Sudden switches in investors' expectations lead to rapid shifts in their portfolios, thereby creating disruptive pressures in foreign exchange and securities markets."

Put in other words, in a M-IMS the degree of discipline that market forces can impose on borrowers can be severe, but the fierce competition among global players entails that such discipline is normally applied too late. This results in periodic phases of excessive lending followed by phases of widespread illiquidity. It is recognized that under such a system more than $1 trillion in private capital has flowed from developed to developing countries since the start of the 1990s, providing a fundamental contribution to growth and the improvement of living standards. Yet for all the benefits and opportunities that large-scale capital flows bring with them, they have also exposed the fragility of the current financial system and its inherent instability.

4. Why an instability-prone IMS?

It may be legitimate at this stage to wonder whether the "revealed preferences" of the international community, or at least of the major industrial countries that are leading it, point in the direction of an instability-prone IMS as the current one appears to be. It may be legitimate but would be unfair, as no country, large or small, has ever put monetary and financial instability in the list of its key policy objectives. Yet throughout history we have witnessed periods in which the prevailing configuration of the IMS was stability-oriented, as in the gold standard and in the early Bretton Wood years, and periods in which it was instability-prone, as in the years between the two world wars. The reasons for such collective choices could best be identified by historians and by political scientists. Without pretending to replace either category, the following factors seem to have played a determinant role in bringing about the current IMS.[3]

The first factor is the refusal of the United States, following the collapse of the Bretton Woods system, to accept ever again any external constraint on its domestic policies. This policy stance was loudly expressed by the U.S. Administration and Congress, which saw the exchange-rate regime of Bretton Woods as unfair to the United States because it allowed Japan and the major industrial countries in Europe to keep undervalued exchange rates, accumulate trade surplus compared to the United States, and "export" unemployment to America. In the negotiations that eventually led to the Jamaica Agreement of 1976, the U.S. government asked (successfully) that the right to float the currency be officially recognized in the IMF Articles of Agreement and that no obligations would be imposed on IMF members to intervene to stabilize its exchange rate.[4] In this way the exchange-rate regime lost its anchor, and all other major currencies were forced to float as well or had to look for alternative ways to anchor their policies. In practice, only in the European Community did monetary stability, both internal and external (price and exchange-rate stability), remain a key policy objective and the German mark became the anchor currency for the entire continent. The linkages with the U.S. dollar and the Japanese yen in their respective spheres of influence (Latin America and Asia) remained in fact much looser.

The second guiding factor in the evolution toward the present IMS has been the rise to power in the United States and the United Kingdom of politicians like Ronald Reagan and Margaret Thatcher deeply committed to the pursuit of free-market policies both domestically and internationally. In the monetary and financial field this philosophy has resulted in what has been called the "house-in-order" approach, according to which if every country would follow sound, noninflationary policies at home, there would be no payment imbalances in the world and therefore no need for "systemic" arrangements to deal with them. Although never fully shared by the other G-7 members, the house-in-order approach has left its mark on the course of negotiations and debates on international monetary reform, representing a sort of veto on the introduction of any "international" arrangement to deal with what was regarded as an essentially "domestic" problem of each individual country.

The quickening pace of financial integration on a global scale and the increasing frequency of episodes of financial instability has led to a partial revision of the house-in-order approach. It is now broadly accepted that there may be market imperfections (such as inadequacies in financial disclosure, accounting standards, and supervisory regimes) that lead to an undervaluation of risks by intermediaries and hence to excessive lending. Thus, in addition to the pursuit of sound domestic policies, the emphasis was put on the need to strengthen financial market structures and to remove the information asymmetries that may distort the working of market forces in the allocation of financial flows.

5. Toward reforming the international financial architecture

A critical review of the systemic implications of the operation of globalized financial markets by the major industrial countries in the G-7 and the G-10 began in the aftermath of the 1992 and 1993 crisis of the EMS. Although a study conducted by the G-10 deputies (1993) showed that the crisis had witnessed the massive involvement of global intermediaries and the mobilization of speculative flows of unprecedented magnitude, the crisis was attributed to intra-European imbalances and hence considered to be essentially a regional affair. Roughly at the same time, following a seminar on the IMS organized by Banca d'Italia to honor the memory of Rinaldo Ossola, the editors of the proceedings (Kenen, Papadia, and Saccomanni, 1994, p. 13) concluded that "no contributor [to the seminar] defends the present international monetary system as the best of all possible regimes. The strongest defences one can find are that it is functioning reasonably well and, more emphatically, that there is no obvious way to improve it."

At the 1994 G-7 Summit in Naples, the leaders of the Seven declared themselves broadly satisfied with the current international setting but paid lip service to the fiftieth anniversary of the Bretton Woods system by promising to reconsider the adequacy of the monetary arrangements in light of the challenges of the next millennium. By the time of the 1995 summit in Halifax, however, the Mexican crisis had erupted, shaking financial markets throughout Latin America with repercussions even in so-called high-yielding countries as far away as Italy, Spain, and Sweden. The objective of strengthening the international financial architecture was then put on the agenda of the G-7 meetings of finance ministers and central bank governors. Progress toward establishing the new architecture has been gradual and achieved partly in response to further episodes of financial instability. A shift away from the house-in-order school toward a more "deliberately managed" approach gradually materialized.

Initially, efforts were concentrated on strengthening the IMF's instruments and resources to enable it to provide financial assistance to countries in crisis more rapidly and in larger amounts. Thus, an emergency financing mechanism was established in the IMF in September 1995. In 1996 the new arrangements to borrow (NAB) were concluded among the IMF and 26 members providing additional financial resources to the IMF. In December 1997 a new Supplemental Reserve Facility was established as a reaction to the Korean crisis. Progress on the institutional and regulatory aspects of the architecture has been slower and partial. The main achievements have been in the field of banking supervision and securities regulation with the approval in 1996 of the so-called Core Principles of Effective Banking Supervision drafted by the Basle Committee on Banking Supervision (BCBS) of the G-10 and with the report on the Objectives and Principles of Securities Regulation drafted by the International Organization of Securities Commissions (IOSCO) in 1998.

With the deepening and spreading of the Asian financial crisis, efforts by the G-7 since 1998 have become more systematic and coordinated, moving along two main directions: identifying all the relevant elements of the international financial architecture and linking those elements in a consistent strategy. In this endeavor the G-7 has benefited from the work done together with a number of so-called systematically relevant countries of Asia, Latin America, and Eastern Europe, in the context of an informal grouping also known as the G-22.[5] At the G-7 Summit in Cologne in June 1999, G-7 leaders approved a report prepared by their finance ministers entitled "Strengthening the International Financial Architecture" (G-7, 1999). The report identifies five main components of a strengthened IFA and outlines the changes in institutional arrangements required to manage it.

5.1. The elements of a strengthened international financial architecture

The five components of the IFA are enhancing transparency and promoting best practices, strengthening financial regulation in industrial countries, strengthening macroeconomic policies and financial system in emerging markets, improving crisis prevention and management and involving the private sector, and promoting social policies to protect the poor and most vulnerable elements of society. In the following sections, the IFA components are briefly summarized and evaluated.

5.1.1. Transparency and best practices.   This section comprises a wide spectrum of suggestions for changing current reporting and management practices by all categories of market participants.

- *Greater transparency and accountability.*   Transparency is needed to ensure that information about existing conditions, decisions, and actions is made accessible, visible, and understandable to economic agents. Transparency contributes to the efficient allocation of resources by ensuring that market participants have sufficient information to identify and evaluate risks. Moreover, transparency can influence market expectations, thereby helping to stabilize markets during periods of uncertainty. Greater transparency is required from the private sector, national authorities, and international financial institutions. Disclosure of information should be timely, complete, and consistent. Particularly relevant is information about the international exposure of banks, institutional investors, and major corporations. Monetary authorities are required to publish information about their reserve positions (foreign-exchange liquidity position, including forward books) and on external indebtedness. International financial institutions are also encouraged to disclose their evaluations about the economic and financial policies and structures of member countries.

- *Greater reliance on standards of sound practices and codes of conduct.*   In addition to the principles for banking supervision and securities regulation, standards and policies that foster the development of stable and efficient financial systems need to be identified and introduced in a broad range of activities. Standards of sound practices to be applied by countries, banks, financial intermediaries and corporations should cover, *inter alia*, methods and coverage of official statistics on economic and financial developments, policy formulation and execution, accounting techniques and methods, corporate governance, and internal audit and controls.

5.1.2. Stronger financial regulation in industrial countries.   The G-7 recognize that for every "bad borrower" there is a "bad lender" and that situations of financial instability may arise because of inadequate evaluation of risks leading to an excessive extension of credit. Such excessive risk taking, combined with high degrees of leverage, can propagate and magnify the negative effect of tensions in banking and financial activities.

The G-7 identify three critical areas that should be addressed by industrial countries to rectify inadequacies and to close loopholes in the regulatory framework by

- Improving risk assessment and risk management, through increased supervisory oversight of risk-management practices and strengthened capital adequacy;
- Assessing the implications of the activity of highly leveraged institutions (HLI), such as hedge funds, particularly on market dynamics in general and in relations to emerging countries; and
- Evaluating the implications of the activity of offshore financial centers (OFC) as a potential source of financial instability and encouraging OFC to comply with international supervisory standards.

These areas are interconnected as highly leveraged institutions are almost by definition institutions devoted to conduct very risky business and are frequently located in offshore financial centers. The HLI category includes hedge funds but not exclusively: in fact, practically every international bank or securities house also runs its own internal hedge fund or undertakes similar risky activities in their "proprietary trading."

5.1.3. Strengthening macroeconomic policies and financial systems in emerging countries.
This is the most extensive chapter of the G-7 as it deals with the full spectrum of macroeconomic and financial policies of emerging countries. In addition to the general prescription of adopting sound monetary and fiscal policies, the report emphasizes a number of specific areas as deserving particular attention by emerging countries:

- *Choice of the exchange-rate regime.* While recognizing that there is no ideal regime for all countries and that different regimes may be suitable in different circumstances, the report stresses the point that stability depends on the exchange-rate regime being backed by consistent macroeconomic policies and supported by robust financial systems. This general advice is accompanied by two clear warnings: (1) there would be no "large-scale official financing for a country intervening heavily to support a particular exchange-rate level except where that level is judged sustainable and certain conditions have been met," and (2) the IMF should encourage countries to change their policies "in order to help avoid moves towards unsustainable positions." In substance, emerging countries are invited to adopt a floating exchange-rate regime, as fixed exchange rates are seen as an inducement to excessive foreign-currency borrowing by providing an implicit guarantee against exchange-rate risk.
- *Prudential supervision.* There is a firm commitment by the G-7 to work together with the relevant international financial institutions (IFIs) and international regulatory bodies to promote improved supervision of banking and financial systems. Emerging countries are invited to collaborate with the IMF and the World Bank in the field of financial-sector reforms and to make "rapid progress towards full compliance with existing international codes." In this context, the governments of emerging countries are invited to "narrow the scope of their guarantees of private obligations so as to make sure that creditors do not lend to private entities with the expectation that they will be protected from adverse outcomes."
- *Capital flows.* There is a clear commitment to review the "appropriate pace and sequencing of capital account liberalization" and to "further studying the benefits and costs of market-based prudential measures aimed at curbing excessive capital inflows, including those used by the Chilean authorities." This is a significant reversal from earlier positions of unqualified support for the principle of capital liberalization.[6] Such a new stance is also accompanied

by the strong call for the "IMF and other relevant institutions to cooperate with national authorities to create a better system for monitoring cross-border capital flows," with the aim "to verify the sustainability of debt structures, especially of foreign short-term exposures." This is an implicit admission that there has been some degree of complacency by the international community over the massive inflow of funds into emerging economies.

- *Debt management.* Emerging countries are invited to adopt best practices in the field of debt management elaborated in cooperation with relevant IFIs. Such practices include (1) greater reliance on long-term debt, if possible denominated in domestic currency; (2) removal of biases that encourage short-term private borrowing in foreign currencies (such as a fixed exchange-rate regime); (3) promotion of debt strategies that minimize exposure to liquidity and rollover risks rather than short-term borrowing costs; and (4) in primary producing countries, promotion of hedging of exposure to commodity prices volatility, through arrangements that provide greater contractual risksharing between debtors and creditors.

In substance, emerging countries are urged to adopt medium-term debt-management strategies and to rely to a greater extent on market techniques for risk management and sharing.

5.1.4. Improving crisis prevention and management and involving the private sector.
This is one of the most sensitive issues covered in the G-7 report. It envisages a framework for preventing crises without introducing moral hazard and for ensuring that, when debt crises occur, they are managed in an orderly and cooperative fashion, without the traumas normally associated with unilateral debt defaults. The key element of the framework is the involvement of private creditors in all aspects of debt-management strategies:

- *Crisis prevention.* The report recognizes that recourse to official financial assistance under certain conditions can play an important role in preventing crises and limiting the risk of contagion. However, the G-7 urge emerging countries to develop mechanisms for a more systematic dialogue with their main creditors and to use market-based tools aimed at preventing crises and facilitating adjustment to shocks. Innovative financial arrangements that are recommended include private contingent credit lines and debt instruments containing rollover options. Moreover, emerging countries are encouraged to "use collective action clauses in sovereign debt contracts, along with other provisions that facilitate creditor coordination and discourage disruptive legal action." More generally, debtor countries are urged to establish sound and efficient bankruptcy procedures and strong judicial systems to promote transparency, predictability, and equity in their insolvency regimes.
- *Crisis resolution.* The G-7 report outlines a framework for the orderly management of debt crises based on the principles that crisis resolution must

not undermine the commitment of countries to meet their obligations and that market discipline works only if creditors bear the consequences of the risks they take. The G-7 framework essentially establishes a link between the provision of official financial assistance and the commitment by debtor countries to obtain from private creditors new funds, the maintenance of exposure levels, or the restructuring of outstanding obligations. In exceptional circumstances where debt-service arrears occur, debtor countries are urged to seek a cooperative debt restructuring under the supervision of the IMF. If the policies to deal with the crisis are judged appropriate, the IMF may apply its policy of "lending into arrears" or authorize the introduction of capital or exchange controls.

5.1.5. Promoting social policies to protect the poor and most vulnerable elements of society. This chapter deals with the highly contentious issue of whether the strategies recommended by the international financial institutions to manage financial crises have aggravated the conditions of the underprivileged segments of society in emerging countries. The G-7 report is rather guarded in its analysis and recommendations but eventually recognizes that more attention is to be devoted, in adjustment programs sponsored by IFIs, to the need of maintaining adequate levels of social spending to shield, to some extent, the poor from the impact of crises. At the same time, there is a strong call for the elaboration of a code of good practices in social policies to be drafted by the United Nations and the main IFIs to which emerging countries should adhere in the formulation and implementation of social policies.

5.2. Organizational and institutional assets of IFA

The G-7 report devotes an important chapter to organizational and institutional issues: How many architects, masons, and bricklayers are required to build a stable and efficient international financial architecture? Who will supervise the construction site?

The explicit answer of the G-7 report is that the new IFA will imply a sort of general mobilization of all international financial institutions, regulatory agencies, and groupings of market participants. While the G-7 report places the traditional Bretton Woods institutions (the IMF and the World Bank) at the top of the pyramid of the IFA hierarchy, the Bank for International Settlements (BIS) (and its panoply of specialized committees on banking supervision, global financial system, and payments and settlement systems) and the Organization for Economic Cooperation and Development (OECD) are also assigned specific tasks in the drafting of codes of best practices in their respective fields of competence. A third layer of "mobilized" institutions includes official or semiofficial groupings such as the International Organization of Securities Commissions (IOSCO), the International Association of Insurance Supervisors (IAIS), and the International Accounting Standards Commission (IASC). In the layer of private groupings, a role is implicitly assigned to the International Institute of Finance (IIF), a body representing the interests of international commercial banks, and the International Security Market Association (ISMA).

The G-7 report, however, endorses or proposes new arrangements for dealing with the challenges of the global financial system. Three main changes are particularly relevant: the reform of the IMF Interim Committee, the creation of the Financial Stability Forum, and the creation of a new group for informal dialogue among the G-7 and a number of "systematically relevant countries" in the emerging world.

5.2.1. Reform of the IMF Interim Committee. The reform of the IMF Interim Committee is more a question of form than of substance. The Committee will retain its ministerial rank but will shed its "interim" nature to become a permanent body. With the name of International Monetary and Financial Committee (IMFC), it will become the key advisory body of the IMF and will have an enhanced status compared with that of the Development Committee. The deliberations of the IMFC will be prepared by ad-hoc meetings of deputies that will single out policy issues to submit to ministers for consideration. A more substantive reform of the Interim Committee, as proposed by its earlier chair, Carlo Azeglio Ciampi of Italy, did not receive unanimous support. According to the Ciampi proposal, the reformed Interim Committee should have built on its nature of IMF body with maximum representativeness to become the chief coordinator for all initiatives of relevance for the IMS.

5.2.2. Creation of the Financial Stability Forum. The creation of the Financial Stability Forum (FSF) provides an important forum for coordination of supervisory policies on the banking and financial systems of the G-7. In fact, it brings together around the same table representatives of finance ministries, bank supervisors, and financial regulators of the G-7 countries, plus representatives of the IMF, World Bank, the BIS, the OECD, and relevant groupings such as IOSCO and IAIS. The task of the FSF is to look after the section of international financial architecture that deals with strengthening financial supervision on the side of the creditor countries of the industrial world (see Section 5.1.2. above). The main novelty of the FSF is that government officials are now directly involved at an international level in dealing with issues of financial stability that, at domestic level, fall mainly under the responsibility of independent central banks.

5.2.3. Creation of a new international group for informal dialogue. The establishment of a new international group, called the Group of 20 (G-20: the G-7 countries, a representative of the European Union, a representative of the IMF and the World Bank, and 11 major emerging economies—Argentina, Australia, Brazil, China, India, Mexico, Russia, Saudi Arabia, South Africa, Korea, and Turkey), is one of the most controversial decisions taken by the G-7 and one likely to revive debates and quarrels about the ultimate goals of the major industrial countries, and of the United States in particular, regarding the institutional structure of the IMS. The main issues to be clarified are the implications of the mandate of the new Group for its relationships with the revamped IMFC. The communiqué issued on September 25, 1999, at the end of the last meeting of the ministers and governors of the G-7 reads as follows: "We propose to establish a new mechanism for informal dialogue in the framework of the Bretton Woods institutional system, to broaden the dialogue on key economic and financial policy issues among systematically significant economies and promote co-operation to achieve stable and sustainable world economic growth that benefits all." These indications seem to imply for the G-20 an intermediate ranking, just below the G-7 but above the IMFC. This is likely to raise problems as the IMFC is an official body of the IMF and, through its constituencies, represents directly or indirectly all 182 IMF members: it therefore enjoys a legitimacy and representativeness that is unparalleled. Although the IMF is used to receive "indications" from the G-7, its memberships might resent a similar supervisory role for a new group comprising a few emerging countries hand-picked by the G-7, which represent only themselves. Similar problems have arisen in connection with the work of the so-called G-22 (which had to increase its participants to 26 and later to 33), but that forum was clearly of a temporary nature and with a specific objective (to study international financial instability), while the G-20 is expected to be a permanent addition to the constellation of groupings and has a rather broad, if still vague, mandate.

6. A quick visit to the IFA construction site

Where do we stand on the international financial architecture? Is IFA still just a blueprint or a construction underway? The answer to these questions is mixed, as progress differs in the five building blocks of the IFA.

6.1. Transparency and best practices

In the field of transparency and best practices an impressive amount of work has been conducted by practically all relevant IFIs and international groupings. The IMF alone has implemented four major initiatives in the last two years: the General Data Dissemination Standard (GDDS) and the Special Data Dissemination Standard (SDDS) in the field of statistical data compilation and reporting (the latter standard applying to countries having or seeking access to international capital markets), the Code of Good Practices on Fiscal Transparency, and the Code of Good Practices on Transparency in Monetary and Financial Policies (setting standards of transparency for the procedures of policy formulation and execution). Under the hospitable roof of the BIS, the Basle Committee on Banking Supervision is actively promoting the adoption by emerging countries of its Core Principles on Banking Supervision. Moreover, the Committee on the Global Financial System is studying ways to improve disclosure by market participants, including a modal template of exposures and risk profile by institutions engaged in trading, investment, and lending activity. Also IOSCO and IAIS have established Core Principles for Supervision in their respective areas of responsibility. The OECD has recently approved Core Principles on Corporate Governance and is cooperating with the World Bank and other IFIs to encourage the broadest adoption by emerging and industrial countries.

This list does not pretend to be exhaustive or to give full credit to all the initiatives underway. It simply points to the fact that the process is now in the implementation phase, where it is essential for individual countries to take the necessary action to introduce the standards, the codes, and the practices into their domestic legislation. This can only be a lengthy and gradual process that will have to be monitored by all relevant partners. Adoption of the codes could be the subject of surveillance by the IMF and other international financial institutions in the context of consultations with member countries. Similarly, financial intermediaries could take into account in their lending decisions the borrower's attitude toward international standards and its record of implementation. For countries seeking access to organized capital markets, an "accreditation procedure" could be envisaged, whereby the relevant regulatory agencies would ascertain, possibly with the cooperation of major financial intermediaries, the compliance of the applicant with internationally agreed standards and practices.

6.2. Financial regulation in industrial countries

Regarding financial regulation in industrial countries, initiatives to strengthen and update the existing regulatory framework are well underway: at the Bank for International Settlements (BIS), International Organization of Securities Comissions (IOSCO), International Association of Insurance Supervisors (IAIS), the Joint Forum on Financial Conglomerates made up of the these institutions, and the newly established Financial Stability Forum. Of particular relevance is the revision of the capital accord undertaken by the BCBS to make it more sensitive to risk, including credit risk involved in lending to emerging countries and in short-term lending. Equally relevant is the work undertaken by the FSF on the activity of highly leveraged institutions and offshore centres and its implications for international financial stability. The FSF is also examining, within a broad framework of risk management, the role that could be played by measures to contain capital inflows.

Also in this area, while analysis and review are well underway, implementation will be left to individual countries. This should not pose major problems as the regulatory frameworks in industrial countries are already in place and are broadly fit to incorporate the proposed changes. However, a major issue may arise regarding the division of responsibilities among government agencies and independent authorities in the broad area of financial-stability supervision. Different institutional arrangements are in force in the major industrial countries, and the issue is under review in many of them. The model that the G-7 governments seem to propose, as in the case of the FSF, is one in which regulatory agencies and authorities, independent or not, are all participating in a coordination process conducted by government officials. The implications that this model for international supervision may have for the organization of domestic supervision may be far-reaching and would have to be carefully evaluated by each individual country.

6.3. Prescriptions for emerging countries

The numerous prescriptions for emerging countries are of a more general nature, and their implementation will be realized in the context of the ongoing policy dialogue with the IMF, the World Bank, and other relevant international financial institutions. The overall impression is that the general principles outlined in the G-7 report concerning macro policies, exchange-rate regimes, capital account liberalization, and financial systems will be implemented on a case-by-case basis taking into account the particular economic and structural circumstances of each country. The pace of implementation is therefore likely to differ from country to country. In most cases, the required changes constitute a radical reform involving a broad spectrum of policies and institutions. The pressure for reform that can be brought to bear by the IMF or the World Bank and by foreign lenders has obvious limitations that can be overcome only through a strong and widespread political consensus in the countries themselves. In the recent episodes of financial crises in Asia, some structural reforms have been rapidly introduced in a member of countries under the pressure of events, but the pace of implementation slowed down as soon as macroeconomic and financial conditions improved.

Under these circumstances it is difficult to identify *ex ante* what would be the impact of such individual actions at the level of the IMS—for instance, in a crucial area such as the choice of the exchange-rate regime. At this stage, the vague prescription by the G-7 could result in both a move toward freely floating exchange rates and greater reliance on currency-board arrangements involving rigid links with one of the key reserve currencies. Moreover, it is not obvious *ex ante* that an exchange-rate regime polarized around such "corner solutions" would be more stable than the current one. This indetermination is unfortunate because emerging countries have good justifications for pegging their currencies (the "fear of floating" analyzed by Calvo and Reinhart, 1999) but have also suffered from using the "wrong peg" (for example, an appreciating dollar). The only way to deal with this predicament is to address the issue of the choice of the exchange-rate regime for emerging countries in the broader context involving arrangements for the key reserve currencies (on this point, see Section 8 below).

6.4. Crisis prevention and resolution

In the field of crisis prevention and resolution, the progress is also mixed. A major step forward in crisis prevention was the establishment in April 1999, by the IMF, of a new instrument, the contingent credit lines (CCL), designed to protect emerging countries in good economic and financial standing from the contagion of financial-market turbulence. The establishment of the CCL has somewhat papered over the deep differences of views among the G-7. Some countries saw it as a dangerous further step toward the establishment of a formal lender-of-last-resort function in the IMF, which could only foster moral hazard in international financial activities.[7] Other countries felt that the CCL was an essential ingredient of the strategy to contain financial instability. In the end, the CCL has been saddled with so many constraints and preconditions that it may well remain unutilized in its present form.

On insolvency regimes, work has been done by the United Nations Commission on International Trade Law (UNCITRAL), which has adopted a model law on the treatment of cross-border insolvencies. The World Bank is assisting emerging countries in the long-run effort to introduce bankruptcy laws and courts.

Various difficulties are hampering progress regarding the introduction in sovereign bond contracts of clauses that would facilitate cooperative solutions in the case of debt problems (the so-called collective action clauses). Here the main obstacle is that no debtor likes the idea of including in its liabilities the hint that these may not be honored in full. It is feared that such clauses may increase the risk premium that borrowers have to pay to raise funds in international capital markets. Although some emerging countries have included such clauses in their bond issues without any visible increase in risk premia, it has been suggested that the widespread adoption of this technique would come about only if industrial countries took the initiative of including them in their own debt instruments. This idea has plunged the proposal into a political quagmire from which it may never resurface.[8] The improved situation of many emerging countries in 1999 has probably reduced the urgency of seeking new complex legal formulas, while at the same time private-sector lenders have found "troubling" certain proposals to involve them in involuntary debt-restructuring exercises.[9] Be that as it may, the recent episode of default by Ecuador on its Brady-bond obligations is just a reminder that the emerging countries' crisis is not really over yet.

6.5. Policies to protect the poor

The adoption of policies to protect the poor in case of financial crises is still in its early stage. The World Bank has taken the lead in this field, developing in April 1999 a set of Principles and Good Practices in Social Policy with the aim of identifying and managing the social dimension of crises; the IMF has just renamed its unattractive Enhanced Structural Adjustment Facility (ESAF) with the more captivating title of Poverty Reduction and Growth Facility, signaling an important shift of emphasis toward the achievement of social objectives in IMF-supported programs. Both institutions are deeply committed to achieve significant results in this field and to appear in fundamental agreement with each other (after some difference of views on the appropriate strategy to deal with debt crises attracted widespread attention by analysts and economists). A major debt-reduction initiative for the heavily indebted poor countries (HIPC), promoted by the G-7 at their Cologne Summit in June 1999, was finally endorsed on the occasion of the recent annual meeting of the IMF and the World Bank.

Despite this new sentiment, radical changes in the prevailing approach to dealing with developing countries' macroeconomic adjustment and structural reforms by the Bretton Woods institutions are not be expected in the short run, while the degree of overlapping of responsibilities of the Fund and the Bank is likely to increase in some areas, with potential negative implications for program implementation.

7. Has the IFA reformed the IMS?

The reaction of public opinion to the G-7's work on the international financial architecture has been on the whole positive. While the man and the woman in the street probably would find it difficult to follow this highly technical debate and might have been annoyed by the proliferation of new committees and groups, economists and market participants have appreciated the pragmatism and the concreteness of the exercise. In fact, the G-7 have carefully stayed away from the most radical proposals formulated by a wide spectrum of concerned people, ranging from market participants such as George Soros and Henry Kaufman, to former officials like Fred Bergsten and Paul Volker, to academic economists like Allan Meltzer and Charles Calomiris.[10]

The reason for G-7 moderation was very well explained by Barry Eichengreen in an article published by the *Financial Times* on February 2, 1999: "However compelling the argument that global financial markets require a global financial regulator, global bankruptcy court, global money, and a global central bank, realism requires acknowledging that national governments are not prepared to turn over significant additional powers to a super-International Monetary Fund. Europe has created a single currency and a European Central Bank only after half a century of hard slog. It is fantastic to think that this process could be replicated on a global scale in a few years."

A broad consensus with the G-7 approach, albeit with significant variations, is expressed in recent works by Barry Eichengreen (1999) and Alan Blinder (1999) and in a report by an independent task force coordinated by Morris Goldstein (1999) under the aegis of the Council on Foreign Relations. In particular, there seems to be full agreement in these three analyses on the need for emerging countries to adopt floating exchange-rate regimes, to rely less on foreign-currency borrowing, and to be extremely cautious about capital-account liberalization (which could imply using controls on capital inflows). Regarding financial crises, there is broad support for the idea that prevention is better than cure and for a cooperative approach to crisis management. In this context, the adoption of collective-action clauses in bond contracts is generally seen as a very good idea, which is somewhat surprising given the fact that such a proposal seems to have lost its appeal in both official and private circles. No one questions that the IMF and the World Bank would continue to play a key role, although the Goldstein report advocates a "refocusing of the IMF and the World Bank," and Blinder maintains that "austerity is not always the right medicine" (which is presumably a criticism of the IMF approach). Again, differing views are expressed about the need for additional financial assistance to forestall situations of crisis or to limit contagion. Eichengreen and Blinder seem more open on this issue, while the Goldstein report flatly states that as regards IMF lending "less will do more."

All three sources seem to attach little importance to transparency as a tool for removing market imperfections and information asymmetries. For example, Blinder (1999, p. 58) notes that "although transparency—which is the current rage—is all to the good, no one should expect it to accomplish very much in the way of crisis prevention. Bubbles form and burst even in extremely transparent markets like the New York Stock Exchange." Eichengreen (1999, p. 84) similarly believes that "too much should not be expected of these initiatives. Unavoidably, information asymmetries will remain."

The issue of whether the proposed changes in the international financial architecture would amount to a meaningful reform of the international monetary system is not explicitly addressed in these works. The Goldstein report does include, however, a "dissenting view," signed by a minority of the members of the task force (which includes people like Fred Bergsten, George Soros, and Paul Volker), where it is firmly stated that "Our point is that 'reforming the international financial architecture' without reforming the currency regime is like watching *Hamlet* without the Prince. The international monetary system will continue to be ineffective and crisis prone until that crucial centrepiece of its operation is thoroughly revamped. We urge the G-3 countries to adopt some variant of target zones in the near future."

Such a minority view has been shared in another report, commissioned by the Counseil d'Analyse Economique of the French Government to Bergsten, Davanne, and Jacquet (1999), where it is proposed to manage the relationships among the three main currencies—the dollar, the euro, and the yen—through a mechanism of reinforced surveillance based on "soft" or "mute" target zones for the reciprocal exchange rates. A similar proposal had been made by Pisani-Ferry and Coeuré (1999), who outlined a framework for the early detection of exchange-rate misalignments among the three key currencies and for coordinated policy response by the G-7 countries.

This survey of the immediate reactions to the G-7 initiatives on IFA does not pretend to be exhaustive, but I believe it contains all the main schools of thought on the matter. My own assessment of IFA falls within the range of opinions outlined above. I believe however that the broad issue of how to orient toward monetary and financial stability the present market-led system has not yet been properly addressed.

8.   Two missing pillars

The new international financial architecture does not represent a fundamental change in the way the current market-led international monetary system operates. The level of exchange rates, the creation and distribution of international liquidity, and the timing and the modalities of the adjustment process would still be dictated by market forces, even if all of the new IFA proposals were to be adopted. This does not mean that the proposed changes are useless; they are not. In fact, in most cases they represent necessary improvements that will have beneficial effects on the working of international financial markets. But their implementation will require a long time and a very tight coordination among all the numerous actors that have been summoned on the stage of IFA. Moreover, it is likely that, even in conditions of greater transparency, strengthened financial systems and improved risk-management techniques, the pressure of competition among intermediaries may still bring about the excessive credit expansions followed by sudden credit contractions that are at the root of the boom and bust cycles that have characterized the evolution of the international monetary and financial system since the emergence of globalization.

8.1.   A first missing pillar

In this respect, a first missing pillar in the current reform efforts is a framework for managing the interdependence among the macroeconomic policies of the global powers (United States, European Union, and Japan) and the working of international financial markets. The new IFA, while it assigns to the G-7 the role of *de facto* directorate of the IMS, does not foresee any form of policy coordination among the members of the G-7 themselves to deal with the international repercussions of their domestic policies, in line with internationally agreed objectives of promoting noninflationary growth and financial stability. From this point of view, the proposed changes do not modify in any significant way the "house-in-order" model of international relations, whereby all major countries pursue their uncoordinated (and therefore possibly inconsistent) domestic-policy objectives, leaving to exchange-rate flexibility the task of reconciling *ex post* any *ex ante* policy inconsistency. Moreover, even with the proposed improvements in the institutions and rules that govern the world's financial system, market participants would still continue to take advantage of any profit opportunity that may be opened by policy inconsistencies or by policy signals of the major industrial countries, setting in motion trends in financial flows that may be difficult to predict. To clarify the point, a few examples may be drawn from recent financial history:

- The inclusion of Russia in the G-7 in 1995 (since renamed the G-8) and the entry of Mexico (in 1994) and Korea (in 1996) in the OECD were decisions motivated by foreign-policy or security considerations, but they have been interpreted by financial markets as signals of a higher creditworthiness for these countries (and possibly as an implicit bail-out guarantee) leading to massive capital inflows;

- The low-interest-rate policy together with the weak-yen policy adopted by the Bank of Japan since 1995 was necessary to counter a domestic recession but has turned out to be an extremely cheap source of external financing for massive investment in the U.S. stock market and large lending to emerging countries in Asia;

- The passive acceptance by the G-7 of a sharp reversal of the yen decline in early 1999, despite its negative repercussions on the recovery of the Japanese economy, has led market participants to bet on the further appreciation of the yen as this was considered to be consistent with the U.S. objective of reducing the trade deficit with Japan.[11]

The list could be longer and include earlier examples of aberrant market reactions to policy actions and signals drawn from the experience of the EMS.[12] But the general point is clear: the G-7 countries should accept the "fact of life" that their foreign and economic policy measures or statements are inevitably going to have market implications particularly regarding the level of exchange rates and the creation and distribution of international liquidity. If such effects are undesired, the G-7 should stand ready to "intervene"—that is, take the appropriate policy measures or make the appropriate policy statement, clearly expressing the negative judgment of the major countries on market trends and practices. Such measures would typically include coordinated exchange-market interventions but also other type of actions, including credible statements of future policy response in the monetary, fiscal, or regulatory fields.

The question of whether such "interventions" would be effective in influencing market trends has been analyzed by economists in academia and in official institutions (national and international), mostly with reference to the foreign-exchange market, since the inception of the floating exchange-rate regime in the mid-1970s. The results of the analyses have not succeeded in bringing about a consensus. Deep divisions persist among those who believe that tampering with the working of market forces is wrong and that interventions are ineffective and those who believe that markets need a guidance and that interventions are effective. This is not surprising, given the huge size of the world foreign-exchange markets, the large number of dealers involved, and the attendant difficulties of making unambiguous econometric tests of the impact of foreign-exchange interventions.[13]

In light of these mixed analyses, there has been a widespread reluctance in official circles to attempt to influence market trends because of the fear that monetary authorities would "lose face" if markets failed to comply. The reluctance has been particularly strong in the case of foreign-exchange intervention, based on the rather obvious consideration that official reserves of central banks are much smaller than the size of foreign-exchange markets. But this is not the crux of the matter: no one can expect miraculous and immediate effects from actions involving symbolic amounts of money. What counts is the policy signal that the authorities are broadcasting and that the markets would then process and evaluate as part of their continuous reassessment of risks and returns. In fact, a careful examination of the experience of the last two decades shows that, when certain conditions are met, monetary authorities can indeed influence market trends. The following episodes are relevant:

• The correction of the overvaluation of the U.S. dollar in 1985 and the stabilization of the U.S. dollar in 1986 and 1987, through coordinated foreign-exchange market interventions by the G-5 and G-7;
• The maintenance of the French franc and German mark parity in the EMS in 1992 to 1994 through a combination of coordinated interventions, official supporting statements, and widening of fluctuation margins in the exchange-rate mechanism;
• The correction of the overvaluation of the yen to dollar exchange rate in 1995 through G-7 official statements followed by coordinated intervention;
• The maintenance of currency-board arrangements by Hong Kong and Argentina and the G-7 support to China's exchange-rate policy during the financial crisis of 1997 to 1999; and
• The stabilization of the price of gold in September 1999 following an official policy statement by 15 European central banks.

The detailed analysis of each episode would require a separate paper. However, some conclusions may be drawn from the main features of the intervention strategies, which are generally well known. The conditions under which these policy actions were successful in influencing market trends within a reasonable period of time are the following: the action was either taken in the context of a coordinated effort involving all the countries and authorities concerned or was taken in application of formal institutional arrangements; the action was part of a consistent set of stability-oriented policies; the strategy adopted was clearly and officially explained to the markets to emphasize the consistency between objectives and policy measures and the absence of policy dilemmas; the active participation of central banks was instrumental in fostering the perception by the markets of the noninflationary nature of the action and of its time-consistency.

These ingredients could be used in the context of a "framework for enhanced surveillance"[14] by the G-7 in conjunction with the IMF and explicitly extended to cover both the exchange-rate relationships among the major currencies and the creation and distribution of international liquidity.[15] The Framework does not require the establishment of target zones for exchange rates, which could become a target for speculative attacks, but implies that the G-7, with the assistance of the IMF, should have a view about the appropriateness of exchange rates and should be able to detect the emergence of currency misalignments. The

Framework should also be used to monitor capital flows to emerging countries, with the assistance of the IMF, the World Bank, the BIS, and the representatives of major financial intermediaries and determine whether there is a need for action, including in the regulatory area, to contain excessively risky lending. The action taken in the context of the Framework should meet the conditions listed above. Governments and central banks should take these conditions seriously: markets can be enrolled to support ambitious objectives but cannot be fooled for long. If policy inconsistencies materialize and are not quickly corrected, markets would react severely and no official intervention or statement could influence its course.

8.2. A second missing pillar

A second missing pillar in the IFA project is a market-oriented approach to the financing of the IMF. The IMF obtains its resources through the quota subscriptions of its members. In return, it creates international liquidity as IMF positions are held in the official reserves of creditor member countries. The IMF is also empowered to create international liquidity *ex nihilo* through the issue of Special Drawing Rights (SDR). These features, which reflect concerns about a possible shortage of international liquidity that where widely shared in the 1960s, are no longer needed in the present market-led international monetary system. In fact, what is now feared is that the IMF may create too much international money or become an international lender of last resort, entailing an unacceptable moral hazard. This has resulted in the IMF being systematically denied adequate resources, with replenishments lagging behind recognized liquidity needs.

In a M-IMS, where the markets can always create sufficient liquidity to finance a creditworthy borrower, there is no need for an official source of money creation. The IMF could play a more effective role in recycling existing liquidity, which it could raise in international capital markets.[16] Indeed, the very act of IMF borrowing in the market to tackle an international financial crisis would send an immediate stabilizing signal to markets with a positive impact on expectations. It would make clear that the IMF had the means to prevent a crisis situation in an individual country from degenerating into a systemic instability. A recent study by Lerrick (1999) for the Bretton Woods Committee argues along similar lines and suggests that IMF borrowing in the market could be obtained in large amounts at attractive interest rates.

9. A concluding comment

An international monetary arrangement that would involve, along with the new international financial architecture, the two pillars indicated above would go a long way toward a true reform of the current market-led international monetary system. The reformed system would in fact be "co-managed" by the policy coordination Framework of the major industrial countries and by the market forces. It would entail a more transparent and cooperative relationship between G-7 monetary authorities, the main international financial institutions, and the major financial intermediaries. Under such new system, cases of exchange-rate and financial instability could still materialize, but it would be more difficult for misunderstandings to distort protractedly financial flows and exchange-rate trends; it would be easier for policy inconsistencies to be identified and corrected.

What are the chances that the major countries would agree to include the two missing pillars in their reform efforts? The chances are very small indeed, as the political motivations that are behind the continuing reliance on the house-in-order approach are still very strong.

Nevertheless, the experience of the 1990s shows that the frequency and intensity of financial crises are increasing and that the economic and social costs of each episode are high. Elected governments in major industrial countries should thus have an interest in protecting their citizens from the impact of financial crises and in dispelling the idea that ruthless and uncontrollable markets can determine the fate of currencies, economic systems, and countries. The growing intensity of the opposition voiced by representatives of the "civil society" to the very concept of globalization is an indication that these are politically relevant issues of an urgent nature. If, to tackle them, some degree of policy coordination and some cooperative attitude toward the markets is required, this may be a worthwhile price to pay.

Appendix: List of abbreviations

BCBS	Basle Committee on Banking Supervision
BIS	Bank for International Settlements
CCL	contingent credit line
EMS	European Monetary System
EMU	European Economic and Monetary Union
ESAF	Enhanced Structural Adjustment Facility
EU	European Union
FSF	Financial Stability Forum
GAB	general arrangements to borrow
GDDS	General Data Dissemination Standard
G-IMS	government-led international monetary system
G-5	Group of Five (France, Germany, Japan, the United Kingdom, the United States)
G-7	Group of Seven (G-5 plus Canada and Italy)
G-10	Group of 10 (G-7 plus Belgium, the Netherlands, Sweden, Switzerland)
G-20	Group of 20 (G-7, a representative of the European Union, a representative of the IMF and World Bank, and II major emerging

	economies—Argentina, Australia, Brazil, China, India, Mexico, Russia, Saudi Arabia, South Africa, Korea and Turkey)
HIPC	heavily indebted poor countries
HLI	highly leveraged institution
IAIS	International Association of Insurance Supervisors
IASC	International Accounting Standards Commission
IFA	international financial architecture
IFI	international financial institution
IIF	International Institute of Finance
IMF	International Monetary Fund
IMFC	International Monetary and Financial Committee
IMS	International Monetary System
IOSCO	International Organization of Securities Commissions
ISMA	International Security Market Association
M-IMS	market-led international monetary system
NAB	new arrangements to borrow
OECD	Organization for Economic Cooperation and Development
OFC	offshore financial center
SDDS	Special Data Dissemination Standard
SDR	special drawing rights
UNCITRAL	United Nations Commission on International Trade Law
U.S.	United States

Notes

1. For a more detailed survey of these issues, see Salvatore (1998).
2. The degree of formalization of such codes is different under the two systems: under Bretton Woods, the codes were derived from a treaty ratified by the member states of IMF; under the present market-led international monetary system, the codes are informal and derived by prevailing market practices as accepted by intermediaries and policy makers.
3. The assumption that the current market-led international monetary system is instability-prone because financial intermediaries make profits only when markets are volatile and unstable is not to be taken seriously. It reflects what one might call a "dealing-room" approach where a very narrow time horizon (usually one day) is taken into consideration to determine profits and losses. In a longer-term perspective, and in the context of globalization where profit margins are squeezed by competitive pressures, financial instability can be expected to affect negatively the profitability of intermediaries as it increases the probability of losses and the cost of hedging.
4. These events have been subject of countless books and articles: one of the best is that of Solomon (1982). The position of the U.S. administration and Congress on exchange rates is analyzed in detail by Saccomanni (1988).
5. The G-22 set up three working groups to study issues related to transparency and disclosure, the strengthening of financial systems, and the management of financial crises. The findings of the working groups are summarized in G-22 (1998).
6. A balanced survey of the emerging countries' experience in this difficult area is conducted by Williamson and Mahar (1998).
7. The analytical pitfalls of the concept of international lender of last resort have been clearly exposed by Giannini (1999).

8. This is pity because the proposal, initially put forward three years ago in a G-10 Deputies Report (1996) and subsequently analyzed in greater detail by the G-22 (1998), would probably help reducing the risk premium paid by emerging countries precisely because it reduces the risk of protracted litigation in cases of debt restructuring.
9. On this point, see Institute of International Finance (1999).
10. All these proposals are described in Eichengreen (1999).
11. On the trade and financial issues underlying the dollar and yen evolution, see McKinnon and Ohno (1997) and McKinnon (1999), where the "syndrome of the ever-higher yen" is analyzed.
12. It is sufficient to recall that the approval of the Maastricht Treaty in 1991 was taken by the market as an indication of immediate convergence of bond yields in the EU, setting in motion a huge volume of "convergence trades," which had subsequently to be unwound as various types of obstacles, political and economic, materialized in the EMU process.
13. To provide a summary of the literature in this area, even a brief one, would go beyond the scope of this article. Suffice it to say that in cases where the tests pointed to the ineffectiveness of interventions, a very brief time horizon had been chosen to identify the impact. By contrast, tests pointing to the effectiveness of intervention had generally adopted longer time horizons in other to allow for a pass-through of the impact. On this issue, see Jurgensen (1983), Dominguez and Frankel (1993), Catte, Galli, and Rebecchini (1994), and Levy and Pericoli (1999).
14. The institutional features of the "framework" do not need to be spelled out at this stage. There is a wide spectrum of institutional arrangements experimented in the field of monetary and financial cooperation from which a model framework could be shaped.
15. In making this proposal I have taken into account the conclusions reached in the context of the first conference on this matter organized by the Associazione Guido Carli (see Fratianni, Salvatore, and Savona, 1998).
16. A proposal in this sense was formulated by the Italian government in 1995. On this issue, see Padoa-Schioppa and Saccomanni (1996).

References

Bergsten, F., O. Davanne, and P. Jacquet (1999) "Pour une Gestion Conjointe de la Flexibilité des Changes." In Conseil d'Analyse Économique, *Architecture Financière Internationale*. Paris: La Documentation Française, 9–54.

Blinder, A.S. (1999) "Eight Steps to a New Financial Order." *Foreign Affairs* (September-October): 50–63.

Calvo, G. and C. Reinhart (1999) "The Balance Between Adjustment and Financing." Paper prepared for the IMF Conference on Key Issues in Reform of the International Monetary and Financial System, Washington, DC, May.

Catte, P., G. Galli, and S. Rebecchini (1994) "Concerted Interventions and the Dollar: An Analysis of Daily Data." In P.B. Kenen, F. Papadia, and F. Saccomanni (eds.), *The International Monetary System*. Cambridge: Cambridge University Press, 201–239.

Dominguez, K.M. and J.A. Frankel (1993) *Does Foreign-Exchange Intervention Work?* Washington, DC: Institute for International Economics.

Eichengreen, B. (1999) *Toward a New International Financial Architecture: A Practical Post-Asia Agenda*. Washington, DC: Institute for International Economics.

Fazio, A. (1998) "The International Monetary System." *Open Economies Review* (Special Supplement) 9:701–708.

Fratianni, M., D. Salvatore, and P. Savona (1998) "Ideas for the Future of the International Monetary System: Conclusions and Remarks." *Open Economies Review* (Special Supplement) 9:689–700.

G-7 (1999) *Report on Strengthening the International Financial Architecture*.

G-10 Deputies (1993) *Report on the International Capital Movements and Foreign Exchange Markets*. Basle: Bank for International Settlements.

G-10 Deputies (1996) *Report on the Resolution of Sovereign Liquidity Crises*. Basle: Bank for International Settlements.

G-22 (1998) *Reports on the International Financial Architecture*: (1) *Report of the Working Group on Transparency and Accountability*; (2) *Report of the Working Group Strengthening Financial System*; (3) *Report of the Working Group on International Financial Crises*. Basle: Bank for International Settlements. http://www.bis.org.

Giannini, C. (1999) "Enemy of None but a Common Friend of All? An International Perspective on the Lender-of-Last-Resort Function." *Essays in International Finance*. Princeton University, 214.

Goldstein, M. (ed.) (1999) *Safeguarding Prosperity in a Global Financial System: The Future International Financial Architecture Report of an Independent Task Force*. Sponsored by the Council on Foreign Relations. Washington, DC: Institute for International Economics.

Institute of International Finance (1999) *Letter of Managing Director to the Chairman of the Interim Committee*. September 16. http://www.iif.com.

Jurgensen, P. (1983) *Report of the Working Group on Exchange Market Intervention*. Paris: La Documentation Française.

Kenen, P.B., F. Papadia, and F. Saccomanni (eds.) (1994) *The International Monetary System*. Cambridge: Cambridge University Press, 1–15.

Kindleberger, C.P. (1978) *Manias, Panics and Crashes: A History of Financial Crises*. New York: Basic Books.

Lerrick, A. (1999) *Private-Sector Financing for the IMF: Now Part of an Optimal Funding Mix*. Washington, DC: Bretton Woods Committee, April.

Levy, A. and M. Pericoli (1999) "Episodes of Concerted Intervention in 1993–1998: Some Stylised Facts." Mimeo, Research Department of the Banca d'Italia, Rome.

McKinnon, R. (1999) "Wading in the Yen Trap." *The Economist*, July 24.

McKinnon, R. and K. Ohno (1997) *Dollar and Yen: Resolving Economic Conflict Between the United States and Japan*. Cambridge: MIT Press.

Padoa-Schioppa, T. and F. Saccomanni (1994) "Managing a Market-Led Global Financial System." In P.B. Kenen (ed.), *Managing the World Economy: Fifty Years After Bretton Woods*. Washington, DC: Institute for International Economics, 235–268.

Padoa-Schioppa, T. and F. Saccomanni (1996) "What Role for the SDR in a Market-Led International Monetary System?" In M. Mussa, J.M. Boughton, and P. Isard P. (eds.), *The Future of the SDR in Light of Changes in the International Financial System*. Washington DC: IMF, 378–386.

Pisani-Ferry, J. and B. Coeuré (1999) "The Exchange-Rate Regime Among Major Currencies." Paper prepared for the IMF Conference on Key Issues in Reform of the International Monetary and Financial System, Washington, DC, May 28–29.

Saccomanni, F. (1988) "On Multilateral Surveillance." In Paolo Guerrieri and P.C. Padoan (eds.), *The Political Economy of International Cooperation*. London: Croom Helm, 58–86.

Salvatore, D. (1998) "International Monetary and Financial Arrangements: Present and Future." *Open Economies Review* (Special Supplement) 9:375–416.

Solomon, R. (1982) *The International Monetary System: 1945–1981*. New York.

Williamson, J. and M. Mahar (1998) "A Survey of Financial Liberalization." *Essays in International Finance*. Princeton University, 211.

Open economies review **11:S1** 43–61 (2000)
© 2000 *Kluwer Academic Publishers. Printed in The Netherlands.*

Capital Flows, Exchange Rates, and the New International Financial Architecture: Six Financial Crises in Search of a Generic Explanation

ROBERT Z. ALIBER
University of Chicago, Chicago, Illinois

Keywords: Bretton Woods, exchange-rate regimes, capital flows, market failure, international monetary system, international financial architecture

JEL Classification Numbers: F33, F34

Abstract

Exchange-rate history can be divided into two periods: the Bretton Woods period and the period of floating exchange rates since the early 1970s. In this second period, financial crises and the roles played by institutions, rules, and commitments in international finance have been of central importance. Many proposals for changing the international financial architecture have been presented to reduce the likelihood of crises, but the source of the problem is in variable capital flows and the floating exchange-rate system. Based on six major financial crises of the last 25 years, the wide range in movements in the exchange rate, which might also be inferred from differences in national inflation rates, reflects changes in the ex-ante cross-border capital flows. As long as currencies are floating, economic conditions among countries are likely to be more variable and diverse: the greater variability in economic conditions suggests greater variability in capital flows.

Introduction

The financial crisis that began with the debacle in the Mexican peso in the last several months of 1994 and then continued with the sharp depreciation of the Thai baht, the Korean won, and the Brazilian real has raised questions about the adequacy of international monetary arrangements and the role of the International Monetary Fund (IMF). It also brought forth numerous proposals for reform under the buzzword of the *new international financial architecture*. The mai-tai effect has followed the tequila effect.

One aspect of these events has been the severe impact of the sharp depreciation of currencies on the solvency of firms and banks in the capital-importing countries. Another aspect has been the relation of currency depreciation in these various foreign countries. The cliché about falling dominoes has been resurrected, and terms like *the flight to quality, the contagion effect*, and *competitive exchange-rate depreciation* have been applied to market developments.

Another feature of these events has been the extensive overshooting of currency values: the Korean won traded at 900 won to the U.S. dollar prior to the crisis and then depreciated to 1800; since then the won has appreciated to 1200 won. Similar patterns are evident in most of the currencies in Southeast Asia, although the rebounds of these other currencies have not been as extensive as in Korea.

The crisis led to a proposal for an increase in the capital of the International Monetary Fund. About the same time, questions were raised about its policies, the competence of its management, and the fit between its activities and those of the World Bank.

A variety of proposals have been developed by national governments, various committees, and other observers to cope with these developments. The situation is somewhat remindful of the second half of the 1960s when there was a plethora of plans to resolve the *Triffin paradox*—namely, whether the structure of payment arrangements permitted various foreign countries to achieve their international reserve targets without forcing the United States to incur persistent payment deficits.

But there are major differences. One is that in the 1960s there was almost universal agreement on the definition of the problem (even if there was far less agreement on the solutions), whereas there seems little if any agreement today on the identification of the problem that merits institutional reform. Thirty years ago there was a grand debate on international monetary reform; now there is little evidence of such a debate. The second difference is that most of the earlier plans were developed by academicians, while many of those in the international financial establishment initially resisted the identification of the problem. Now, in contrast, many of the proposals have originated in national capitals; very few academicians are participating in the discussion.

The range of proposals for the new financial architecture range from taxes on capital movements to the conversion of the International Monetary Fund into an international central bank along the lines suggested by Keynes at Bretton Woods.

It is somewhat ironic that few of those at Bretton Woods in the 1940s would recognize the institution that they designed. Their focus had been to devise a set of rules to ensure that changes in currency values would be orderly to sharply reduce the likelihood of changes in exchange rates that might be construed as beggar-thy-neighbor policies comparable to those that they believed characterized the interwar period. The initiative toward a formal set of rules on exchange rates reflected U.S. concern that as the largest country in the system the United States had to be concerned about the free-rider tendency of some other countries that might manage their currency values to enhance domestic employment. This view about the exchange-rate component of the IMF system appears to have been accepted without much debate at Bretton Woods. Instead, the debate focused on the role of the Fund as a source of credit and whether the Fund would have its own currency and unit of account or whether instead the Fund would manage a pool of member-country currencies. The credit role of the Fund was a necessary arrangement to induce countries to accept constraints on the way they might manage the foreign-exchange values of their currencies.

The irony is that the Fund's involvement with systemic issues like the exchange-rate arrangement has been ignored by its management for the last 20 years. The institution has evolved into another foreign aid agency for the Polands and the Indonesias of the world. Each crisis appears to provide the opportunity to ask for more money and new facilities.

If a poll were taken of economists and officials in Washington about the merits of the Bretton Woods agreements, most would approve of the role of the IMF as a source of credit and technical advice even though most would reject the premise that led to the establishment of the Bretton Woods system—namely, the desirability of a treaty-based system to regulate the management of the currency values of the member countries.

The exchange-rate history of the post–World War II years breaks nicely into two periods: the Bretton Woods period of pegged exchange rates of the 1950s and the 1960s and the period of floating exchange rates since the early 1970s. While the adoption of the system of floating exchange rates was facilitated by arguments advanced by a most distinguished group of economists, the move almost certainly was inevitable given the differences both in the U.S. and German inflation rates and what were deemed acceptable rates of inflation in Washington and in Frankfurt.

The 25-plus years since the move off parities for national currencies is the most extensive ever with floating exchange rates, as measured by both the length of the period and the number of countries that have permitted their currencies to float. The data on national inflation rates and movements in exchange rates do not confirm most of the economic arguments advanced by the proponents of floating exchange rates in the 1950s and the 1960s. Instead, the observations about "destabilizing speculation" that Nurkse used to characterize the movement of exchange rates in the interwar period could be applied to describe these movements in the last 25 years, although now the terms used are *overshooting* and *vicious and virtuous circle*.

This article appraises several of the proposals for the new financial architecture after an identification of the source of the problem that needs fixing. Section 1 is a synopsis of the international monetary developments of the last 50 years and especially of the period since the breakdown of the Bretton Woods system of pegged exchange rates. Section 2 examines the scope of the changes in both exchange rates and changes in trade balances and raises the question of market failure. Two themes introduce this section: currency volatility and the value of foreign investment. The recent concern about the shortcomings of the international monetary arrangements highlights the impacts on the foreign-currency values of the capital-importing countries when the volume of capital flows declines sharply or when the direction of these flows is reversed.

Section 3 of the article first reviews the roles of institutions, rules, and commitments in international finance and then summarizes the variety of proposals for changing the international financial architecture. One set of proposals involves arrangements that would deter international capital flows; the *Tobin tax* might be the generic term. The motive for this set of proposals is to reduce the likelihood of crises. A second set of proposals would enhance the information available to the various participants involved in international capital flows. The presumption is that the source of the problem is that the borrowers and the lenders, but primarily the lenders, get into difficulty because the information set is incomplete; reserves may be overstated, and indebtedness often is underestimated. The third set of proposals includes those that would enable the borrowers to more effectively cope with the variability of these flows. Section 4 of the article provides my conclusions.

1. A synopsis of international monetary developments: 1950 to 2000

A review of economists' views about the contemporary international monetary events is a humbling experience. One of the dominant views of the late 1940s and throughout the 1950s was that the dollar shortage would be a persistent feature of postwar economic life. There were two elements in the argument: one was that productivity in the United States would remain significantly higher than productivity in most other industrial countries, and the second was that the United States would be more successful than most of these countries in achieving a low inflation rate. Books about the dollar shortage continued to appear throughout the 1950s.

The U.S. dollar shortage began to disappear at the end of 1949, following the devaluation of the various European currencies by 30 percent or more. The dominant feature of the next 20 years was a persistent U.S. payment deficit: U.S. gold holdings declined, and foreign official and foreign private holdings of U.S. dollar securities increased.

Three separate problems seemingly occurred at more or less the same time. One was the shortage of gold and other international reserve assets. The second was that the German mark and the Japanese yen were becoming increasingly undervalued. The parities for each currency had been set in 1949, when each was still occupied and when much of their productive potential had been (temporarily) destroyed during the last several years of World War II and with the rearrangement of national borders. The third was the increase in the U.S. inflation rate associated with the excess demand associated with the war in Vietnam.

There were two different types of explanations for this shift in the U.S. payment position: one was a set of sector-specific arguments, including more rapid productivity gains in tradable goods industries in Europe and Japan than in the United States and a higher inflation rate in the United States than in other industrial countries, and the second was the excess demand for domestic money or international money by agents in these same countries.

The major economic debate of the 1960s was the cause of the persistent U.S. payment deficit and particularly whether the cause was country specific and somehow reflected the profligate nature of U.S. financial policies or whether instead the cause was systemic and reflected either the excess demand for domestic money or the demand for international reserves on the part of agents in the countries with the payment surpluses.

Despite the persistent U.S. payment deficit, the United States continued to have current-account surpluses. The "definitional interpretation" was that the U.S. capital-account deficit was larger than the current-account surplus. The behavioral interpretation was that the United States had a current-account surplus because it had a capital-account deficit. But if agents in various foreign countries had an excess demand for U.S. dollar securities, the United States had to have a deficit on either its current account or its capital account.

There was an extended impasse about whether the United States or France, Germany, and Japan should take the initiative in changing parities. The U.S. view was that the countries with excessively large payment surpluses should revalue their currencies; most had effectively devalued their currencies earlier, and so symmetry suggested a revaluation was appropriate. The view in foreign capitals was that the United States should devalue the U.S. dollar—that is, raise the U.S. dollar price of gold because the source of the problem was that the United States had allowed its inflation rate to escalate.

The impasse about the change in exchange-rate arrangements was broken by measures taken in mid-August 1971 at the Camp David weekend: the U.S. Treasury's gold window was formally closed, and a 10 percent surcharge was levied on dutiable imports. The timing of these changes appears to have been prompted by the concern that one or several foreign central banks might seek to buy gold from the U.S. Treasury.

The concern of the U.S. authorities was that any U.S. initiative to increase the U.S. dollar price of gold would not lead to an improvement in the U.S. international payment position because a number of foreign countries would follow any U.S. initiative to increase the U.S. dollar price of gold and leave unchanged the price of the U.S. dollar in terms of the foreign-exchange value of their currencies. Since the German mark had been floating since May 1970, the concern primarily was with the Japanese response. The message was that the surcharge would be lifted only after the countries with the payment surpluses—and particularly Japan—had permitted their currencies to float.

This episode provides insight into the Bretton Woods rules as they applied to different countries. The Fund could induce changes in domestic policies of individual countries because it had the ability to withhold credit, but the Fund could not really be effective in its criticism toward the largest member. Nor could the Fund force those countries with excessively large payment surpluses to revalue their currencies.

The 1971 Smithsonian agreement was an attempt to patch together a slightly modified set of pegged exchange rates. There was a very modest debate about exchange-market arrangements; parities were renamed, and support limits widened.

The effective appreciation of other currencies in terms of the U.S. dollar was about 12 percent, and it appears as if both the U.S. authorities and the foreign authorities believed the scope of this realignment was appropriate.

The Smithsonian agreement lasted little more than one year. The arrangement broke down as the U.S. inflation rate began to increase as the price ceilings adopted at Camp David were relaxed.

While the transition from the pegged exchange-rate arrangement to a floating exchange-rate arrangement probably was inevitable given the differences in U.S. and German inflation rates, the change was facilitated by a powerful set of arguments that had been developed by the proponents of floating exchange rates. The principal argument was that when currencies were no longer pegged, changes in exchange rates would more or less track the difference in national inflation rates, so the difference between the market exchange rate and the real or price-level adjusted exchange rate would be smaller than when currencies were pegged. A second argument was that the foreign-exchange market would be "efficient" or at least "not inefficient": the forward exchange rates would be an unbiased forecast of the spot exchange rates on the dates that each forward exchange contract matured. A third argument was that there would be fewer foreign-exchange crises. The fourth argument is that the international reserve-adequacy issue would disappear because central banks would no longer need to acquire reserve assets.

When the German mark and the Japanese yen began to appreciate by much more than was consistent with the differences between their inflation rates and the inflation rate in the United States, the story was that exchange-market participants would take some time to "get used to the new system."

At the end of the 1970s, there was a marked shift into "hard assets" and away from U.S. dollar securities. The depreciation of the U.S. dollar in terms of the currencies of other industrial countries was four or five times larger than the change that would have been predicted on the basis of the difference between the U.S. rate and their inflation rate.

The scope of the appreciation of the German mark and the Japanese yen was a major surprise. There were several other surprises in the 1970s. One was the virulence of world inflation, unprecedented as a peacetime event. The several oil shocks were largely unanticipated.

The second surprise was the large amplitude of the movements in the exchange rates relative to the values that would have been predicted based on the contemporary movements in the differentials in national inflation rates.

The third surprise was the sharp increase in the level of international reserve assets. The proponents of floating exchange rates had suggested that the demand for these assets would decline sharply once currencies were no longer pegged.

Another surprise in the 1970s was the surge in bank loans to Mexico, Brazil, Argentina, and other developing countries and the flip side of this increase, the increase in the external indebtedness of these countries by nearly $700 billion. The popular story was that members of the Organization of Petroleum Exporting Countries (OPEC) had large payment surpluses, which they used to finance the purchase of deposits in the major international banks. The banks in turn then made large loans to Mexico, Brazil, Argentina, and others. Unfortunately for this explanation, the increase in bank loans to these (MBA) countries was three times larger than the increase in OPEC holdings of international reserve assets.

One of the modest debates in the 1970s was about the Reserve Substitution Account: whether IMF member countries could swap U.S. dollar securities for a claim on the IMF, which would have been an indirect way for these countries to secure a form of exchange-rate guarantee on the U.S. dollar securities that they had acquired to limit the appreciation of their currencies.

The surprises continued in the 1980s with the developing-country debt shock, which effectively led to the external bankruptcy and in some cases the formal domestic bankruptcy of the governments. Another surprise in the first half of the decade was the sharp appreciation of the U.S. dollar relative to the values predicted on the basis of the difference between the U.S. inflation rate and the contemporary inflation rates in Germany and in Japan. A third surprise was the sharp change in the U.S. international investment position: at the beginning of the 1980s the United States had been the world's largest creditor country, and by the end of the decade the United States had become the world's largest debtor country. (There was a very small decline in the U.S. net international creditor position in the 1970s.)

The U.S. dollar began to depreciate in the mid-1980s, months before the so-called Plaza accord. The U.S. trade deficit declined modestly.

One of the big surprises in the 1980s was the surge in asset prices in Tokyo with the reflected less extensive increases in asset prices in Taipei and Seoul and Hong Kong. Real estate prices increased by a factor of 10 in the decade in Japan, and stock prices by a factor of seven. One interpretation was that these asset-price increases reflected an equilibrium adjustment to sharp decline in the inflation rate; an alternative interpretation was that these increases were part of a "bubble."

The 1980s was "a dreadful decade" in that the MBA countries were seeking to adjust to their excess indebtedness.

One of the major political surprises at the end of the 1980s was the fall of the Berlin Wall and the resulting reunification of the two Germanies. What had been West Germany began to make large financial transfers to what had been East Germany. One consequence was that the large current-account surplus that West Germany had had with the world became transformed into a smaller current-account deficit as its current-account surplus was redirected toward what had been East Germany.

The first surprise of the 1990s was the crisis in the exchange-rate mechanism of September 1992. There was a ripple of the devaluations of the currencies on the periphery of Europe relative to the German mark and the French franc.

The second crisis was the Mexican foreign-exchange crisis of 1994 and 1995. The administration of President Salanias was both extremely ambitious and extremely successful in its initiatives toward privatization, import liberalization, and macrostabilization. This combination of arguments led to a surge in capital flows to the developing countries, since renamed the *emerging-market countries*.

The third crisis of the 1990s was the Asian financial crisis that began with the depreciation of the Thai baht in June 1997 and continued with the depreciations of the Indonesian rupiah, the Malaysian ringit, and the Korean won. IMF credits to the five troubled Asian countries totaled more than $100 billion. The irony is that the World Bank had previously published *The East Asian Miracle,* which made no effective mention that these countries had been experiencing an extended period of Ponzi finance. Each—with the exception of Korea—had a bubble in its real estate market. Some of the countries in the neighborhood that were not capital importers also were experiencing bubbles in their asset markets.

There were two several unique aspects of the foreign-exchange crises in these countries. One was the sharpness of the real depreciation of their currencies and the scope of overshooting. Thus the Korean won depreciated from 900 won to the U.S. dollar to 1800 won and then appreciated to 1200 won. The second aspect was that the combination of the sharp depreciation and the revaluation losses incurred by both banks and nonbank firms and the surge in interest rates meant large losses for banks.

2.   Capital flows, changes in exchange rates, and market failure

The first issue discussed in this section involves the causes of the very large movements in exchange rates relative to those that would have been predicted based on the contemporary (or lagged) differential in national inflation rates. The second issue involves the welfare gains and losses from cross-border investments and particularly changes in these investments in both the capital-exporting country and the capital-importing country.

The case for floating exchange rates developed in the 1950s and the 1960s had five major arguments. The first was that the deviations between the market exchange rate and the real or price-level adjusted exchange rate would be smaller when currencies were floating than when they were pegged because the foreign-exchange value of currencies would change continuously and by relatively small amounts. When currencies were pegged, in contrast, the real exchange rates might deviate from the parities because of monetary or structural shocks. Because the monetary authorities were reluctant to alter the parity by less than 15 or 20 percent, there might be extended periods of significant overvaluation and undervaluation.

A second argument advanced by the proponents of floating exchange rates was that the exchange market would be "efficient" or "not inefficient," in the sense that the forward exchange rates would be effective forecasts of the spot exchange rates on the dates that each forward exchange contract matured. The forward exchange rate has no predictive power with respect to the change in the spot exchange rate during the term to maturity of the forward contract. During the first half of the 1980s, both the German mark and the Japanese yen were at forward premium in the forward market, yet both currencies more or less continuously depreciated.

The third argument was that choice of the monetary policy or more broadly macro policy would no longer be constrained when currencies were no longer pegged. Hence, the United States would no longer be obliged to sell gold and other reserve assets because other countries might demand these assets. Similarly, central banks would no longer be obliged to sell their currencies. The exchange rate would be the buffer that would adjust to shocks, and, as a result, shocks that would occur in one country would be less readily transmitted to other countries.

The fourth argument was that the demand for international reserve assets would decline once currencies were no longer pegged, since central banks would have no need to support their currencies in the foreign-exchange market. In fact, central-bank intervention in the foreign-exchange market has been much more extensive.

The fifth argument was that there would be fewer foreign-exchange crises.

In retrospect the validity of the second, third, fourth, and fifth arguments depended on the validity of the first argument.

The first argument has been proven invalid because the extensive variability in cross-border capital flows has led to much larger movement in exchange rates than would have been forecast on the basis of the contemporary difference in national inflation rates.

Given the large *ex ante* demand of investors to buy securities denominated in a foreign currency, the change in the exchange rate can be analyzed in terms of the transfer problem associated with Keynes.

Keynes's concept of the transfer problem distinguished the financial side of foreign investment from the real side, where the real side involved changes in the current-account balances. His skepticism about the size of reparations levied on the Germans by the Allies after World War I reflected his concern that the combination of the real appreciation of the French franc and the expansive demand policies in France together with the real depreciation of the German mark and the deflationary policies in Germany would be insufficient to generate a French current-account deficit and a German current-account surplus comparable to the size of the intended financial transfer.

One of the major stylized facts is that the scope of current-account imbalances on average has been larger when currencies have been floating than when they were pegged. Similarly, the variability of the current-account balances generally has been larger when currencies have been floating than when they have been pegged.

Water flows downhill, and capital flows toward higher rates of return—most of the time. Since uncertainty about exchange rates almost certainly is larger when currencies are floating than when they are pegged, then the inference is that the differential between domestic and foreign returns when currencies are floating almost certainly is larger than when currencies are pegged and are pegged by more than enough to compensate for the increase in the uncertainty. The differential return argument has two components—the differential in interest rates and anticipated changes in exchange rates.

One reason that the differential in anticipated returns is higher when currencies are floating than when they are pegged is that the differential in anticipated inflation rates is likely to be greater; similarly the difference in anticipated returns is higher. Investors typically move funds from areas where real interest rates are low and declining to areas where real interest rates are high and increasing.

One reason that the difference in anticipated returns is higher is that the differential in anticipated inflation rates is generally higher. Indeed, the variability in inflation rates leads to the variability in interest rates. There are two arguments here: the anticipated inflation rate and the interest rates.

The cross-border movement of funds is affected by the changes in the differential in anticipated inflation rates and changes in the differential in interest rates and changes in the anticipated exchange rates.

The volatility of exchange rates in the last 25 years reflects the variability of capital flows. Investors move funds from areas of low anticipated returns to areas of higher anticipated returns. The difference in anticipated returns between the two areas reflects a combination of two arguments: the difference in interest rates (or yields) on comparable securities denominated in different currencies and the anticipated change in the exchange rate. Thus, in the first half of the 1980s investors moved funds into U.S. dollar securities both because interest rates on U.S. dollar securities were higher than interest rates on comparable securities denominated in the German mark and because the appreciation of the U.S. dollar was anticipated. In retrospect the appreciation of the U.S. dollar accounted for about 80 percent of the excess return on the U.S. dollar securities relative to the return on comparable foreign securities.

At times the exchange-rate argument and the interest-rate argument are additive in their impacts on capital flows, and at other times they are offsetting, although not necessarily fully offsetting (indeed, if the two arguments were fully offsetting, capital would not flow). The magnitude of the exchange-rate argument almost always is larger than the interest-differential argument.

In the late 1970s there was an increase in the capital flow from the United States as the U.S. inflation rate accelerated, and the United States developed a small current-account surplus. In the first half of the 1980s, the U.S. dollar appreciated in response to the increase in the capital flow to the United States, and by the middle of the decade the United States had developed a current-account deficit that was 4 percent of U.S. GNP.

The popular interpretation of the surge in the U.S. trade and current-account deficits and of the turnabout in the U.S. international payments position was the U.S. fiscal deficit. The story line was that the surge in the U.S. fiscal deficit attributable to the supply-side-inspired tax cuts led to a surge in interest rates on U.S. dollar securities, which in turn induced investors to increase their demand for these securities. Before they could buy these securities, they first had to buy U.S. dollars in the foreign-exchange market. And so the U.S. dollar appreciated.[1]

The variability of the exchange rate is a market response to the desire of investors to alter the currency composition of the securities in their portfolios. Before these investors can buy these securities, they first must buy the foreign currency in the foreign-exchange market. The currency necessarily appreciates to induce a larger trade deficit (or a smaller trade surplus) in the capital-importing countries. The change in the exchange rate is necessary so that the *ex post* change in the current-account balance will equal the *ex post* change in the capital-account balance. In effect the transfer problem is at work, and relative prices have to change (which occurs as a result of the changes in the exchange rate) so the transfer of real resources from the capital-exporting to the capital-importing country can be effected.

The reason that changes in capital flows drive the exchange rate is that the change to induce a change in the current-account balance must be comparable to the change in the capital-account balance. Because the current-account balance must change whenever there is a change in the *ex ante* capital flow of a given size each period, it necessarily follows that the deviation between the market exchange rate and the equilibrium exchange rate will be larger when currencies are floating than when they are pegged. When currencies are pegged, the same or a comparable capital flow will lead to a change in reserves of the capital-importing country in the first instance; in the second instance, the change in the current-account balance may reflect the changes in national income.

Because of these changes in exchange rates, productive resources must shift between the tradable-goods sector and the nontradable-goods sectors in both the capital-importing countries and the capital-exporting countries. These shifts incur costs of unemployment of resources.

Keynes had raised the question, "Does foreign investment pay?" in the mid-1920s. He used the bankruptcy of the New York City subway to illustrate the distinction between social costs and benefits of foreign investment and the private costs and benefits of foreign investment. His story was that when the subway tanked, the Americans had the subway while the British investors held securities whose market value had declined significantly below their purchase price.

While fault might be directed at the conclusion drawn from Keynes's example, his initiative highlights attention on the wedges between the social costs and benefits of foreign investment and the private costs and benefits of these same investments. One possible wedge between private and social costs is created by losses on foreign investments, and another by taxes in the country in which the investment had been made. A third wedge involves the externalities of the impact of the marginal investor on the returns achieved by inframarginal investors. One component of this wedge is the impact of the marginal investor's decision to purchase (or sell) a foreign security on the value of the foreign currency in the foreign-exchange market.

The cliché "vicious and virtuous circle" highlights that capital flows may facilitate growth in real income in the capital-importing country. Changes in national income may attract capital from the foreign countries, or alternatively, the movement of capital may induce the changes in income.

Consider six episodes of major capital flows in the last 25 years. At least five of these episodes have been associated with crisis in the foreign-exchange market:

- The bank loans to the developing countries in the 1970s,
- The capital flows from the United States in 1978 and 1979,
- The capital flows to the United States in the 1980 to 1985 period,
- The reduction in the capital flows to the United States in the 1985 to 1988 period,
- The capital flows to Mexico and other Latin American countries in the early 1990s, and
- The capital flows to Korea and the other Asian countries in the mid-1990s.

Four of these episodes are associated with booms in the capital-importing countries. Consider first the surge in bank loans to the MBA countries in the 1970s. Real income growth in these countries was high because of the combination of the increases in commodity prices and export volumes. Real interest rates on the loans denominated in the U.S. dollar were declining. The combination of the real income argument and the real interest-rate argument increased the debt-servicing capability of the capital-importing countries.

Consider the surge in the capital outflow from the United States in the late 1970s. The story was an increase in the U.S. inflation rate and a decline in real interest rates on U.S. dollar securities; investors sold U.S. dollar securities.

Consider the surge in the capital flow to the United States in the first half of the 1980s. Throughout this period the inflation rate in the United States was higher than the inflation rates in Germany and Japan. Investors bought U.S. dollar securities both because of high level of interest rates on U.S. dollar securities and the downward revision in the anticipated U.S. inflation rate. Although the interest rates on these securities began to decline in 1982 and hence the interest-rate differential declined, the capital flows to the United States were increasing.

Consider the decline in the capital flow to the United States that began in the second half of the 1980s. Investors bought fewer U.S. dollar securities even as interest rates on these securities were increasing; interest rates may have been increasing because demand of foreign investors for these securities was declining.

Consider the surge in the capital flow to Mexico in the early 1990s in response to the major initiatives of privatization, import liberalization, and macrostabilization. The inflation rate in Mexico declined sharply, and real interest rates were exceptionally high. Foreign portfolio investors were attracted to the high real interest rates on securities denominated in the peso. Others were attracted to equities of newly privatized firms. Mexico's current-account deficit increased to 7 percent of GNP; Mexico needed $25 billion of new foreign money each year to maintain the foreign-exchange value of the peso consistent with its gliding peg exchange.

Consider the surge in the capital flow to Korea, Thailand, Indonesia, and the nearby countries in response to *The East Asian Miracle*. Partly because of a bubble in their real estate markets, rates of growth of real income were exceptionally high. Foreign investors were attracted to the anticipated high rates of return associated with high rates of economic growth.

Three of these crises involved the United States, three involved developing countries. The surge in the capital flows to the developing countries was a response to the high rates of economic growth; however, the capital flows to these countries were at rates that were unsustainable.

The increase in the capital outflow from the United States in the late 1970s was a typical development in response to an increase in the inflation rate and a decline in real interest rates. The same pattern is evident in the French franc in 1924 to 1926 and the British pound in 1975 and 1976.

Similarly, the surge in the capital flow to the United States in the first half of the 1980s is a typical response to the adoption of a convincing anti-inflationary policy. Comparable developments occurred in the French franc in the second half of 1926, in the British pound in 1977 and 1978, and in a number of other industrial countries in the last decade—Canada, Australia, and even Germany.

Capital flows to these countries are a response to the sharp increase in interest rates associated with the anti-inflationary monetary policy and to the downward revision in the anticipated inflation rate. At some levels currency appreciation associated with the capital inflow may attract a group of investors that are "momentum players." The currencies *always* "overshoot" because the capital inflow primarily is a stock adjustment; as this adjustment is completed, the capital flow diminishes, and the currency depreciates.

These large overvaluations and undervaluations of the currencies of the industrial countries have predictable stock market consequences. During the period of the capital inflow (although not necessarily at the beginning of this period) stock prices are likely to be increasing in response to the increase in the supply of credit and the decline in interest rates on domestic securities. In contrast, during the period of the currency depreciation, stock prices are likely to decrease because interest rates will move upward as investors move funds from domestic securities to foreign securities.

The wealth effects associated with the changes in the capital flows and the induced changes in exchange rates also operate in the emerging-market countries.

However, the impacts of a change in the capital flow of a given size in the emerging market countries are different because the public bond markets and the equity markets account for a much smaller part of private wealth, and so a larger share of wealth adjustment occurs in the markets for bank loans.

One big difference between the capital flows to the developing countries in the 1970s and the 1990s is the composition of borrowers. Thus in the 1970s the principal borrowers in the developing countries were the governments, whereas in the 1990s the principal borrowers were private firms. In the 1980s the governments in most of the MBA countries went bankrupt.

The impact of changes in capital flows on the foreign-exchange values of individual countries causes the social costs and benefits to differ from the private costs and benefits. Individual investors fail to recognize the impact of their transactions on the foreign-exchange value of individual currencies. Similarly, they fail to recognize the costs of the shift of resources between tradables and nontradables as the real exchange-rate changes.

The domestic impacts of the inflow of capital tend to enhance the economic performance, and to some extent the inflow of capital appears like a partial self-fulfilling prophecy. Equity markets in many of the developing countries are modest in size, and so the purchase of domestic equities by foreign investors can, because of the price effects, attract additional foreign buyers.

Moreover, the sudden reduction in the volume of capital flows to an individual developing country necessitates a sharp increase in interest rates. Unemployment surges. Real income in Mexico declined by 7 percent. Real income in some of the Asian countries may have declined by 5 percent.

There are two possible sources of market failure:

- Investors may fail to realize that the financial data that motivate the capital flows are not likely to be sustained for an indefinite future. In the 1970s, for example, it appears that the bank lenders acted as if they believed that commodity prices would continue to increase at a rapid rate so that GNP growth in the commodity-producing countries would remain high. Oil prices were expected to increase so that the real price of oil would increase at 3 percent a year forever.
- Investors may fail to recognize that the cross-border capital flows have a substantial stock adjustment component in response to any change in the yield differential. As this adjustment is completed, the capital flow diminishes, and the currency begins to depreciate.

The rationale for the commitment to the pegged exchange-rate arrangements in the Bretton Woods arrangements had two legs: the first was that uncertainty about exchange rates in the future would deter trade and investment, and the second was that some countries might manage the foreign-exchange value of their currencies to enhance domestic income and employment, presumably at the expense of income and employment in their trade partners. The second concern is identified with export-led growth and the desire of Japan and a number of its neighbors, as well as most countries in the European Union, to achieve payment surpluses.

The analogy between the welfare aspects of trade flows and capital flows breaks down in several regards. Although there are similarities, in that changes in trade barriers cause adjustment costs, the one-time costs associated with changes in trade barriers must be offset against the (present value of the) gains associated with an increase in the volume of trade.

The financial debacles in the MBA countries in the early 1990s, in Mexico in 1994 and 1995, and in Korea and the other Asian countries in the 1997 and 1998 period resulted primarily from the sudden reduction in the capital inflows. These countries needed a continuing inflow of new foreign money each year to finance their current-account deficits. In addition, each of the countries needed to refinance maturing short-term debt. (Korea's problem in 1997 was primarily a refinance problem; its current-account deficit was relatively small.)

The source of the financial problem is that a significant part of the capital inflow to these countries is a stock adjustment; investors respond to "new news" by reallocating a portion of their wealth among securities denominated in different currencies. The inflow of capital is "good news"; the price of the currency in the foreign-exchange market and the price of debt and of equities all increase. But to the extent the capital inflow is partly a stock adjustment, the foreign-currency value will decrease as the stock adjustment is completed.

The variability in the cross-border capital flows incurs social costs in both capital-importing and capital-exporting countries as the size of the current-account balances adjusts to changes in the amount of the cross-border flow of capital each period. These costs can be exceptionally high when the capital inflow to an emerging-market country declines.

3.   The proposals for a new financial architecture

The range of proposals under the new financial architecture is extensive. Most of these proposals can be placed in one of three groups—proposals that would deter or regulate capital flows, proposals that would enhance information to the agents involved in international capital flows and especially to the lenders or investors, and proposals that would facilitate coping with the adverse effects of sudden shifts in the magnitude of capital flows either by enhancing some aspect of the credit arrangements of the IMF or by facilitating adjustment to an excess-debt burden. A fourth set of proposals involves changes in the management of the International Monetary Fund while the institutional arrangements remain more or less unchanged.

Some of these proposals, if implemented, would reduce the volume of capital flows for any given set of the differential in anticipated returns on domestic investment and on foreign investment. Other proposals, if implemented, might lead to a larger volume of these flows, on average, although the impact of the adoption of the proposal on the variability of the capital flows is not clear.

One set of proposals would reduce the volume of capital flows either by taxes or by exchange controls. The Tobin tax would reduce the after-tax return on foreign investment relative to the after-tax return on domestic investments. (The traditional debate about the distinction between social returns and private returns on private investment highlights that the impact of income taxes on the foreign investment of private individuals creates a wedge between social returns and private returns. The Tobin tax creates a wedge between the after-tax returns to private investors on foreign investment and on domestic investment.)

The Chilean experience reserve requirements on inflow of capital often are cited as evidence of the success of these controls. There is some skepticism that the controls were as effective as the advertisement.

Those who propose this set of measures appear to believe that the source of the problem is that the investors are fair-weather friends and readily reverse the flows. Perhaps some investors reverse their holdings of securities denominated in particular currencies if the news becomes less attractive. The implication of the model discussed in the previous section is that change in the foreign-exchange value of a country's currency is triggered by the stock adjustment by investors in the currency denomination of securities in their portfolios.

If taxes or regulations were adopted to deter the inflow of foreign capital, then the pace of the capital flows would be smaller. The current-account deficit of the capital-importing countries would increase less rapidly, and the stock adjustment would occur more slowly. The capital-importing country still might have an adjustment problem, but the necessary adjustment might occur later or it might be smaller.

The second set of proposals centers on more complete information: *greater transparency* is one of the buzzwords. The motive for these proposals is that the net debtor position is somewhat understated in a stock sense or in a flow sense. The rationale is that if the agents involved in capital flows were fully cognizant of the volume of these flows, they would be more cautious because they would recognize that they would be increasingly vulnerable to a shock. The lenders would be concerned about their potential losses because the borrowers may not be able to repay, and the borrowers would be concerned that they could be thrown into bankruptcy because of the large revaluation loss or because the lenders would curtail credit.

It is impossible to be against more complete information or against greater transparency (even though information and transparency are not costless). Consider the Mexican crisis of 1994 and 1995. Some skeptics have suggested that the Mexican government was not fully forthcoming about the "true" state of its foreign-exchange reserves. Perhaps the source of the problem is that capital inflows had positioned Mexico so that it needed $25 billion of new foreign money each year. Once the Mexican current-account deficit had increased to 7 percent of GNP, a crisis seemed inevitable because external debt could not continue to increase more rapidly than GNP for an extended period. Similarly, the developing-country debt crisis of the early 1980s had little, if anything, to do with information or with transparency; the source of the problem was the (mistaken) assumption that the real prices of primary products could increase without limit.

A third set of proposals involves enhancing the capital of the international financial institutions so they will be better able to cope with shocks. More effective prudential regulation would fit into this ball park. To the extent the Korean won and other currencies have "overshot," there is a liquidity problem. Most of the countries had both a liquidity problem and an adjustment problem. For reasons that are somewhat opaque, the Fund proved slow in recognizing the scope of the liquidity problem.

The striking aspect of the discussion about new international financial architecture is the lack of attention to the causes of market failure.

4. Conclusions

In the 1960s there was a grand debate about international monetary reform in response to the identification of the Triffin paradox. Today there are numerous proposals for modifying international financial arrangements, almost certainly stimulated by the severe financial crisis in Mexico in 1994 and 1995 and the Asian financial crisis of 1997 and 1998. The debate—to the extent there is a debate—seems sterile because there is so little agreement on the source of the problem.

This article identified six major international financial crises of the last 25 years, including the developing-country debt crisis of the early 1980s (which followed a 10-year period when bank loans to these countries increased at a rate of 30 percent a year) and three crises involving the U.S. dollar: one in the late 1970s, the second in the early 1980s when the U.S. dollar was appreciating, and the third in the second half of the 1980s as the U.S. dollar began to depreciate.

The wide range of movement in the market exchange rates relative to the rates that might be inferred from contemporary (or lagged) change in differentials in national inflation rates reflects changes in the *ex ante* cross-border capital flows. Before investors can alter the currency denomination of the securities in their portfolios, they must first buy the currency in the foreign-exchange market. The currency appreciates so the country can generate a larger current-account deficit; this change in the current-account balance is necessary so that a real transfer can occur that is more or less the counterpart of the intended financial transfer. The model is that of the transfer problem identified by Keynes in response to World War I reparations. Changes in relative prices and in relative incomes are necessary to induce the required changes in the current-account balances; otherwise the financial transfer is unregulated. Most of the requisite change is in relative prices, and most of this change is likely to occur as a result of changes in exchange rates.

The variability of capital flows both to and from the United States, between the United States and other industrial countries, and between industrial countries as a group and the developing countries is the source of the variability in exchange-rate movements. Changes in capital flows respond to changes in rates of growth of national income and to changes in inflation rate and changes in real interest rates.

There is a form of market failure in that individual investors fail to recognize the impact of their purchases of a foreign security on the foreign-exchange value of the country's currency and on asset prices in the capital-importing countries. Asset prices tend to increase in countries experiencing an increase in the inflow of foreign capital; similarly, the currency tends to appreciate. Conversely, the currency depreciates as the capital inflow declines.

A large part of the cross-border flow of capital represents a stock adjustment as investors reallocate their wealth between domestic securities and foreign securities. As the stock adjustment to a change in the information set is completed, investors reduce their demand for foreign securities.

Most of the proposals that fall under the heading of the new international financial architecture fail to recognize that the source of the problem is the combination of the variability of capital flows and the floating exchange-rate system. As long as currencies are floating, economic conditions among countries are likely to be both more variable and more diverse. The greater variability in economic conditions suggests greater variability in capital flows.

Acknowledgments

Discussions with Nick Sargen and J.J. Polak have been very helpful.

Note

1. There are several problems with the "twin-deficits" explanation. One is that the explanation is inconsistent with the timing of the appreciation of the U.S. dollar. A second is that interest rates on U.S. dollar securities began to decline even as the U.S. fiscal deficit began to increase. A third is that the fiscal-balance story cannot be readily extended to periods when the U.S. dollar has depreciated.

References

Askari, H. (1999) "Twenty-Five Years of Post-Bretton Woods Experience: Some Lessons." *Banca Nazionale del Lavoro Quarterly Review* 208:3–38.

Brown, B. (1988) *The Flight of International Capital: A Contemporary History*. London: Routledge.

Calomiris, C.W. and A.H. Meltzer (1999) "Fixing the IMF." *National Interest* 56:88–96.

Council of Economic Advisors (1999) *Economic Report of the Presiden*. Washington, DC: CEA.

De Vries, M.G. (1976) *The International Monetary Fund: 1966–1971*, Vol. 1, *Narrative*. Washington, DC: IMF.

Dornbusch, R. (1988) "Doubts About the McKinnon Standard." *Journal of Economic Perspectives* 1:105–112.

Eichengreen, B. (1990) *Elusive Stability: Essays in the History of International Finance, 1919–1939*. Cambridge: Cambridge University Press.

Eichengreen, B. (1999a) "International Architecture Reform Scorecard." *International Economy* 3:34–35.

Eichengreen, B. (1999b) "A Practical Fix." *International Economy* 3:30–33.

Eichengreen, B. (1999c) *Toward a New International Financial Architecture: A Practical Post-Asia Agenda*. Washington, DC: Institute for International Economics.

Federal Reserve Bank of Boston (1984) *The International Monetary System: Forty Years After Bretton Woods*. Proceedings of a Conference Held in May 1984, Conference Series No. 28. Boston: Federal Reserve Bank of Boston.

Feldstein, M.S. (1988a) "Distinguished Lecture on Economics in Government: Thinking About International Economic Co-ordination." *Journal of Economic Perspectives* 2:3–14.

Feldstein, M.S. (ed.) (1988c) *The United States in the World Economy*. Chicago: University of Chicago Press.

Feldstein, M.S. (1988b) *International Economic Cooperation*. Chicago: University of Chicago Press.

Friedman, M. (1961) "The Case for Floating Exchange Rates." In *Essays in Positive Economics*. Chicago: University of Chicago Press.

Goldstein, M. (1995) *The Exchange Rate System and the IMF*. Washington, DC: Institute for International Economics.

Haldane, A.G. (1999) "Private Sector Involvement and Public Policy." Mimeo, London.

Horsefield, K.J. (1969) *The International Monetary Fund: 1945–1965*. Vol. 2, *Chronicle*. Washington, DC: IMF.

Hul Haq, M., I. Kaul, and I. Grunberg (1996) *The Tobin Tax: Coping with Financial Volatility*. New York: Oxford University Press.

James, H. (1996) *International Monetary Co-operation Since Bretton Woods*. Washington, DC: IMF.

Kapstein, E.P. (1994) *Governing the Global Economy*. Cambridge: Harvard University Press.

Kemp, M.C. (1969) *The Pure Theory of International Trade and Investment*. Englewood Cliffs, NJ: Prentice-Hall.

Kindleberger, C.P. (1987) *International Capital Movements*. Cambridge: Cambridge University Press.

Krueger, A.O. (1998) "Whither the World Bank and the IMF?" *Journal of Economic Literature* 4:1983–2020.

Krugman, P. (1990) *Exchange Rate Instability*. Cambridge, MA: MIT Press.

League of Nations (1943) *International Currency Experience*. Geneva: League of Nations.

Marston, R.C. (1995) *International Financial Integration*. Cambridge: Cambridge University Press.

McKinnon, R.I. (1988) "Monetary and Exchange Rate Policies for International Financial Stability: A Proposal." *Journal of Economic Perspectives* 1:83–104.

Mikesell, R.F. (1994) *The Bretton Woods Debates: A Memoir*. Princeton: Essays in International Finance, 192.

Rogoff, K. (1999) "International Institutions for Reducing Global Financial Stability." Mimeo, Cambridge, MA.

Saber, N. (1999) *Speculative Capital: The Invisible Hand of Global Finance*. London: Pearson.

Shelton, J. (1994) *Money Meltdown: Restoring Order to the Global Currency System*. New York: Free Press.

Sohmen, E. (1966) *Floating Exchange Rates*. Cambridge, MA: MIT Press.

Solomon, R. (1999) *Money on the Move: The Revolution in International Finance Since 1980*. Princeton: Princeton University Press.

The East Asian Miracle: Economic Growth and Public Policy (1993) A World Bank Policy Research Report, Oxford University Press.

Williamson, J. (1999) "On McKinnon's Monetary Rule." *Journal of Economic Perspectives* 1:13–120.

Open economies review 11:S1 63–67 (2000)

Comment on Aliber's "Capital Flows, Exchange Rates, and the New International Financial Architecture: Six Financial Crises in Search of a Generic Explanation"

MICHELE FRATIANNI
Indiana University, Kelley School of Business, Bloomington, Indiana

Introduction

Robert Aliber's article makes two main and interrelated points. The first is that today's discussion on reforming the international monetary system is puny compared to the grand debate of the 1960s that tried to provide a solution to the Triffin paradox. Current discussion, instead, is ad hoc and is aimed at fixing specific crises rather than looking at the system as a whole. Aliber characterizes today's debate as sterile "because there is so little agreement on the source of the problem." The second is that private decentralized decisions by investors involve some type of market failure in that these "investors fail to recognize the impact of their purchases of a foreign security on the foreign-exchange value of the country's currency and on asset prices in the capital-importing countries. Asset prices tend to increase in countries experiencing an increase in the inflow of foreign capital; similarly, the currency tends to appreciate. Conversely, the currency depreciates as the capital inflow declines."

Let's take the two points in reverse order.

1. Exchange rates and capital flows: Three scenarios

Exchange rates are influenced primarily by capital flows. These flows respond to national differences in perceived real rates of interest, economic growth, and inflation rates. In a world of flexible exchange rates, a net inflow of capital implies a current-account deficit—a net outflow a current-account surplus. Start with a situation in which a country (say, Mexico) is in current-account equilibrium. Say that George Soros deems that real rates of return, adjusted for risk, are higher in Mexico than elsewhere and buys $5 billion worth of pesos. Assume also that Soros has such a reputation to convince many other investors to buy pesos for $25 billion. The peso appreciates, if not nominally then in real terms, and Mexico swings into a current-account deficit. Soros, the next day, looks at the current-account deficit and realizes that it is much higher that he initially anticipated: he did not count on the *herd* effect. He reverses his transaction because he believes that the deficit is not sustainable; other investors follow suit. The peso declines in value, and the current account returns to its initial equilibrium solution. Is there a market failure other than the fact that Soros's trading creates an externality? In this model the current account returns to equilibrium. The only market failure may be of the type identified by Jeremy Stein (1987): more speculators may create a negative externality in the sense of lowering the quality of information to all traders. Stated differently, the reputation of Soros as a trader leads to herd behavior, which in turn leads to exchange-rate overshooting. The policy prescription to correct the negative externality is to disclose more, better, and more timely information.

Two comments on this scenario. First, a rational Soros would have to know that as he moves so do others and consequently ought to adjust his move. Second, the remedy for excessive price movements may well be capital controls, with its attendant costs.

Now let's complicate the scenario as follows. This time Soros invests not in Mexican share prices but in deposit liabilities of Mexican banks. These banks invest the funds in the local economy. The critical assumption is that local banks overreach, either by selecting deliberately risky projects or by not understanding banking. A good example of the latter was the heavy increase in consumer loans by Mexican banks in the pre-1994 crisis. The capital outflow from Mexico not only caused a currency devaluation but also left banks with bad loans. A banking crisis unfolded, and the Mexican government rescued the banks. Here, market failure resides in a poorly supervised banking system. The IMF (1998, p. 78) has surveyed currency and banking crises for a group of 50 countries over the period 1975 to 1997 and concludes that "it is not surprising that countries appear to have banking and currency crises at around the same time. In these instances, banking crises preceded currency crises more often than the other way around."

Clearly, not all currency crises occur with banking crises. In fact, currency crises were more numerous in the first half of the period (1975 to 1986) than in the second half (1987 to 1997), whereas the opposite was true for banking crises. The speed and extent of financial market liberalization has had a material impact on banking crises.

The policy prescription for the joint occurrence of currency and banking crises is to tighten up supervision at home before capital flows into the country, as well as to impose more, better, and more timely information disclosure.

Let's consider a third and final scenario. This time, capital flows out of Mexico not because of Soros's actions but because of an unanticipated external event: say, a rise in world interest rates. The policy solution to this problem is that lenders must accept a rescheduling or a partial default of Mexican debts. Since Mexico is not at fault, the *correct* prescription is not to penalize Mexico without at the same time rescuing private creditors.

2. Solutions

There is no shortage of proposals, these days, on how to deal with currency and financial crises. The U.K. government would like to merge the International Monetary Fund, the World Bank, and the Bank for International Settlements into one big supranational regulator. The French government would prefer to strengthen the Interim Committee of the Finance Ministers. Canada leans toward debt relief engineered through an IMF-sanctioned pause in debt payments. George Soros, the currency speculator and financier, would welcome the creation of an International Credit Insurance Agency. Jeffrey Sachs, the Harvard economist, sees more value in an International Bankruptcy Court. Allan Meltzer, of Carnegie-Mellon University, favors an international lender of last resort. Robert Litan, of the Brookings Institution, would impose an automatic reduction of the principal for withdrawing or failing to rollover interbank deposit claims (for a longer list of proposals, see Eichengreen, 1999, app. A).

The latest proposal (as of September 1999) comes from the report of an independent task force sponsored by the U.S. Council on Foreign Relations (1999). Here are the report's seven recommendations:

- The IMF should refuse to defend unsustainable pegged exchange rates;
- Emerging economies should avoid excessive reliance on capital flows through transparent and nondiscriminatory taxes;
- All countries ought to include collective action clauses in their sovereign bond contracts to promote fair burden sharing between official and private creditors;
- The IMF should lend at favorable terms to those countries that take effective steps in reducing crisis vulnerability;
- The IMF and World Bank should get back to basics and concentrate on crisis prevention and macroeconomic policies;
- The IMF should abandon big financial rescue packages and return to normal lending limits; and
- A special global meeting of finance ministers should look into reforms of the international financial system.

These recommendations are quite sensible and reflect a consensus among academic experts, financial market participants, and policy makers. Aliber would characterize them as ad-hoc. This panel, like others before, does not propose a grand design; it delegates the search for a solution to finance ministers. Aliber clearly favors a systemic solution, but he too does not provide one. It may well be that a grand design is not in the cards because the premises are not there. Take, for example, a Bretton Woods–type architecture, without capital controls. Would it be feasible? How many countries would be willing to accept U.S. leadership, provided that the United States was willing to exercise it? If not the United States, would we have collegial leadership?

The European Economic and Monetary Union (EMU) and the euro are now a reality that is bound to alter fundamentally the international monetary system, pushing it away from the existing structure where one international money, the U.S. dollar, is dominant and toward an oligarchical structure where the role of international money will be shared by a few currencies—the dollar, the euro, and possibly the yen. Each of these currencies will form a gravitational center to which clusters of *domestic* monies will be attracted. The dollar sphere of influence today stretches to Latin America, South and East Asia, Iraq, Bahrain, Qatar, Saudi Arabia, and United Arab Emirates. That of the euro will most likely encompass Central and Eastern Europe, the African Financial Community (Communauté Financière Africaine, CFA) zone, and parts of the Middle East and North Africa. These maps will have uncertain boundaries. A deepening and widening of the North American Free Trade Agreement (NAFTA) and the European Union (EU) will enlarge the sphere of influence of both currencies; trade wars will restrict them. The prediction on the yen area is more problematic. The deep and still unresolved financial crisis in Japan works against the enlargement of the yen; deregulation of its financial markets, with the attendant decline in transaction costs, goes in the opposite direction. Asian countries have preferred the dollar to the yen as anchor currency, but the recent currency crisis in the region may call for a rethinking of this strategy. Predictions on the size of the yen are more difficult than for the dollar and the euro.

The EMU has a currency of its own with the potential to challenge the U.S. dollar in international money and financial markets. Like the United States, the EMU may be in the desirable position to borrow abroad by issuing debt in its own domestic currency and, consequently, relax the borrowing external constraint. This was not possible for each of the member countries of the EMU before the introduction of the euro.

The hierarchical structure that was successful in the gold standard—Bretton Woods—and the European monetary system cannot be duplicated in a multipolar world: the United States and the EMU, for example, are so large that neither is likely to subordinate monetary policy to the other. What are the chances that two or three currency areas may coordinate monetary policies? On a first look, the case for coordination appears ambiguous, resulting from two conflicting forces—the openness of the economy and the reduction of relevant players in desiring a cooperative solution. A large EMU works in favor of coordination because fewer players imply lower decision-making costs in reaching a cooperative solution. The openness of the economy, on the other hand, works against cooperation and in favor of benign neglect because the EMU will be as closed as the U.S. economy. Using the experience of the Federal Reserve System, which takes monetary policy decisions more on domestic than international considerations, one arrives at the prediction that also the decisions of the European Central Bank will be heavily influenced by domestic (that is, inside EMU) considerations. This line of argumentation, however, ignores the fact that large countries initiate cooperation because large countries reap a large share of the total benefits and do not suffer from free-riding problems. Collective-action theory would predict that the incentives for an exchange-rate agreement would be higher in a multipolar world than under current conditions.

In sum, the paucity of global thinkers on reforming the international monetary system may reflect awareness that there is no dominant solution. National incentives to implement large designs are smaller than they were in the aftermath of World War II. The reduction in relative economic and financial power of the United States has reduced this country's incentive to lead. The increase in relative economic and financial power of the EU does not automatically translate into more desire for cooperation. Indeed, there is little evidence that the Group of Three (Germany, Japan, and the United States) has any stomach for currency management. This fact is so obvious to have prompted a group of the above-mentioned Task Force Report to write a dissenting view, whose central message is (Task Force Report, 1999, p. 129). "The international monetary system will continue to be ineffective and crisis prone until that crucial centerpiece of its operation is thoroughly revamped. We urge the G-3 countries to adopt some variant of target zones in the near future." This is the background against which grand-design architects must build a reformed international monetary system.

References

Eichengreen, B. (1999) *Towards a New International Financial Architecture: A Practical Post-Asia Agenda*. Washington, DC: Institute for International Economics.

International Monetary Fund (1998) *World Economic Outlook*. Washington, DC: IMF, May.

Stein, J.C. (1987) "Informational Externalities and Welfare-Reducing Speculation." *Journal of Political Economy* 95(6):1123–1145.

U.S. Council on Foreign Relation Task Force (1999) *Safeguarding Prosperity in a Global Financial System: The Future International Financial Architecture*. Washington, DC: Institute for International Economics.

Open economies review **11:S1** 69–109 (2000)
© 2000 *Kluwer Academic Publishers. Printed in The Netherlands.*

Some Lessons for Regulation from Recent Bank Crises

DAVID T. LLEWELLYN
Loughborough University, Loughborough, Leicestershire

Keywords: bank crises, bad banking practices, incentives, moral hazard, monitoring, supervision, regulation

JEL Classification Numbers: G21, G28

Abstract

Recent bank crises in developed and developing countries have underlined the question of a good "regulatory regime," which is a wider concept than the set of prudential principles and business rules established by external regulatory agencies. The role of external regulation in fostering a safe and sound banking system is limited. The incentive's structure for private banks and the efficiency of monitoring and supervision have to play a great role. Liberalization of markets can have bad effects in the transitional period, but advantages can be enormous after the system starts to work correctly. The main lesson of recent bank crises is that there needs to be more effective surveillance of financial institutions both by supervisory authorities and by markets. Effective regulation (internal and external) and supervision of banks and financial institutions have the potential to give a major contribution to the stability and robustness of financial system.

Introduction

Our objective is to consider the experience of recent banking crises in both developed and developing countries and to draw lessons, especially with respect to the design of an optimum regulatory regime. This is done by setting out a series of general principles designed to lower the probability of banking distress. The concept of a regulatory regime is considerably wider than the prevailing set of prudential and conduct of business rules established by external regulatory agencies. It is widened to include the nature of the incentive structures operating within banks, the role of monitoring and supervision (by private and official agents), the disclosure regime and the role of market disciplines, and corporate governance arrangements within banks. It also includes the arrangements for official intervention in the event of bank distress. Just as the causes of banking crises are multidimensional, so the principles of an effective regulatory regime must also incorporate a wider range of issues than just externally imposed rules on bank behavior.

A central theme is that, while external regulation has a role in fostering a safe and sound banking system, this role is limited. Equally and increasingly important are the incentive structures faced by private banking agents and the efficiency of the necessary monitoring and supervision of banks by official agencies and the market. External regulation is only one component of regimes to create safe and sound banking systems. It is further argued that over time and as the market environment in which banks operate becomes more complex, two structural shifts are needed within the regulatory regime: (1) external regulation needs to become less prescriptive, more flexible, and more differentiated among different institutions, and (2) more emphasis needs to be given to incentive structures and the contribution that regulation can make to creating appropriate incentive structures.

It is also necessary within the regulatory regime to include the arrangements for intervention in the event of bank distress and failures, not the least because they have incentive and moral-hazard effects that potentially influence future behavior by banks and their customers and the probability of future crises. These arrangements also have important implications for the total cost of intervention (for example, initial forbearance often has the effect of raising the eventual cost of subsequent intervention) and the distribution of those costs between taxpayers and other agents. Different intervention arrangements also have implications for the future efficiency of the financial system in that, for instance, forbearance may have the effect of sustaining inefficient banks and excess capacity in the banking sector.

For instance, it has frequently been argued (e.g., Drage and Mann, 1999) that, in the recent case of Southeast Asia, the injection of funds by the International Monetary Fund (IMF) and World Bank (which in effect replaced private finance) effectively bailed out investors and, by shielding them from the full losses of their actions, may have had the effect of encouraging imprudent lending in the future, which in turn may subsequently raise the probability of banking crises. It has also been claimed that the aftermath of the Mexico crisis sent a signal to investors that they are less likely to sustain losses by investing in short-term securities.

The focus of the article is wider than the banking crises recently experienced by countries in Latin American and Southeast Asia. There are also significant lessons to be learned from the experience in more long-standing developed countries such as the Scandinavian banking crises in the early 1990s.

The outline of the article is as follows. It begins with a brief overview of recent banking crises and the economic costs that emerge. Section 2 considers the common elements in banking crises. This is followed in Section 3 by a discussion of the multidimensional nature of recent crises and focuses on the macroeconomy, the legacy of preliberalization, the role of bad banking practices, perverse incentive structures and moral hazard, ineffective regulation, weak monitoring and supervision, weak market discipline on banks, and unsound corporate governance arrangements. This is followed (in Section 4) by a review of the impact of liberalization with a distinction made between the transitional effects associated with the shift from one regime to another and the steady-state characteristics of a deregulated financial system. The characteristics of a robust financial system are outlined in Section 5. The final section draws together the implications of the previous analysis of the nature and origin of banking crises by setting out a set of principles for a regulatory regime designed to lower the probability of distress in the banking sector. These are organized in six components: regulation, incentive structures, monitoring and supervision, intervention, market discipline, and corporate governance.

1. Recent banking crises

A recent IMF study of banking crises around the world begins as follows: "A review of the experiences since 1980 of the 181 current Fund member countries reveals that 133 have experienced significant banking-sector problems at some stage during the past fifteen years (1980–1995)" (Lindgren, 1996). Crises in the banking sector (in both developing and industrial economies) are clearly not random, isolated events. Around the world, banks in many countries have had very high levels of nonperforming loans, there has been a major destruction of bank capital, banks have failed, and massive support operations have been necessary. This represents a greater failure rate among banks than at any time since the great depression of the 1930s. They have involved substantial costs. In around 25 percent of cases the cost has exceeded 10 percent of gross national product (for example, in Spain, Venezuela, Bulgaria, Mexico, Argentina, and Hungary).

The main causes of recent crises have been those that have always attended commercial banking problems: poor risk analysis by banks, weak internal credit-control systems, connected lending, insufficient capital, ineffective regulation, weak monitoring and supervision by regulatory agencies, and weak internal governance. These factors have frequently been aggravated by a volatile conduct of economic policy and structural weaknesses in the macroeconomy. In other words, the origins of crises are both internal to banks and external. To focus myopically on one side misses the essential point that systemic crises have both macro and micro origins.

Almost always and everywhere banking crises are a complex interactive mix of economic, financial, and structural weaknesses. For an excellent survey of the two-way link between banking systems and macro policy, see Lindgren, Garcia, and Saal (1996). The trigger for many crises has been macroeconomic in origin and often associated with a sudden withdrawal of liquid external capital from the country. As noted by Brownbridge and Kirkpatrick (1999), financial crises have often involved triple crises of currencies, financial sectors, and corporate sectors. Similarly, it has been argued that East Asian countries were vulnerable to a financial crisis because of "reinforcing dynamics between capital flows, macro-policies, and weak financial and corporate sector institutions" (Alba et al., 1998, pp. 275–290). The link between balance of payments and banking crises is certainly not a recent phenomenon and has been extensively studies (e.g., Kaminsky and Reinhart, 1998; Gadlayn and Valdes, 1997; Sachs, Torrell, and Velesco, 1996).

Almost invariably, systemic crises (as opposed to the failure of individual banks within a stable system) in the financial system are preceded by major macroeconomic adjustment. This often leads to the economy moving into recession. Most financial crises have been preceded by sharp fluctuations in the macroeconomy and often in asset prices. However, it would be a mistake to ascribe banking crises and financial instability entirely to macroeconomic instability. While macro instability may be the immediate and proximate cause of a banking crisis, such a crisis usually emerges because the instability in the macroeconomy reveals existing weaknesses within the banking system. It is also usually the case that the seeds of the problem (such as overlending, weak risk analysis, and control) were sown in the earlier upswing of the cycle. The downswing phase reveals previous errors and overoptimism. The mistakes made in the upswing emerge in the downswing. Such weaknesses include, for instance, poor, weak, or inappropriate incentives in the system, weak internal-risk analysis, inefficient management and control systems within banks and financial firms, poor regulation and supervision of financial institutions, and so on. In Southeast Asia, for instance, a decade of substantial economic growth up to 1997 concealed the effects of questionable bank lending policies.

A common experience in countries that have experienced serious banking problems is that expectations have been volatile and asset prices (including property) have been subject to wild savings. A sharp (sometimes speculative) rise in asset prices has been followed by an equally dramatic collapse. An initial rise in asset prices induces overoptimism and sometimes euphoria, which in turn lead to increased demand for borrowed funds and an increased willingness by banks to lend.

Analysis of financial crises throughout the world indicates very powerfully that two common characteristics are weak internal-risk analysis, management, and control *systems* and weak (or even perverse) *incentives* within the financial system generally and financial institutions in particular. These need to be addressed if a robust and stable financial system is to be created. In particular, the conclusion is that an unstable or unpredictable macroeconomic environment is neither a necessary nor a sufficient condition for banking crises to emerge: it is an illusion to ascribe such crises to faults in the macroeconomy alone. The fault also lies internally within banks.

2. Some common elements in banking distress

While each banking crisis has unique and country-specific features, they also have a lot in common. Several conditions tend to precede most systemic banking crises:

- Rapid growth in bank lending within a relatively short period;
- Urealistic expectations and euphoria about economic prospects in the economy;

- A sharp and unsustainable rise in asset prices (part of euphoria speculation), leading to unrealistic demands for credit and willingness of banks and other lenders to supply loans;
- Concentrated bank portfolios often with a high property content (that is, while project risks may be properly assessed, portfolio risk is often not);
- Excessive interconnected lending within banking groups;
- Government involvement in loans and loan decisions, which may have the effect of weakening incentive structures, eroding discipline on lenders (an implicit guarantor), and involving undue political influence or insider relationships;
- Inappropriate risk premia being charged in lending interest rates,
- Insufficient attention being given to the value of collateral, most especially if rapid balance-sheet growth occurs in a period of asset-price inflation; and
- Weak conduct of monetary policy in a context of high and volatile rates of inflation.

In the final analysis, weak internal-risk analysis, management, and control systems are at the root of all banking crises. Instability elsewhere should not conceal or be used to excuse weaknesses in this area of bank management. Further, when these weaknesses are present, they frequently manifest themselves in excessive lending on property projects. Many banking crises around the world have been associated in part with overlending on property projects. This is partly because, in periods of rapid asset-price inflation, property appears to be an attractive lending proposition. However, it is in essence speculative lending, and the bubble bursts when the overcapacity in the property sector becomes evident. In other words, when internal-risk analysis, management, and control systems are weak and when euphoria supplants analysis, the problem will frequently be focused on property lending, which, in essence, is speculative in nature.

Banking crises also often follow major changes in the regulatory regime that create unfamiliar market conditions. Periods of rapid balance-sheet growth—especially if it occurs after a regime shift and in a period of intense competition where market-share considerations dominate bank behavior—almost inevitably involve banks incurring more risk. There are several reasons for this: banks begin to compete for market share by lowering their risk thresholds; risks are underpriced to gain market share; control systems tend to weaken in periods of rapid balance-sheet growth; growth itself generates unwarranted optimism and a balance-sheet growth momentum develops; and portfolios become unbalanced if new lending opportunities are concentrated in a narrow range of business sectors. When, as is often the case, fast-growth strategies are pursued by all banks simultaneously, borrowers become overindebted and more risky, which in turn increases the vulnerability of the banks from whom they are borrowing.

3. A multidimensional problem

The recent banking crises in Southeast Asia have, as always, been complex and their causes multidimensional. While evident macro-policy failures and volatile and structurally weak economies have been contributory factors, it is also the case that fundamentally unsound banking practices, perverse incentive structures and moral hazards, and weak regulation and supervision have also been major contributory factors. A myopic concentration on any single cause will fail to capture the complex interactions involved in almost all banking and financial crises.

This also suggests that the response to avoid future crises equally needs to be multidimensional, involving the conduct of macro policy, the conduct of regulation and supervision, the creation of appropriate incentive structures, the development of market discipline, and the internal governance and management of financial institutions. As a prelude to a consideration of the principles to reduce the probability of future banking fragility, the remainder of this section briefly considers in turn the main components of recent banking crises. While the experiences of these countries vary in detail, there is a remarkable degree of commonalty among them, including, to some extent, the experience of financial fragility in some developed economies. A discussion of the factors behind the Scandinavian banking crises of the early 1990s is given in Andersson and Viotti (1999) and Benink and Llewellyn (1994).

Reflecting the multidimensional aspect of financial distress, the main causal factors in recent banking crises are now considered under eight headings: (1) volatility in the macroeconomy, (2) the inheritance of structural weaknesses in the economy, (3) bad banking practices, (4) hazardous incentive structures and moral hazard within the financial system, (5) ineffective financial regulation, (6) weak monitoring and supervision by official agencies, (7) the absence of effective market discipline against hazardous bank behavior due partly to the lack of transparency and the disclosure of relevant information, and (8) structurally unsound corporate governance mechanisms within banks and their borrowing customers.

We find that the recent distress of banks in Southeast Asia is a product of a volatile economy (with strong speculative elements) combined with bad banking practices, weak regulation, ineffective supervision both by the official agencies and the market, and hazardous incentive structures. All of this induced excessive lending and risk taking by banks.

3.1. The macroeconomy

Although growth in the countries of Southeast Asia had been strong for many years before the onset of the crises, structural weaknesses in some of the economies of the region was also evident. In many cases, exceptionally high investment rates concealed inefficiencies in the allocation of investment funds

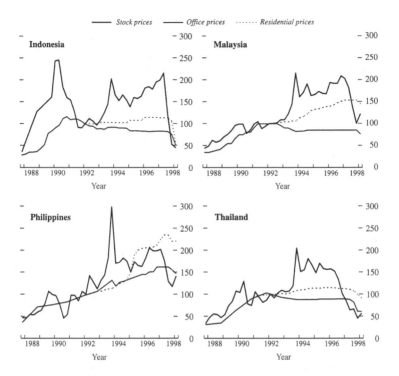

Figure 1. Real estate and stock prices in selected Asian countries.
Source: Adams et al. (1998).
Note: March 1992 = 100. Real estate and stock prices in local currencies, except for Indonesia, where prices are in U.S. dollars.

in the economy. Investment plans were often undertaken without reference to realistic assessment or measurement of expected rates of return. The financial and solvency position of many large investing companies was also seriously overstated by inaccurate accounting procedures.

Many financial crises have often been preceded by sharp and speculative rises in real and financial asset prices (see, for instance, the experience of Indonesia, Malaysia, Philippines, and Thailand in Figure 1 and Tables 1 and 2). Such sharp and unsustainable rises in asset prices have a bearing on subsequent financial distress through several channels. As already noted, the main route is through the effect on the demand and supply of bank credit.

A key factor in the macroeconomic background to recent banking crises has been the dependence on short-term capital inflows intermediated via the banking system. Table 3 shows the pattern of private capital flows to Asian countries over the 1990s and the dependence of the crisis countries (Indonesia, Korea, Malaysia, Philippines, and Thailand) on volatile banking flows (the dominant component of the "other" category in Table 3). The vulnerability to such volatile flows is shown in the $73 billion turnaround in 1997 when a net inflow

Table 1. Stock market price index.

Country	1990	1991	1992	1993	1994	1995	1996	1997
Korea	696.00	610.00	678.00	866.00	1027.00	882.00	651.00	376.00
Indonesia	417.00	247.00	274.00	588.00	469.00	513.00	637.00	401.00
Malaysia	505.00	556.00	643.00	1275.00	971.00	995.00	1237.00	594.00
Philippines	651.00	1151.00	1256.00	3196.00	2785.00	2594.00	3170.00	1869.00
Singapore	2254.00	1490.00	1524.00	2425.00	2239.00	2266.00	2216.00	1529.00
Thailand	612.00	711.00	893.00	1682.00	1360.00	1280.00	831.00	372.00
Hong Kong	3024.00	4297.00	5512.00	11888.00	8191.00	10073.00	13451.00	10722.00
Taiwan	4350.00	4600.00	3377.00	6070.00	7111.00	5158.00	6933.00	8187.00

Table 2. Stock market price index (property sector).

Country	1990	1991	1992	1993	1994	1995	1996	1997
Indonesia		119.00	66.00	214.00	140.00	112.00	143.00	40.00
Malaysia	113.00	113.00	126.00	369.00	240.00	199.00	294.00	64.00
Philippines	32.00	34.00	39.00	81.00	80.00	87.00	119.00	59.00
Singapore	230.00	280.00	250.00	541.00	548.00	614.00	648.00	357.00
Thailand	74.00	82.00	168.00	367.00	232.00	192.00	99.00	7.00
Hong Kong	32.00	453.00	554.00	1392.00	862.00	1070.00	1682.00	941.00
Taiwan	61.00	71.00	57.00	137.00	109.00	59.00	55.00	55.00

of $41 billion in 1996 was followed by a $32 billion net outflow in the following year. A substantial proportion of the short-term capital inflow was intermediated by domestic banks incurring short-term liabilities against foreign banks. The vulnerability of the crisis countries to an external illiquidity problem became substantial, and this was a pattern evident in crises faced by other countries (see Cole and Kehoe, 1996, and Sachs, Torrell, and Velesco, 1996). The issue is discussed in more detail in Corsetti, Pesenti, and Rabini (1998).

Overall, strong economic growth was, at least at the margin, intermediated by domestic banks incurring foreign-currency liabilities to foreign banks on the basis of short-term interbank lines.

3.2. *The inheritance*

Many of the crisis countries have had a long tradition of substantial government involvement and ownership in the banking system. This has frequently meant that funds have been channeled to ailing industries under overt or covert political pressure. Bisignano (1998) argues that such selective credit allocation has been a factor retarding the development of effective risk-analysis and

Table 3.　Private capital flows to asian countries.

	1990	1991	1992	1993	1994	1995	1996	1997
Total net private capital inflows	19.10	35.80	21.70	57.60	66.20	95.80	110.40	13.90
Net foreign direct investment	8.90	14.50	16.50	35.90	46.80	49.50	57.00	57.80
Net portfolio investment	−1.40	1.80	9.30	21.60	9.50	10.50	13.40	−8.60
Other	11.60	19.50	−4.10	0.10	9.90	35.80	39.90	−35.40
Net external borrowing from official creditors	5.60	11.00	10.30	8.70	5.90	4.50	8.80	28.60
Affected countries net private capital inflows[a]	24.90	29.00	30.30	32.60	35.10	62.90	72.90	−11.00
Net foreign direct investment	6.20	7.20	8.60	8.60	7.40	9.50	12.00	9.60
Net portfolio investment	1.30	3.30	6.30	17.90	10.60	14.40	20.30	11.80
Other	17.40	18.50	15.40	6.10	17.10	39.00	40.60	−32.30
Affected countries net external borrowing from official creditors	0.30	4.40	2.00	0.80	0.70	1.00	4.60	25.60

Sources: IMF; International Financial Statistics; World Economic Outlook database.
[a]Indonesia, Korea, Malaysia, the Philippines, and Thailand.

management systems in banks. In effect, banks were not acting as market-orientated financial intermediaries but as a channel for the public-policy support of industries that would not have received the scale of support through market mechanisms. In addition, the close connections between banks and industrial corporations and the general influence of government in the economy and the support of certain industries created the climate that neither borrowers nor the banks would be allowed to fail. This in turn aggravated a tendency toward imprudent lending. The issues are discussed further in Martinez (1998).

This is not a problem restricted to the less developed countries of Southeast Asia. Suzuki (1986) has argued that heavy involvement of government in the financial intermediation process carries three potential hazards: capital may be allocated inefficiently and on nonmarket criteria, it may undermine the effectiveness of monetary policy, and it may undermine fiscal discipline.

The inheritance problem also included weak corporate-sector structures with powerful links between companies in a way that could avoid normal market discipline on corporate behavior. This in turn was aggravated in many cases by weak corporate governance arrangements and the nonfeasibility for the market in corporate control to operate, both of which again muted normal market disciplines.

Before the financial liberalization process was instigated, many of the crisis countries operated on the basis of quite rigid public control or direction. Some of the subsequent problems emanated from losses (which were often concealed) incurred during the previously repressed financial regime. It is also evidently the case that the true financial condition of many banks had been concealed in the preliberalization period because of weak loan classification standards and an expectation that banks would be supported in the event of difficulty. In many Latin American countries, accounting standards were very lax, to the extent that banks were reporting positive net income even during a banking crisis (see Rojas-Suarez and Weisbrod, 1995). Such questionable accounting practices are not exclusive to developing countries (Kim and Cross, 1995). In some cases, banks seem to be able to determine loan-loss provisions on the basis of managing the level of declared capital rather than to reflect the true quality of loans (Beatty, Chamberlain, and Magliola, 1993).

3.3. Bad banking practices

Several elements of bad banking have also played a central role in the emergence of financial fragility and the subsequent failure of banks but were concealed during the optimism generated during the previous period of rapid economic growth. Mention may be made in particular of the following:

- Banks operated on the basis of low capital ratios, which were sometimes below minimum levels required by the regulatory authorities and which were not forced to be addressed by the regulators.
- Substantial foreign-currency exposures were incurred because foreign-currency borrowing was cheap, because the alleged commitment to a fixed exchange rate was not questioned, and because of the general expectation of bailouts in the event of difficulty.
- Very rapid growth was experienced in bank lending. As already noted, a common feature of bank crises (including in advanced economies) is that they are preceded by a period of very rapid growth in bank lending. This is shown for the crisis countries of Southeast Asia in Tables 4 and 5, which show the high rates of growth in bank lending to the private sector and the sharp rise in the proportion of bank lending to gross domestic product (GDP). Periods of rapid growth in bank lending frequently conceal emerging problems: it is more difficult to distinguish good from bad loans (Hausmann and Gavin, 1996), banks often lend to areas with which they are not familiar, herding behavior develops, credit standards are weakened in a phase of euphoria, and some of the lending is based on speculative rises in asset prices. This has also been noted in the Scandinavia banking crises of the early 1990s (Benink and Llewellyn, 1994).
- Weak risk-analysis and management systems were in place within banks.
- Excessively concentrated portfolios often had a substantial exposure to property and real estate either directly in the form of loans or indirectly through the collateral offered by borrowers (the exposure to property of seven countries of Southeast Asia is given in Table 6).

Table 4. Bank lending to private sector (percent growth).

Country	1991	1992	1993	1994	1995	1996	1997
Korea	20.78	12.55	12.94	20.08	15.45	20.01	21.95
Indonesia	17.82	12.29	25.48	22.97	22.57	21.45	46.42
Malaysia	20.58	10.79	10.8	16.04	30.65	25.77	26.96
Philippines	7.33	24.66	40.74	26.52	45.39	48.72	28.79
Singapore	12.41	9.77	15.15	15.25	20.26	15.82	12.68
Thailand	20.45	20.52	24.03	30.26	23.76	14.63	19.8
Hong Kong		10.17	20.15	19.94	10.99	15.75	20.1
China	19.76	20.84	43.52	24.58	24.23	24.68	20.96
Taiwan	21.25	28.7	19.46	16.18	10	6	8.92

Table 5. Bank lending to private sector (percent of GDP).

Country	1990	1991	1992	1993	1994	1995	1996	1997
Korea	52.54	52.81	53.34	54.21	56.84	57.04	61.81	69.79
Indonesia	49.67	50.32	49.45	48.9	51.88	53.48	55.42	69.23
Malaysia	71.36	75.29	74.72	74.06	74.61	84.8	93.39	106.91
Philippines	19.17	17.76	20.44	26.37	29.06	37.52	48.98	56.53
Singapore	82.2	83.34	85.06	84.14	84.21	90.75	95.96	100.29
Thailand	64.3	67.7	72.24	80.01	91	97.62	101.94	116.33
Hong Kong		141.84	134.2	140.02	149	155.24	162.36	174.24
China	85.51	87.87	86.17	95.49	87.12	85.83	91.65	101.07
Taiwan	100.41	108.99	126.43	137.23	146.89	149.49	146.05	146.23

Table 6. Banking system exposure to property.

	Property Exposure	Collateral Valuation
Korea	15–25%	80–100%
Indonesia	25–30	80–100
Malaysia	30–40	80–100
Philippines	15–20	70–80
Singapore	30–40	70–80
Thailand	30–40	80–100
Hong Kong	40–55	50–70

Source: J.P. Morgan, *Asian Financial Markets* (January 1998).

- Bank lending was done on the basis of an unsustainable rise in asset prices.
- Substantial connected lending was done by banks to companies within the same group and on the basis of poor (or nonexistent) risk assessment and nonmarket criteria.
- Loans failed to incorporate risk premia in their interest rates. The Bank for International Settlements has noted (BIS, 1998) that in many crisis countries the lending margin was low (and was declining during the period of rapid growth) relative to operating costs, which indicates that insufficient risk premia were being charged.
- Inaccurate accounting standards and weak loan classification and provisioning had the effect of overstating the value of bank loans and hence the true capital position of banks.

An interesting perspective on the effect of excessive bank lending is given by an IMF team (Adams et al.,1998). Bank-lending growth was substantially in excess of the growth of GDP in the distress countries of Southeast Asia (Figure 2). This produced high leverage ratios (ratio of credit to the private sector relative to GDP). The IMF study notes that in many of the countries of the region (and particularly those where bank distress was most marked: Korea, Malaysia, and Thailand) the loan-leverage ratios rose to levels that were higher than those in industrial countries with more developed financial infrastructures (Figure 2). Several studies (e.g., Demirguc-Kunt and Detragiache, 1998; Kaminsky and Reinhart, 1999; Benink and Llewellyn, 1994) show that rapid credit growth and high and sharply rising leverage are significant determinants of banking crises in both developing and developed countries. The authors of the IMF study

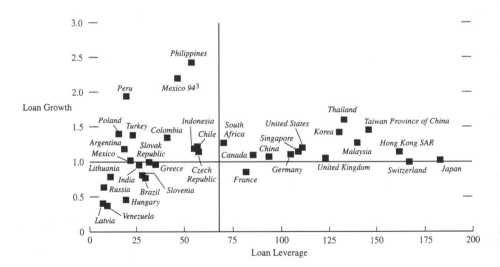

Figure 2. Financial-sector lending; Growth and leverage, 1990 to 1996.
Source: Adams et al. (1998).

suggest that with respect to Figure 2 countries in the early stages of economic development are normally in the northwest quadrant (high loan growth with low leverage) but that as they advance in their development they are expected to converge to the border between the southeast and northeast quadrants. The figure shows, however, that Korea, Thailand, and Malaysia each had both high growth rates of bank lending and high leverage ratios. A somewhat different picture emerges for the Philippines (very high growth rate of bank lending but comparatively low leverage ratio) and Indonesia with a modest growth rate of bank lending and a modest leverage ratio.

3.4. Hazardous incentive structures and moral hazard

A central theme of this article is that the incentive structures and moral hazards faced by decision makers (bank owners and managers, lenders to banks, borrowers, and central banks) are major issues to consider in the regulatory regime. Some analysts ascribe much of the recent banking crises to various moral hazards and perverse incentive structures such as fixed exchange-rate regimes, anticipated lender-of-last-resort actions, what are viewed as bailouts by the IMF, the ownership structure of banks and their corporate customers, and safety-net arrangements.

Mora-hazard effects, while important, may nevertheless also be exaggerated. For instance, Brealey (1999) argues against the adverse incentive effect of IMF lending on the grounds that investors did in fact lose value, and also points, to the reluctance of governments to resort to IMF facilities because of the resultant conditionality that is applied. It is also argued (Adams et al., 1998) that investors in Southeast Asia were motivated not by any alleged safety net but by the "star-performance" status of the economies. While potential moral-hazard effects may be exaggerated, this is not to deny the central importance of identifying the incentive structures implicit in regimes and the potential moral hazards that can arise.

There is a particular issue with respect to the incentive structure of state-owned or state-controlled banks, as their incentives may be ill defined if not hazardous. Such banks are not subject to the normal disciplining pressures of the market, their "owners" do not monitor their behavior, and there is no disciplining effect from the market in corporate control. Political interference in such banks and the unwitting encouragement of bad banking practices can itself become powerful ingredients in bank distress. Lindgren, Garcia, and Saal (1996) found, for instance, that banks that are, or were recently, state-owned or -controlled were a factor in most of the instances of unsoundness in their sample of banking crises.

Several adverse-incentive structures can be identified in many of the countries that have recently experienced distressed banking systems:

- The expectation that the government's commitment to the exchange value of the domestic currency was absolute induced imprudent and unhedged foreign-currency borrowing both by banks (though these were sometimes hedged) and companies.

- Expectations of bailouts or support for industrial companies (which had at various times been in receipt of government support) meant that the bankruptcy threat was weak.
- This may also have affected foreign creditors.
- A strong belief in the role of the lender-of-last-resort led to expectations that banks would not be allowed to fail. The IMF notes that the perception of implicit guarantees was probably strengthened by the bailouts in the resolution of earlier banking crises in Thailand (1983 to 1987), Malaysia (1985 to 1988) and Indonesia (1994).
- The effect of close relationships between banks, the government, other official agencies and industrial corporations often meant that relationships (such as lending) that would normally be conducted at arm's length became intertwined in a complex structure of economic and financial linkages within sometimes opaque corporate structures. This also meant that corporate governance arrangements, both within banks and their borrowing customers, were often weak and ill defined.

3.5. Ineffective regulation

The many elements of weak regulation in the origin of banking crises in recent years aggravated the effect of the other dimensions to the distress:

- Capital-adequacy regulations were often either not in place or were not effectively enforced.
- Regulatory requirements for capital, while conforming to the letter of international agreements, were nevertheless set too low in relation to the nature of the risks in the economy and the risks being incurred by banks: capital-adequacy regulation often did not accurately reflect the banks' risk characteristics (BIS, 1998).
- The rules with respect to classification of loan quality and provisions were often too lenient and ill specified, with the result that provisions were insufficient to cover expected losses, and earnings and capital were overstated (Brownbridge and Kirkpatrick, 1999; Folkerts-Landau et al., 1995).
- Rules with respect to exposure to single borrowers were often too lax (or not enforced).
- Regulation and supervision with respect to concentrated exposures (such as property) were too lenient.
- Poor accounting standards enabled banks to evade prudential and other restrictions on insider lending (Rahman, 1998).
- Many governments and regulatory authorities were slow and hesitant to act in the face of impending solvency problems of banks. Such regulatory forbearance was often due to the fact that regulatory authorities had substantial

discretion as to when and whether to intervene and were often subject to political pressure of one kind or another.

3.6. Weak monitoring and supervision

As with all companies, banks need to be monitored. In addition to the standard principal-agent issues, banks are universally monitored and supervised by official agencies (such as central banks). In practice, "some form of supervisory failure was a factor in almost all the sample countries" (Lindgren, Garcia, and Saal, 1996, p. 312). In many countries, supervisory agencies did not enforce compliance with regulations (Reisen, 1998). In Korea and Indonesia, in particular, banks did not comply with regulatory capital-adequacy requirements and other regulations (UNCTAD, 1998). In particular, connected lending restrictions were not adequately supervised, partly because of political pressure and the lack of transparency in the accounts of banks and their corporate customers.

A further aspect of this supervisory failure was that supervisory intensity did not adjust in line with the liberalization of the financial system and the new business operations and risk characteristics of banks that emerged in a more deregulated market environment. This is discussed in more detail in the next section. This was also the case with Scandinavian countries when, in the second half the 1980s, banks responded aggressively to deregulation. The nature and intensity of official supervision needs to reflect the nature of the regulatory regime. In practice, while the latter changed, this was not accompanied by sufficiently intensified supervision.

3.7. Weak market discipline for banks

Monitoring is not conducted only by official agencies whose specialist task it is. In well-developed financial regimes, the market also monitors the behavior of financial firms. The disciplines imposed by the market can be as powerful as any sanctions imposed by official regulatory agencies. However, in practice, the disciplining role of the markets (including the interbank market, which in many jurisdictions is able to impose powerful discipline through the risk premium charged on interbank loans) was weak in the crisis countries of Southeast Asia. This was due predominantly to the lack of disclosure and transparency of banks and the fact that, for reasons already noted, little reliance could be placed on the quality of the accountancy data provided in bank accounts. In many cases standard accountancy and auditing procedures were not applied rigorously. In some cases there was willful misrepresentation of the financial position of banks and nonfinancial companies. Overall, market disciplines can work effectively only on the basis of full and accurate disclosure and transparency.

Effective competition in the banking system (and especially if this includes competition from foreign banks) can also impose its own discipline and instill good business practice. In general, a competitive banking system is essential

for long-term efficiency and soundness. Monopoly rents may engender ineffi-
ciency, most especially if the monopolies are state-owned or -controlled.

   A further dimension relates to the potentially powerfully disciplining power of
the market in corporate control, which, through the threat of removing control
from incumbent managements, is a discipline on managers to be efficient and
not endanger the solvency of their banks. As put in a recent IMF study: "An
open and competitive banking market exerts its own form of discipline against
weak banks while encouraging well-managed banks" (Lindgren, Garcia, and
Saal, 1996, p. 312).

3.8. Unsound corporate governance arrangements

In the final analysis, all aspects of the management of a bank are corporate governance issues. This means that if banks behave hazardously this is, to some
extent, a symptom of weak internal corporate governance. This may include, for
instance, a hazardous corporate structure for the bank, lack of internal control
systems, weak surveillance by (especially nonexecutive) directors, and ineffective internal audit arrangements. Corporate governance arrangements were
evidently weak and underdeveloped in banks in many of the distress countries.

   Some ownership structures of banks in the private sector can produce bad
corporate governance. In some cases, particular corporate structures (for example, banks being part of larger conglomerates) encourage connected lending
and weak risk analysis of borrowers. This has been found to be the case in a
significant number of bank failures in the countries of Southeast Asia and Latin
America. Some corporate structures also make it comparatively easy for banks
to effectively conceal their losses and unsound financial positions.

3.9. Assessment

The central theme of this section has been that recent banking crises have been
multidimensional and a complex mix of several interacting pressures and weaknesses. A myopic focus on particular causal components is likely to produce
a distorted picture and also to produce inadequate policy and reform proposals. The experience of many countries has demonstrated the lethal cocktail
of fundamental and structural weaknesses in the economy, hazardous incentive structures, weak and ineffective regulation, inadequate official supervision,
and an inability or unwillingness of the market to impose discipline on banks.
It follows that reform needs to proceed along several channels simultaneously,
which in itself makes the reform process more demanding and challenging.

4.   Liberalization: Stock adjustment versus steady state

Many financial crises have been associated with changes in the regulatory
regime and a process of liberalization in particular. For decades, the economies

of Southeast Asia were highly regulated with interest-rate ceilings, limitations on lending growth by financial institutions, restrictions on foreign entry into the banking system, and so on. At various times during the 1990s, these restrictions were relaxed, and the pace of financial liberalization accelerated.

Williamson and Mahar (1998) show that almost all of their sample of 34 economies (both industrialized and developing) that undertook financial liberalization over the 1980s and 1990s experienced varying degrees of financial crisis. Similarly, Kaminsky and Reinhart (1998) found that in the majority in their sample of countries that had experienced banking crises, the financial sector had been liberalized during the period of five years. They conclude that financial liberalization helps predict banking crises across a range of countries. Goldstein and Folkerts-Landau (1993) observe a general pattern of deregulation inducing more competition to be followed by increasing financial fragility.

While in both developed and less developed countries banking distress has often followed periods of deregulation and liberalization, a distinction needs to be made between the *transitional* effect of moving from one regulatory regime to another and the characteristics of a *steady-state* liberalized financial system. The instabilities that may occur in the transition period do not necessarily carry over into the new steady state.

4.1. The transitional phase

The universal evidence is that financial liberalization enhances efficiency in the financial system and that financial repression distorts the incentives for saving and investment. However, financial liberalization often brings problems most especially in the transition period.

One effect of increased competition that results from liberalization is often to erode the economic rents of financial firms associated with the previously noncompetitive environment. This reduced profitability may induce financial institutions into taking more risk.

In the stock-adjustment phase (that is, during the period when the new regime is being introduced) uncertainty may be created as financial firms are unfamiliar with the requirements of the new regime. Previously protected institutions need to adapt behavior, though this may occur only with a considerable lag. New behavior patterns need to be learned. Some mistakes during the process of financial liberalization occur because banks do not adjust quickly enough to the new regime. Behavior that is appropriate under one regime may be totally inappropriate in another (see Benink and Llewellyn, 1994, for a more formal discussion).

In the first instance, liberalization may also increase inflationary pressure as balance-sheet restraints are lifted and financial firms increase their lending very rapidly in a relatively short period. This is often associated with a sharp rise in asset prices within a relatively short period. The implication is that financial liberalization needs to be accompanied by an appropriate stabilization policy to reduce the potential impact on inflation, which can distort lending decisions.

In countries that have liberalized their financial systems after decades of controls, banks responded in a remarkably similar way by substantially increasing the volume of lending in a short period. As a result of increased competitive pressures, banks tend to lower *equilibrium* and *disequilibrium* credit rationing and risk thresholds (Llewellyn and Holmes, 1991), bank lending margins are squeezed, and bank profitability at first rises due to this expansion but later deteriorates sharply due to massive loan losses.

The rapid growth in lending during the stock-adjustment phase may also increase risk because banks' internal control systems are weak. This is compounded when banks adopt market-share strategies in a strongly expanding loans market.

In general, periods of substantial growth of bank lending are likely to involve banks moving into more risky business and adopting a higher risk profile (OECD, 1992). The removal of controls often unleashes a pent-up demand for credit, and suppliers of credit are freed to compete, which in some cases leads to a relaxation of standards (see also Schinasi and Hargreaves, 1993). There are many reasons why risks might rise in a period of a sharp growth in lending following a period of deregulation: economic rents created by regulation are suddenly removed, more risky business appears to be profitable, and credit rationing is eroded. The same competitive pressures may also make it difficult, in the short-run, for banks to incorporate higher risk premia in loan rates, with the results that bank loans are underpriced.

The initial stock-adjustment reaction often involves a phase of overreaction by lenders as balance-sheet structures are taken beyond long-run sustainable positions. There are several reasons for this: reactions times in financial markets are short, adjustments can be made quickly, and the financial system is characterized by oligopolistic competition. As a result, competitive pressures seem to force firms to move together—sometimes described as a herd instinct. Some analysts have ascribed it to a property of the incentive structure within banks in that, in a world of uncertainty, the desire to avoid personal blame for mismanagement is liable to make risk-averse bank managers subject to peer-group pressure to follow the same policy.

The rise in interest rates that often follows the process of liberalization leads to an erosion of credit rationing and interest-rate ceilings imposed by financial firms. This in itself may both increase risk and reduce the profitability of banks.

Liberalization may also reveal inherent weaknesses in the banking system both with respect to structure and the traditional way of conducting business.

If supervision is not intensified at the same time as the financial system is liberalized, the financial system may become crisis prone. In liberalizing their financial systems, the countries of Southeast Asia ignored the risks posed by rapid liberalization, which is not accompanied by significant strengthening of regulation and supervision of bank behavior (Furman and Stiglitz, 1998). In this, they followed the earlier experience of the Scandinavian countries (Benink and Llewellyn, 1994). Bisignano (1998) suggests that it represented a combination of "excess momentum" by the private sector and "excess inertia" by the regulatory authorities. Put another way, there is a tradeoff between regulation and supervision in that if regulation is eased to allow banks to conduct more business, there is an increased requirement for effective supervision of the way that business is conducted. There are many examples, in both developing and developed countries, where liberalization was not accompanied by more intensive supervision.

However, many of these problems are ones of transition. A distinction needs to be made between what happens during a *stock-adjustment* phase of liberalization and the characteristics of a *steady-state*, deregulated financial system. The evidence powerfully indicates that a liberalized financial system is more efficient and contributes more substantially to economic development. However, when moving from one regime to another (especially from a highly controlled financial system to a more market-oriented system) instability may be created as new behavior patterns need to be learned. The fact that instability may occur during the transitional, stock-adjustment period does not mean that a deregulated financial system is inherently unstable or even less stable than a regulated regime. Many of the financial crises experienced in recent years have been associated with the uncertainties and mistakes during the *transitional* phase during which liberalization measures were adopted. The crisis is often a function of the uncertainty associated with regime changes (as the system moves from one regime to another) rather than the inherent characteristics of the new regime *per se*. A deregulated system is not to be discredited because of the problems sometimes associated with moving toward it.

The policy implication is that care is needed in the process of liberalization and that supervision of financial institutions needs to move in pace with liberalization. Deregulation without enhanced supervision is likely to be hazardous irrespective of the long-run benefits of liberalization and the erosion of financial repression. Liberalization is often not accompanied by necessary changes in regulation and supervision, corporate governance reforms, and enhanced market monitoring and control.

4.2. The steady state

However, there is an argument that while some of the financial distress is associated with the transition from one regime to another, a more competitive market environment is potentially more risky than an uncompetitive market structure. This is because the value of the banking franchise is reduced by competition. The more valuable the franchise, the less likely are owners to risk losing it. Keeley (1990), for example, analyzes how deregulation and increased competition can induce banks to behave with less regard to risk because it lowers the value of the banking franchise. Similar conclusions are found in Caprio and Summers (1993) and Demsetz, Saidenberg, and Strahan (1997). Using data to proxy bank franchise values, Hellman, Murdock, and Stiglitz (1995) examine the relationship between bank franchise values and financial-market Liberalization as a test of the argument that moral hazard increases as banks' franchise values fall. Their results confirm that banking crises are more likely to occur in countries with a liberalized financial sector and that franchise values tend to be lower when financial markets are liberalized.

In many previous cases, highly regulated regimes acted as a protection to financial institutions by effectively limiting competition. The extent of the economic rents that were created in this regime were probably underestimated by the regulatory authorities. In many cases, they underestimated the extent to which deregulation and liberalization would increase competition in the banking industry even though that was one of the public-policy objectives. These errors inhibited appropriate responses in the areas of prudential regulation and monitoring and supervision.

5. Robust financial system

Given this experience it is instructive to consider the basic characteristics of a robust financial system—that is, one that satisfies the test of markets. Basically, robustness refers to the ability of the financial system to remain stable and efficient under a wide range of market conditions and shocks. We may identify three particular elements in this: *flexibility* (the ability of the financial system to operate in all circumstances and to change the way it operates as market conditions alter), *resilience* (the ability to continue to function in the face of external shocks including instability in the macroeconomy), and *internally stable* (the ability of the financial system not to generate its own shocks or magnify shocks in the macroeconomy).

Regulation can contribute toward a robust financial system through six main routes: by prescribing risk-taking activity and establishing certain basic prudential standards (such as minimum capital-adequacy requirements), by affecting inventive structures and limiting moral hazard within the financial system, by requiring a high degree of information disclosure and transparency, by establishing a robust basic financial infrastructure, by setting corporate governance standards and structures, and by monitoring and supervising financial institutions. These are discussed in some detail in later sections.

5.1. The infrastructure

A central prerequisite for a robust financial system is to create an institutional setting and financial infrastructure for sound credit culture and effective market functioning. This includes aspects such as legal arrangements, information disclosure and availability, and the basic tools of sound accountancy and auditing. Several particular elements are identified:

- A strong legal framework to ensure that property rights are well defined and easily and reasonably costlessly exercisable (this implies creating a legal environment where the terms and conditions of contracts are observed and the rights and obligations of all agents involved in loans or transactions in financial assets are well-defined, understood, and enforceable without undue delay or cost);
- A legal framework for the pledging of collateral and the ability to take possession of collateral (without these conditions moral hazard and adverse incentives are created with bank borrowers);
- Clearly defined bankruptcy laws and codes, along with effective enforcement mechanisms;
- Good-quality, timely, and relevant information disclosure available to all market participants and regulators so that asset quality, creditworthiness, and the condition of financial institutions can be assessed (this includes timely publication of relevant financial data on the soundness of financial institutions and the adoption of comprehensive and well-defined accounting principles that conform to agreed international standards);
- Effective rating agencies operating independently of government authorities;
- Robust payment, settlement, and custody arrangements and systems; and
- A wide variety of financial instruments (including derivatives) and markets that can assist financial institutions in the management of risks.

These considerations relate to the basic infrastructure of a financial system, and many require public-policy initiatives by public agencies with responsibility for systemic stability. Lindgren, Garcia, and Saal (1996) found that an inadequate legal framework was a common characteristic in the sample of developing and transition economies that had experienced banking crises.

6. The regulatory regime

Having discussed some of the common origins of banking distress, we turn now to consider a set of principles to reduce the future probability of crises. In the final analysis, regulation is about changing the behavior of regulated institutions. One of the key questions is the extent to which behavior is to be altered by externally imposed *rules* or through creating *incentives* for firms to behave in a particular way. The arguments against reliance on detailed and prescriptive rules are outlined in Goodhart et al. (1998). Regulation can be endogenous within the financial firm as well as exogenous. A major issue, therefore, is whether regulation should proceed through externally imposed, prescriptive, and detailed rules or by the regulator creating incentives for appropriate behavior.

Financial systems are changing substantially to an extent that may undermine traditional approaches to regulation and most especially the balance between regulation and supervision and the role of market discipline. In particular, globalization, the pace of financial innovation and the creation of new financial instruments, the blurring of traditional distinctions between different types of financial firm, the speed with which portfolios can change through banks trading in derivatives and other products, and the increased complexity of banking business all create a fundamentally new—in particular, more competitive—environment in which regulation and supervision are undertaken. They also change the viability of different approaches to regulation, which, if it is to be effective, must constantly respond to changes in the market environment in which regulated firms operate.

A robust financial system requires three particular properties: (1) proper decision making and control within financial institutions with effective risk analysis, management, and control systems; (2) an efficient regulatory and supervisory regime for financial institutions; and (3) sound incentive structures for all parties, including regulators. These three dominant themes may, on the face of it, seem fairly obvious. However, when the detailed implications are considered, they are not so obvious. Some of the measures designed to achieve what is required are difficult to implement, and the transactions costs of change can be substantial.

A sustained theme in this article is that a regulatory regime is to be viewed more widely than externally imposed regulation on financial institutions. Regulation is only one of six key components: regulation, incentive structures, monitoring and supervision (private and official), intervention and sanctions, market discipline, and corporate governance. Under current conditions (such as globalization) it would be a mistake to rely wholly, or even predominantly, on external regulation, monitoring, and supervision by the "official sector" of the regulatory regime. The world of banking and finance is too complex and volatile to be able to rely on a simple set of prescriptive rules for prudent behavior.

The key to optimizing the effectiveness of a regulatory regime is the portfolio mix of the six core components. All are necessary, but none alone is sufficient. Particular emphasis is given to incentive structures because, in the final analysis, if these are perverse or inefficient, no amount of formal regulation will prevent problems emerging in the banking sector. In practice, there needs to be a switch in emphasis from prescriptive regulation to creating appropriate incentive structures.

Having established the general framework of the "regulatory regime," the following sections outline a set of general principles designed to reduce the probability of banking distress. They are focused on each of the six core components: regulation, incentive structures, monitoring and supervision, official intervention in the event of bank distress, the role of market disciple, and corporate governance arrangements.

6.1. Regulation

Goodhart et al. (1998) argue that there is always an inherent danger of overregulation because consumers perceive regulation to be a costless activity (and hence is overdemanded) and regulatory agencies tend to be risk averse (which means that regulation may be oversupplied). The case for regulation of banks depends on various market imperfections and failures (especially externalities and asymmetric information), which, in the absence of regulation, produce suboptimal results and reduce consumer welfare. In other words, the objective of regulation should be limited to correcting identified market imperfections and failures. Six main principles are suggested.

6.1.1. The objectives of regulation need to be clearly defined and circumscribed. Financial regulation should have only a limited number of objectives. In the final analysis the objectives are to sustain systemic stability and to protect the consumer. Regulation should not be overloaded by being required to achieve other and wider objectives, such as social outcomes. Constructing effective and efficient regulation is difficult enough with limited objectives, and the more it is overburdened by wider considerations, the more likely it is to fail in all of them.

6.1.2. The rationale of regulation and supervision should be limited. The rationale for regulation lies in correcting for identified market imperfections and failures, incorporating externalities, achieving economies of scale in monitoring, breaking gridlock, and limiting the moral hazard associated with safety nets (see Llewellyn, 1999). Regulation, in general, and regulatory measures, in particular, need to be assessed according to these criteria. If they do not satisfy any of these criteria, particular regulatory measures should be abandoned.

6.1.3. Regulation should be seen in terms of a set of contracts. Laws, regulations, and supervisory actions provide incentives for regulated firms to adjust their actions and behavior and to control their own risks internally. They can usefully be viewed as *incentive contracts* within a standard principal-agent relationship where the principal is the regulator and the agent is the regulated firm. Within this general framework, regulation involves a process of creating incentive-compatible contracts so that regulated firms have an incentive to behave in a way consistent with the objectives of systemic stability and investor protection. Similarly, there need to be incentives for the regulator to set appropriate objectives, to adopt well-designed rules, not to overregulate, and to act in a timely fashion (for instance, in the face of pressure for forbearance). If incentive contracts are well designed, they will induce appropriate behavior by regulated firms. Conversely, if they are badly constructed and improperly designed, they might fail to reduce systemic risk (and other hazards that regulation is designed to avoid) or have undesirable side effects on the process of financial intermediation (such as imposing high costs). At center stage is the issue of whether all parties have the right incentives to act in a way that satisfies the objectives of regulation.

6.1.4. The form and intensity of regulatory and supervisory requirements should differentiate between regulated institutions according to their relative portfolio risk and efficiency of internal control mechanisms. While the objective of competitive neutrality in regulation is something of a mantra, this is not satisfied if unequal institutions are treated equally. In this respect, equality relates to the risk characteristics of institutions. It might be argued that to maintain competitive neutrality two banks with different risk characteristics and quality of risk-management systems should be treated equally because they are both banks and in competition with each other. However, in terms of satisfying the objectives of regulation, a suboptimum outcome will emerge if they are subject to the same regulatory requirements. One of the hazards of a detailed and prescriptive rule-book approach is that it may fail to make the necessary distinctions between nonhomogeneous firms because the same rules are applied to all; it reduces the scope for legitimate differentiations to be made. The adoption of an internal model's approach, such has been introduced by the Group of 10 (G-10) countries (the governments of nine IMF countries—Belgium, Canada, France, Italy, Japan, the Netherlands, Switzerland, the United Kingdom, and the United States—and the central banks of two others, Germany and Sweden) after the Market Risk Amendment of the Basle accord, recognizes this point. Other considerations that should govern the setting of minimum capital-adequacy requirements for individual banks include the quality of management; the quality, reliability, and volatility of the bank's earnings; and the bank's liability and liquidity profile.

6.1.5. In some areas the regulator could offer a menu of contracts to regulated firms requiring them to self-select into the correct category. There is an information, and possibly efficiency, loss if a high degree of conformity in the behavior of regulated firms is enforced. If, alternatively, firms have a choice about how to satisfy the regulator's stated objectives and principles, they would be able to choose their own, least-cost, way of satisfying these objectives. The regulator could offer a menu of self-selecting contracts rather than the same one to all institutions. Equally, banks could offer their own contracts. An example of this approach is the variable add-on in the *multiplication factor* of the Basle internal models approach. Since this add-on varies with the performance of a value-at-risk (VaR) Model during back-testing procedures, a bank has the choice between using a simple (less precise) model with a higher capital requirement for market risk or incurring costs in developing a better model and benefit from a lower capital requirement. However, empirical tests of VaR Models show that the fixed part of 3 in the Basle multiplication factor is already so high that there is little incentive to use the best models because of the relatively small variable add-on (between 0 and 1). Our suggestion, therefore, is to lower the fixed part of the multiplication factor and to increase the variable part.

Another approach that could be adopted for more qualitative measures of internal control and risk-management quality is risk-related examination schedules. Here, financial institutions can be given a risk rating (say, between 0 and 10) on the basis of a series of internal control indicators. The higher the rating, the greater the perceived overall risk and the more frequent and intrusive would be on-site examinations. A more far-reaching proposal is the precommitment approach, which gives a bank the possibility to preannounce a maximum trading loss and incur regulatory penalties or other incentives in proportion to the extent to which preannounced maximum losses are exceeded (this is discussed below).

6.1.6. Capital regulation should create incentives for the correct pricing of absolute and relative risk. If differential capital requirements are set against different types of assets (for example, through applying differential risk weights), the rules should be based on actuarial calculations of relative risk. If risk weights are incorrectly specified, perverse incentives can be created for banks because the implied capital requirements are more or less than justified by true relative-risk calculations. A major critique of the current Basle capital requirements is that the risk weights bear little relation to relative-risk characteristics of different assets and that the loan book carries a uniform risk weight even though the risk characteristics of different loans within a bank's portfolio vary considerably.

6.2. Incentive structure

Emphasis has been given to the central importance of incentives within banks and the role that regulation can have in positively creating appropriate incentives. As banking crises frequently occur when there are weak incentives to act prudently, a necessary ingredient of a robust and stable financial system is the creation of appropriate and efficient incentives and disciplining mechanisms for all market participants and most especially bank owners, bank managers, and financial system supervisors. These are now briefly considered.

6.2.1. There should be appropriate incentives for bank owners. Bank owners play an important role in the monitoring of bank management and their risk taking. In the final analysis, bank owners absorb the risks of the bank. There are several ways in which appropriate incentives for bank owners can be developed:

- One route is to ensure that banks have appropriate levels of equity capital. Capital serves three main roles as far as incentive structures are concerned: a commitment of the owners to supply risk resources to the business (which they can lose in the event that the bank makes bad loans), an internal insurance fund, and the avoidance of the bank becoming the captive of its bad debtors. In general, the higher is the capital ratio, the more the owners have to lose, and hence the greater the incentive for them to monitor the behaviour of managers. Low capital creates a moral hazard in that, given the small amount owners have to lose, the more likely they are to condone excessive risk-taking in a gamble-for-resurrection strategy. This was evidently the case at times during the savings and loan crisis in the United States.

- Corporate governance arrangements should be such that equity holders actively supervise managers.
- Supervisors and safety-net agencies should ensure that owners lose out in any restructuring operations in the event of failure. Failure to penalize shareholders in the restructuring of unsuccessful banks has been a major shortcoming in some rescue operations in Latin America.
- In some countries (such as New Zealand) the incentive on owners has been strengthened by experimenting with a policy of increased personal liability for bank directors.

6.2.2. There should be appropriate internal incentives for management.
The right incentive structures for the managers of financial institutions are equally as important as those for the owners. In fact, the two should be seen in combination. In the final analysis, all aspects of the behavior of a firm are corporate governance issues. Several procedures, processes, and structures can reinforce internal risk-control mechanisms. These include internal auditors, internal audit committees, procedures for reporting to senior management (and perhaps to the supervisors), and making a named board member responsible for compliance and risk-analysis and management systems. Supervisors can strengthen the incentives for these by, for instance, relating the frequency and intensity of their supervision and inspection visits (and possibly rules) to the perceived adequacy of the internal risk-control procedures and compliance arrangements. In addition, regulators can create appropriate incentives by calibrating the external burden of regulation (such as number of inspection visits and allowable business) to the quality of management and the efficiency of internal incentives.

Specific measures have been designed to create correct incentive structures:

- Strong and effective risk-analysis, management, and control systems should be in place in all financial institutions for assessing risks *ex ante* and asset values *ex post*. Systems and incentives are required for timely and accurate provisioning against bad or doubtful debts. In the final analysis, most bank failures are ultimately due to weaknesses in this area. Regulatory agencies have a powerful role in promoting and insisting on effective systems of internal management and risk control in financial institutions by strict accountability of owners, directors, and senior management.
- Managers should also lose if the bank fails. This requires a high degree of professionalism in bank managers and decision makers and penalties

(including dismissal) for incompetence among bank managers. Remuneration packages may be related to regulatory compliance

- Subject to prudential standards being maintained, proper incentives can be created by the fostering of competition in the financial sector. This can be achieved, for instance, by removing restrictions on business activity, allowing the entry of foreign banks and other financial institutions, and forcing the abandoning of restrictive practices, cartels, and other anticompetitive mechanisms.
- Mechanisms need to be in place to ensure that loan valuation, asset classification, loan concentrations, interconnected lending, and risk-assessment practices reflect sound and accurate assessments of claims and counterparties. This also requires mechanisms for the independent verification of financial statements and compliance with the principles of sound practice through professional external auditing and on-site inspection by supervisory agencies.
- Ownership structures need to foster shareholder monitoring and oversight. This includes private ownership of banks to strengthen the monitoring of management performance and to reduce distortions in incentives for managers.
- Large banks need to be required to establish internal audit committees.

The key is that appropriate internal incentives need to be developed for management to behave in appropriate ways and that the regulator has a role in ensuring that internal incentives are compatible with the objectives of regulation. Combining appropriate incentives for owners and managers contributes to a robust financial system, and, in principle, the market would evolve such incentives. However, experience indicates that, in many areas, and most especially when the competitive environment is changing and the regulatory regime is being adjusted, it is hazardous to rely on the market evolving appropriate incentives.

6.3. Monitoring and supervision

Because of the nature of financial contracts between financial firms and their customers (for example, many are long-term in nature and involve a fiduciary obligation), there is a need for continuous monitoring of the behavior of all financial firms. Because most (especially retail) customers are not, in practice, able to undertake such monitoring and because there are substantial economies of scale in such activity, an important role of regulatory agencies is to monitor the behavior of financial firms on behalf of customers. In effect, consumers delegate the task of monitoring to a dedicated agency.

The key issue is who is to undertake the monitoring. Several parties can potentially monitor the management of banks: bank owners, bank depositors, rating agencies, official agencies (such as the central bank or other regulatory body), and other banks in the market. In general, excessive emphasis has been given to official agencies. There may even be an adverse incentive effect in that, given that regulatory agencies conduct monitoring and supervision on a delegated basis, this may reduce the incentive for others to conduct efficient monitoring. The role of other potential monitors (and notably the market) needs to be strengthened in many, including well-developed, financial systems. This in turn requires adequate information disclosure and transparency in banking operations. There need to be greater incentives for other parties to monitor banks in parallel with official agencies. A major advantage of having agents other than official supervisory bodies to monitor banks is that it removes the inherent danger of having monitoring and supervision being conducted by a monopolist with less than perfect and complete information with the result that inevitably mistakes will be made. Two principles related to official monitoring and supervision are suggested.

6.3.1. Official agencies need to have sufficient powers and independence to conduct effective monitoring and supervision. This means that they need to be independent of political authorities and able to license, refuse to license, and withdraw licenses from banks. They need to have the authority and ability to monitor the full range of banks' activities and business and be able to monitor and assess banks' systems for risk analysis and control. Because of the moral hazard created in some bank structures, the agency needs to have power to establish rules on ownership and corporate structure of banks and to be able to establish minimum requirements for the competency and integrity of bank management.

6.3.2. Less emphasis should be placed on detailed and prescriptive rules and more on internal risk-analysis, -management, and -control systems. Externally imposed regulation in the form of prescriptive and detailed rules is becoming increasingly inappropriate and ineffective. More reliance should be placed on institutions' own internal risk-analysis, management, and control systems. This relates not only to quantitative techniques such as value-at-risk (VaR) Models but also to the management culture of those who handle models and supervise traders. There should be a shift of emphasis toward monitoring risk-control mechanisms and a recasting of the nature and functions of external regulation away from generalized rule-setting and toward establishing incentives and sanctions to reinforce such internal control systems. The recently issued consultative document by the Basle Committee on Banking Supervision (Basle Committee, 1999, p. 41) explicitly recognizes that a major role of the supervisory process is to monitor banks' own internal capital-management processes and "the setting of targets for capital that are commensurate with the bank's particular risk profile and control environment. This process would be subject to supervisory review and intervention, where appropriate."

6.4. *Intervention*

Regulation and supervision sometimes fail, at times to a degree that requires official intervention to maintain systemic stability. The way such intervention is made has signaling and incentive effects for the future behavior of financial institutions. The conditions under which intervention is made, the manner of intervention, and its timing may, therefore, have powerful moral-hazard effects.

Care is evidently needed when devising bank restructuring policies. There also need to be appropriate incentives for intervention agencies. Several principles can be established to guide the timing and form of intervention.

6.4.1. The design and application of safety-net arrangements (lender of last resort and deposit insurance) should create incentives for stakeholders to exercise oversight and to act prudently to reduce the probability of recourse being made to public funds. It is well 0 established that, depending on how deposit insurance schemes are constructed (especially with respect to which deposits are insured and the extent of any coinsurance), serious moral hazard can be created: depositors may be induced to act with less care, under some circumstances they may be induced to seek risky banks on the grounds that a one-way-bet is involved, insured institutions may be induced to take more risk because they are not required to pay the full risk premium on insured deposits, risk is therefore subsidised, banks may be induced to hold less capital, and the cost of deposit protection is passed to others who have no say in the risk-taking activity of the insured bank.

6.4.2. The extent and coverage of deposit insurance schemes should be strictly limited. Maintaining the integrity of the banking system requires that some bank liability holders are to be protected from the consequences of bank failure. But this should be limited because such protection may create adverse incentives. In particular, and in order to avoid the potential moral hazards emerging, coverage should be explicit (rather than assumed) and restricted to comparatively small deposits and there should always be an element of coinsurance to the extent that less than 100 percent of any deposit is insured. There should be a clear and public commitment to the limits imposed.

6.4.3. There needs to be a well-defined strategy for responding to the possible insolvency of financial institutions. A response strategy in the event of bank distress has several possible components:

- Being prepared to close insolvent financial institutions;
- Taking prompt corrective action to address financial problems before they reach critical proportions;
- Closing unviable institutions promptly, and vigorously monitoring weak and/or restructured institutions;

- Undertaking a timely assessment of the full scope of financial insolvency and the fiscal cost of resolving the problem.

6.4.4. There should be a clear bias (though not a bar) against forbearance when a bank is in difficulty.   Regulatory authorities need to build a reputation for tough supervision and, when necessary, decisive action in cases of financial distress. Supervisory authorities may, from time to time, face substantial political pressure to delay action in closing hazardous financial institutions. They may also be induced to "gamble for resurrection" by allowing an insolvent (or near-insolvent) institution to make an attempt to trade out of its difficulty. There are additional dangers of regulatory capture and risk-averse regulators that simply delay intervention to avoid blame. The need to maintain credibility creates a strong bias against forbearance, and a large number of cases of unsuccessful forbearance reinforces this conclusion. However, there are circumstances where this general presumption is appropriately overridden.

6.4.5. Time-inconsistency and credibility problems should be addressed through precommitments and graduated responses with the possibility of overrides.   There is an active debate about rules versus discretion with respect to intervention in the case of distressed or insolvent banks: to what extent should intervention be circumscribed by clearly defined rules (so that intervention agencies have no discretion about whether, how, and when to act), or should there always be discretion simply because relevant circumstances cannot be set out in advance? The danger of discretion is that it increases the probability of forbearance. A rules-based approach, by removing any prospect that a hazardous bank might be treated leniently, also has the advantage that it enhances the incentives for bank managers to manage their banks prudently so as to reduce the probability of insolvency (Glaessner and Mas, 1995). It also enhances the credibility of the regulator's threat to close institutions.

Many analysts have advocated various forms of predetermined intervention though a general policy of structured early intervention and resolution (SEIR). Goldstein and Turner (1996) argue that SEIR is designed to imitate the remedial action that private bond holders would impose on banks in the absence of government insurance or guarantees. In this sense it is a mimic of market solutions to troubled banks. An example of the rules-based approach is to be found in the Prompt Corrective Action (PCA) rules in the United States. These specify graduated intervention by the regulators with predetermined responses triggered by capital thresholds.

A major issue for the credibility, and hence authority, of a regulator is whether rules and decisions are time-consistent. There may be circumstances where a rule or normal policy action needs to be suspended. The priors are that there is a strong case for precommitment and rules of behavior for the regulator. There is also a case for a graduated-response approach since, for example, there is no magical capital ratio below which an institution is in danger and above which it is safe. Other things being equal, potential danger gradually increases as the capital ratio declines. This in itself suggests that there should be a graduated series of responses from the regulator as capital diminishes. No single dividing line should trigger action, but there should be a series of such trigger points with the effect of going through any one of them relatively minor, but the cumulative effect large. No distinction in these graduated responses should be made between losses caused by idiosyncratic or general market developments.

Under a related concept (the "precommitment approach" to bank supervision) banks own assessments of their capital needs (as determined by their own internal risk models) are used as the basis of supervision. At the beginning of each period the bank evaluates its need for capital, and the bank is subsequently required to manage its risks so that its capital does not fall below the precommitment level. Penalties are imposed to the extent that capital falls below the declared levels. There should also be a decision as to what market movements are so extreme as to merit government support to withstand them. Banks would be required to hold capital to meet shocks up to this limit in stress tests of proprietary models.

However, even in a precommitment and graduated response regime there may be cases where predetermined rules are to be overridden. The problem, however, is that if this is publicly known, the credibility of the regulator could be seriously compromised bearing in mind that it is to create and sustain such credibility that the precommitment rule is established in the first place. Can there be any guarantee that such an override would not turn regulation into a totally ad hoc procedure? One solution is to make the intervention agency publicly accountable for its actions and decisions not to intervene.

6.4.6. Intervention authorities need to ensure that parties that have benefited from risk taking bear a large proportion of the cost of restructuring the banking system. This implies, for example, that shareholders should be the first to lose their investment along with large holders of long-term liabilities such as subordinated debt. Also, delinquent borrowers must not be given favorable treatment at public expense.

6.4.7. Prompt action should be taken to prevent problem institutions from extending credit to high-risk borrowers or from capitalizing unpaid interest on delinquent loans into new credit. Execution of this principle is designed to reduce the moral-hazard risk in bank restructurings that arises when institutions with low and declining net worth continue to operate under the protection of public policies designed to maintain the integrity of the banking system. This implies that, when practicable, insolvent institutions should be removed from the hands of current owners, whether through sale, temporary nationalization, or closure.

6.4.8. Society must create the political will to make restructuring a priority in allocating public funds while avoiding sharp increases in inflation. Use of public funds in rescue operations should be kept to a minimum and, whenever used, be subject to strict conditionally. This follows from previous principles in that their execution requires adequate funding to pay off some liability holders with negative net worth. Attempts should always be made to recover public funds over a period of time (by, for instance, asset sales from resolution trusts).

6.4.9. Barriers to market recapitalization should be minimized. A particular barrier that is often encountered relates to the market in corporate control. Governments or regulatory agencies frequently have rules regarding the ownership of banks and the extent to which banks can be taken over through the market in corporate control. There are often particular limitations on the extent to which foreign banks can purchase domestic banks. And yet these are often solutions for an insolvent bank that can be effectively recapitalized by being purchased by a stronger domestic or foreign bank.

6.4.10. Regulators should be publicly accountable through credible mechanisms. Regulatory agencies have considerable power over both regulated firms and the consumer through their influence on the terms on which business is conducted. For this reason agencies need to be accountable and their activities transparent. In addition, public accountability can also be a protection against political interference in the decisions of the regulatory agency and is also likely to create incentives against forbearance. Difficulties can arise when it may be prudent for a central bank's success in averting a bank failure or systemic crisis to remain secret. One possible approach is create an audit agency of the regulator with the regulator being required to report on a regular basis to an independent person or body. The report would cover the objectives of the regulator and the measures of success and failure. The audit authority would have a degree of standing that would force the regulatory agency to respond to any concerns raised. In due course, the reports of the regulator to the agency would be published.

6.4.11. Assessment. In the process of restructuring following a financial crisis, financial-market functioning needs to be restored as quickly as possible while minimizing market disruption. Balance-sheet assets of weak institutions need to be restructured and placed on a sound footing. This should be designed to ameliorate the moral hazard that weak banks become the captive of their bad customers and, in the process, bad loans drive out good loans. In addition, the management and recovery of loans should be separated from the ongoing activity of banks so that a proper focus can be given to the efficient management of the continuing activity of banks.

Lessons can be learned about how to respond to crises when they emerge. The experience of Mexico, for example, demonstrates how a serious banking crisis can be managed and the banks restored to viability. The experience is instructive as an object lesson in how, if appropriate measures are taken, a banking crisis can be transformed. Several policy measures were adopted both to restore the banking system and to prevent (or lessen the probability of) similar crises occurring again:

- Foreign competition in banking was encouraged. There was subsequently a major influx of foreign banks and foreign capital into the banking sector associated with the privatization of banks and the relaxation of entry barriers. As a result, foreign ownership of banks in Mexico now exceeds 20 percent.
- Consolidation of the banking system was supported and encouraged.
- Regulation and supervision was tightened and made more explicit.
- Accountancy and disclosure standards and requirements were tightened.
- Links between bankers and politics were broken.

When a banking crisis emerges, policy strategy has to be able to reconstitute the banking system (including recapitalizing banks) and apply measures designed to significantly lower the probability of a crisis reemerging.

6.5. Market discipline

Within the general framework of monitoring a major dimension is the extent to which the market undertakes monitoring and imposes discipline on the risk taking of banks. A central theme of this article is that, given how the business of banking has evolved and the nature of the market environment in which banks now operate, less reliance should be placed on supervision by official agencies and a greater role should be played by the market. Market disciplines need to be strengthened. The issue is not so much about market versus agency discipline but the mix of all aspects of monitoring, supervision, and discipline.

In its recent consultation document on capital adequacy the Basle Committee has recognized that supervisors have a strong interest in facilitating effective market discipline as a lever to strengthen the safety and soundness of the banking system. It goes on to argue: "market discipline has the potential to reinforce capital regulation and other supervisory efforts to promote safety and soundness in banks and financial systems. Market discipline imposes strong incentives on banks to conduct their business in a safe, sound and efficient manner" (Basle Committee, 1999, p. 42).

Some analysts (e.g., Calomiris, 1997) are skeptical about the power of official supervisory agencies to identify the risk characteristics of banks compared with the power and incentives of markets. Along with others, Calomiris has advocated that banks be required to issue a minimum amount of subordinated and uninsured debt as part of the capital base. Subordinated debt holders would have an incentive to monitor the risk taking of banks. Discipline would be applied by the market as the markets' assessment of risk would be reflected in the risk premium in the price of the traded debt. In particular, because of the nature of the debt contract, holders of a bank's subordinated debt capital do not share in the potential upside gain through the bank's risk taking but stand to lose if the bank fails. They therefore have a particular incentive to monitor the risk profile of the bank compared with shareholders who, under some circumstances, have an incentive to support a high-risk profile.

The merit of increasing the role of market disciplines is that large, well-informed creditors (including other banks) have the resources, expertise, market knowledge, and incentives to conduct monitoring and to impose market discipline. For instance, it has been argued that the hazardous state of BCCI was reflected in market prices and interbank interest rates long before the Bank of England closed the bank.

6.5.1. Regulation should not impede competition but should enhance it and, by addressing information asymmetries, make it more effective in the market place. However well-intentioned, regulation has the potential to compromise competition and to condone (and in some cases endorse) unwarranted entry barriers, restrictive practices, and other anticompetitive mechanisms. Historically, regulation in finance has often been anticompetitive in nature. But this is not an inherent property of regulation. As there are clear consumer benefits and efficiency gains to be secured through competition, regulation should not be constructed in a way that impairs it. Regulation and competition need not be in conflict: on the contrary, properly constructed they are complementary. Regulation can, therefore, enhance competition. It can also make it more effective in the market place by, for instance, requiring the disclosure of relevant information that can be used by consumers in making informed choices.

Discipline can also be exerted by competition. Opening domestic financial markets to external competition can contribute to the promotion of market discipline. There are many benefits to be derived from foreign institutions entering a country. They bring expertise and experience, and because they themselves are diversified throughout the world, what is a macro shock to a particular country becomes a regional shock, and hence they are more able to sustain purely national shocks that domestic institutions are unable to do. It is generally the case that competition that develops from outside a system tends to have a greater impact on competition and efficiency than purely internal competition. Foreign institutions tend to be less subject to domestic political pressures in the conduct of their business and are also less susceptible to local euphoria, which, at times, leads to excessive lending and overoptimistic expectations.

6.5.2. Regulation should reinforce, not replace, market discipline, and the regulatory regime should be structured to provide greater incentives than exist at present for markets to monitor banks. Where possible, market disciplines (such as through disclosure) should be strengthened. This means creating incentives for private markets to reward good performance and penalize hazardous behavior. Regulation and supervision should complement and support, and never undermine, the operation of market discipline.

6.5.3. Regulators should, whenever possible, utilize market data in their supervisory procedures. The evidence indicates that markets can give signals about the credit standing of financial firms, which, when combined with inside information gained by supervisory procedures, can increase the efficiency of the supervisory process. If financial markets are able to assess a bank's market value as reflected in the market price, an asset-pricing model can in principle be used to infer the risk of insolvency that the market has assigned to each bank. Such a model has been applied to U.K. banks by Hall and Miles (1990). Similar analysis for countries that had recently liberalized their financial systems has been applied by Fischer and Gueyie (1995). On the other hand, there are clear limitations to such an approach (see Simons and Cross, 1991), and hence it would be hazardous to rely exclusively on it. For instance, it assumes that markets have sufficient data on which to make an accurate assessment of the risk profile of banks, and it equally assumes that the market is able to efficiently assess the available information and incorporate this into an efficient pricing of banks' securities.

6.5.4. There should be a significant role for rating agencies in the supervisory process.
Rating agencies have considerable resources and expertise in monitoring banks and making assessments of risk. It could be made a requirement, as in Argentina, for all banks to have a rating, which would be made public.

6.5.5. Assessment.
While market discipline is potentially very powerful, it has its limitations. This means that, in practice, it is unlikely to be an effective *alternative* to the role of official regulatory and supervisory agencies:

- Markets are concerned with the private cost of a bank failure and reflect the risk of this in market prices. The social cost of bank failures, on the other hand, may exceed the private cost (Llewellyn, 1999), and hence the total cost of a bank failure may not be fully reflected in market prices.
- Market disciplines are not effective at monitoring and disciplining public-sector banks.
- In many countries, limits are imposed on the extent to which the market in corporate control (the takeover market) is allowed to operate. In particular, there are frequently limits, if not bars, on the extent to which foreign institutions are able to take control of banks, even though they may offer a solution to undercapitalized banks.
- The market is able to efficiently price bank securities and interbank loans only to the extent that relevant information is available. Disclosure requirements are, therefore, an integral part of the market disciplining process.
- It is not self-evident that market participants always have the necessary expertise to make risk assessment of complex, and sometimes opaque, banks.
- In some countries, the market in debt of all kinds (including securities and debt issued by banks) is limited, inefficient, and cartelized.
- When debt issues are very small, it is not always economic for a rating agency to conduct a full credit rating on the bank.

While there are clear limitations on the role of market discipline (discussed further in Lane, 1993), the global trend is appropriately in the direction of placing more emphasis on market data in the supervisory process. The theme is not that market monitoring and discipline can effectively replace official supervision but that it has a potentially powerful role that should be strengthened within the overall regulatory regime. In addition, Caprio (1997) argues that broadening the number of those who are directly concerned about the safety and soundness of banks reduces the extent to which insider political pressure can be brought to bear on bank regulation and supervision. In fact, the recent consultative document issued by the Basle Committee on Banking Supervision (Basle Committee, 1999, p. 60) incorporates the role of market discipline as one of the three pillars of a proposed new approach to banking supervision. The Committee emphasizes that its approach "will encourage high disclosure standards and enhance the role of market participants in encouraging banks to hold adequate capital."

6.6. Corporate governance

A key issue in the management of banks is the extent to which corporate governance arrangements are suitable and efficient for the management and control of risks. Corporate governance arrangements include issues of corporate structure, the power of shareholders to exercise accountability of managers, the transparency of corporate structure, the authority and power of directors, internal audit arrangements, and lines of accountability of managers. In the final analysis, shareholders are the ultimate risk takers, and agency problems may induce managers to take more risks with the bank than the owners would wish. This in turn raises issues of what information shareholders have about the actions of the managers to which they delegate decision-making powers, the extent to which shareholders are represented on the board of directors of the bank, and the extent to which shareholders have power to discipline managers.

The OECD has published a set of Principles of Corporate Governance that apply to all companies, and these are relevant to banks (Table 7 for a summary). With respect to banks the following general principle should apply:

6.6.1. Corporate governance arrangements should provide for effective monitoring and supervision of the risk-taking profile of banks. These arrangements would provide for, *inter alia,* a management structure with clear lines of accountability; independent nonexecutive directors on the board, an independent audit committee, and a four-eyes principle for important decisions involving the risk profile of the bank; transparent ownership structure with internal structures that enabled the risk profile of the bank to be clear, transparent, and managed; and monitored risk-analysis and management systems.

Table 7.   Summary of OECD principles of corporate governance.

The OECD Principles of Corporate Governance are intended to assist member and nonmember governments in their efforts to evaluate and improve their own legal, institutional, and regulatory framework for corporate governance, rather than to provide a prescription for national legislation or regulation. They have been grouped under five headings, which are listed below along with the underlying reasoning:

The rights of shareholders

- Basic shareholder rights should be protected. These include the rights to share in profits, vote on appropriate issues, transfer shares, access relevant and timely information, and have secure registration of ownership.
- Capital structures that allow certain shareholders to obtain a disproportionate degree of control should be disclosed.
- The market for corporate control should be allowed to function efficiently, transparently, and in a manner that is fair for all shareholders.

The equitable treatment of shareholders

- All shareholders of the same class should be treated equally, including minority and foreign shareholders and those with shares held by custodians or nominees.
- Self-dealing and insider trading should be prohibited.
- Members of the board and managers should be required to disclose material interests in transactions or matters affecting the corporation.

The role of stakeholders in corporate governance.

- The rights of stakeholders, as established by law, should be respected, and there should be effective redress when these rights are violated.
- Where stakeholders do participate in the corporate governance process, they should have access to relevant information.

Disclosure and transparency

- There should be timely and accurate disclosure of information on all material regarding the financial situation, performance, ownership and governance of the company. Information channels should be cost-effective for users.
- Information should be prepared, audited, and disclosed in accordance with high quality standards.
- To provide an objective and external control over the disclosure of financial information, an independent auditor should conduct an annual audit.

The role of the board

- The corporate governance framework should ensure strategic guidance and effective monitoring of the company by the board (the OECD includes a list of key functions that the board should fulfill) and the board's accountability to the company and shareholders.
- Board members should have access to accurate, relevant, and timely information.
- Where board decisions may affect various shareholders groups differently, the board should treat all shareholders fairly.
- The board should ensure compliance with applicable law and take into account the interests of stakeholders.
- The boards should be able to exercise objective judgment on corporate matters, independent of management. The appointment of independent nonexecutive directors should be considered.

Source: *Financial Stability Review* (June 1999).

7. Conclusions and assessment

The purpose of this article has been to outline some of the characteristics of a stable financial system. A key conclusion is that, in one way or another, including through regulation and supervision, mechanisms are needed for the creation of appropriate *incentives* for all the major players including regulators and supervisors. If the incentive structure is wrong, banking and financial problems will always eventually emerge.

When judging the effectiveness and efficiency of a regulatory regime five key criteria are established:

- The extent to which it generates appropriate incentives for banks owners and managers,
- Whether it generates correct pricing of absolute and relative risk of bank loans,
- Whether it minimizes existing and new moral hazards,
- The extent to which sufficient differentiations are made between institutions based on overall portfolio risks, and
- The impact on competitive conditions and whether it is competitively neutral as between different competing firms.

Overall, the lessons of recent banking crises are that there needs to be more effective surveillance of financial institutions both by supervisory authorities and the markets. For markets to complement the work of supervisory agencies, good and timely information is needed about banks activities and balance-sheet positions. Regulation, supervision, and information disclosure are not alternatives.

Effective regulation and supervision of banks and financial institutions have the potential to make a major contribution to the stability and robustness of a financial system. However, there are also distinct limits to what regulation and supervision can achieve in practice. It must be recognized that, in practice, there is no viable alternative to placing the main responsibility for risk management on the shoulders of the management of financial institutions. Management must not be allowed to hide behind the cloak of regulation or pretend that, if regulation and supervisory arrangements are in place, this absolves them from their own responsibility. Nothing should ever be seen as taking away the responsibility of internal supervision within banks by shareholders and managers themselves. External regulation and supervision by official agencies must, therefore, not be viewed as an alternative to robust and effective internal supervision processes and responsibilities. In other words, regulation must be both internal and external.

References

Adams, C., D. Mathieson, G. Schinasi, and B. Chadha (1998) *International Capital Markets*. Washington, DC: IMF.

Alba, P., G. Bhattacharya, S. Claessens, S. Ghash, and L. Hernandez, (1998) "The Role of Macroeconomic and Financial Sector Linkages in East Asia's Financial Crisis." Mimeo, World Bank, Washington, DC.

Andersson, M. and S. Viotti (1999) "Managing and Preventing Financial Crises." *Sveriges Riksbank Quarterly Review* 71–89.

Basle Committee (1999) "A New Capital Adequacy Framework." Consultative Paper, BIS, Basle, Switzerland.

Beatty, A., S. Chamberlain, and J. Magliola (1993) "Managing Financial Reports on Commercial Banks." Paper No. 94-02, Wharton Financial Institutions Centre, August.

Benink, H. and D.T. Llewellyn (1994) "De-regulation and Financial Fragility: A Case Study of the UK and Scandinavia." In D. Fair and R. Raymond (eds.), *Competitiveness of Financial Institutions and Centres in Europe*. Boston: Kluwer, 186–201.

BIS (1991) *Annual Report*. Basle: BIS.

BIS (1998) *Annual Report*. Basle: BIS.

Bisignano, J. (1998) "Precarious Credit Equilibria: Reflections on the Asian Financial Crisis." Mimeo, BIS, Basle, Switzerland.

Brealey, R. (1999) "The Asian Crisis: Lessons for Crisis Management and Prevention." *Bank of England Quarterly Bulletin* (August):285–296.

Brownbridge, M. and C. Kirkpatrick (1999) "Financial Sector Regulation: Lessons of the Asian Crisis." *Development Policy Review* 20:40–60

Bruni, F. and F. Peterno (1994) "Market Discipline of Banks Riskiness: A Study of Selected Issues." *Journal of Financial Services Research* 313.

Calomiris, C. (1997) *The Postmodern Safety Net*. Washington, DC: American Enterprise Institute.

Caprio, G. (1997) "Safe and Sound Banking in Developing Countries: We're Not in Kansas Anymore." Policy Research Paper No. 1739, World Bank, Washington, DC.

Caprio, G. and L. Summers (1993) "Finance and Its Reform." Policy Research Paper No. 1544, World Bank, Washington, DC.

Cole, H. and T. Kehoe (1996) "A Self-fulfilling Model of Mexico's 1994–95 Debt Crisis." *Journal of International Economics* 41:309–330.

Corbett, J., G. Irwin, and D. Vines (1999) "From Asian Miracle to Asian Crisis: Why Vulnerability, Why Collapse?" In D. Gruen and L. Gower (ed.), *Capital Flows and the International Financial System*. Sydney: Reserve Bank of Australia, 190–213.

Corsetti, G., P. Pesenti, and N. Rabini (1998) "What Caused the Asia Currency and Financial Crisis?" Temi di Discussione. Rome: Banca d'Italia, December.

Demirguc-Kunt, A. and E. Detragiache (1998) "Financial Liberalisation and Financial Fragility." World Bank Annual Conference on Development Economics.

Demsetz, R., M. Saidenberg, and P. Strahan (1997) "Agency Problems and Risk-Taking at Banks." Federal Reserve Bank of New York Research Paper No. 9709.

Dewatripont, M. and J. Tirole (1994) *The Prudential Regulation of Banks*. Cambridge, MA: MIT Press.

Drage, J. and F. Mann (1999) "Improving the Stability of the International Financial System." *Financial Stability Review* (June):40–77.

Fischer, K. and J. Gueyie (1995) "Financial Liberalisation and Bank Solvency." Working Paper, University of Laval, Quebec.

Folkerts-Landau, D., J. Schinasi, M. Cassard, V. Ng, C. Reinhart, and M. Spencer (1995) "Effects of Capital Flows on the Domestic Sectors in APEC Countries." In M. Khan and C. Rheinhart (eds.), *Capital Flows in the APEC Region*. IMF Occasional Paper No. 122. Washington, DC: IMF.

Furman, J. and J. Stiglitz (1998) "Economic Crises: Evidence and Insights from East Asia." Working Paper, Brookings Institute, Washington, DC.

Gadlayn, I. and R. Valdes (1997) "Capital Flows and the Twin Crises: The Role of Liquidity." IMF Working Paper No. 97/87. IMF, Washington, DC, July.

Glaessner, T. and I. Mas (1995) "Incentives and the Resolution of Bank Distress." *World Bank Research Observer* 10(1) (February):53–73.

Goldstein, M. and D. Folkerts-Landau (1993) "Systemic Issues in International Finance." *World Economic and Financial Surveys*. Washington, DC: IMF.

Goldstein, M. and P. Turner (1996) "Banking Crises in Emerging Economies." BIS Economic Papers No. 46, BIS, Basle, Switzerland.

Goodhart, C., P. Hartmann, D.T. Llewellyn, L. Rojas-Suarez, and S. Weisbrod (1998) *Financial Regulation: Why, How and Where Now?* London: Routledge.

Hall, S. and D. Miles (1990) "Monitoring Bank Risk: A Market Based Approach." Discussion Paper. Birkbeck College, London, April.

Hausmann, R. and M. Gavin (1996) "The Roots of Banking Crises: The Macro-economic Context." Working Paper, IADB, Washington, DC.

Hellman, T., K. Murdock, and J. Stiglitz (1995) "Financial Restraint: Towards a New Paradigm." In K. Aoki and I. Okuno-Fujiwara (eds.), *The Role of Government in East Asian Economic Development*. Oxford: Oxford University Press.

IMF (1993) "Deterioration of Bank Balance Sheets." *World Economic Outlook* 2.

Kaminsky, G. and C. Reinhart (1998) "The Twin Crises: The Causes of Banking and Balance of Payments Problems." International Finance Discussion Papers No. 554, Board of Governors, Federal Reserve System, Washington, DC.

Kaminsky, G. and C. Reinhart (1999) "The Twin Crisis: Causes of Banking and Balance of Payments Problems." *American Economic Review* (June):423–500.

Keeley M. (1990) "Deposit Insurance, Risk and Market Power in Banking." *American Economic Review* (December):1183–1201.

Kim, M. and W. Cross (1995) "The Impact of the 1989 Change in Bank Capital Standards on Loan Loss Provisions." Mimeo, Rutgers University.

Krugman, P. (1999) *The Return of Depression Economics*. London: Allen Lane.

Lane, T. (1993) "Market Discipline." IMF Staff Papers, IMF, Washington, DC, March.

Lindgren, C.J., G. Garcia, and M. Saal (1996) *Bank Soundness and Macroeconomic Policy*. Washington, DC: IMF.

Llewellyn, D.T. (1999) "The Economic Rationale of Financial Regulation." Occasional Paper No. 1, Financial Services Authority, London.

Llewellyn, D.T. and M. Holmes (1991) "Competition or Credit Controls?" Working Paper No. 117, Institute of Economic Affairs, London.

Martinez, P. (1998) "Do Depositors Punish Banks for Bad Behavior? Examining Market Discipline in Argentina, Chile and Mexico." Policy Research Working Paper, World Bank, Washington, DC, February.

OECD (1992) *Banking Under Stress*. Paris: OECD.

Rahman, M. (1998) "The Role of Accounting and Disclosure Standards in the East Asian Financial Crisis: Lessons Learned." Mimeo, UNCTAD, Geneva.

Reisen, H. (1998) "Domestic Causes of Currency Crises: Policy Lessons for Crisis Avoidance." Technical Paper No. 136, OECD Development Centre, Paris.

Rodrik, D. (1999) *The New Global Economy and Developing Countries: Making Openness Work*. Washington, DC: Overseas Development Council.

Rojas-Suarez, L. and S. Weisbrod (1995) "Financial Fragilities in Latin America: 1980s and 1990s." Occasional Paper No. 132, IMF, Washington, DC.

Sachs, J., A. Torrell, and A. Velesco (1996) "Financial Crises in Emerging Markets: The Lessons from 1995." Brookings Papers 1, Brookings Institution, Washington, DC.

Schinasi, G. and M. Hargreaves (1993) "Boom and Bust in Asset Markets in the 1980s: Causes and Consequences." *IMF World Economic Outlook* (December).

Shafer, J.R. (1987) "Managing Crisis in the Emerging Financial Landscape." *OECD Economic Outlook* 9:55–77.

Simons, K. and S. Cross (1991) "Do Capital Markets Predict Problems in Large Commercial Banks?" *New England Economic Review* (May):51–56.

Stiglitz, J. (1999) "Must Financial Crises Be This Frequent and This Painful?" In R. Agenor et al. (eds.), *The Asian Financial Crisis: Causes, Contagion and Consequences*. Cambridge: Cambridge University Press.

Suzuki, Y. (1986) *Money, Finance and Macroeconomic Performance in Japan*. New Haven: Yale University Press.

UNCTAD (1998) *Trade and Development Report*. Geneva: United Nations.

Volker, P. (1999) "Problems and Challenges of International Capital Flows." In D. Gruen and L. Gower (eds.), *Capital Flows and the International Financial System*. Sydney: Reserve Bank of Australia, 11–17.

Williamson, J. and M. Mahar (1998) "A Survey of Financial Liberalisation." Princeton Essays in International Finance No. 211, Princeton.

Open economies review 11:S1 111–116 (2000)
© 2000 *Kluwer Academic Publishers. Printed in The Netherlands.*

Comment on Llewellyn's "Some Lessons for Regulation from Recent Bank Crises"

JEFFREY R. SHAFER
Salomon Smith Barney, New York

Introduction

The subject of what lessons to draw from recent systemic financial crises in which banks played a central role is extremely important. Indeed, it may be the most important issue to address in attempting to build a world in which the benefits of full participation in competitive global financial markets, especially by emerging economies with great untapped economic potential, can be secured without catastrophic disruption. David Llewellyn sketches, but sketches convincingly, I believe, the case for putting the banking system at the heart of virtually all of the major economic disruptions of the last 20 years in both the most advanced and the emerging economies.

The questions involved are also exceedingly difficult. Some of the reasons for this are evident from Llewellyn's assessment: multiple factors do indeed interact to create banking crises with serious macroeconomic fallout. Monocausal theories simply do not stand up to experience. In addition, banks in any economy are subjected to strong political, as well as economic forces. The performance of banking systems cannot be analyzed in purely *market* terms. But they must be analyzed in *economic* terms, which means focusing on incentives in political processes, the regulatory structure and within the firms, as well as in markets. Llewellyn rightly puts incentives at the center of his view.

Llewellyn's article presents us with a lot of good material to digest. It lists eight main causes of banking crises and addresses the question of whether these problems are the transitional consequences of financial liberalization or steady-state features of a liberal regulatory environment. Finally, the article identifies six components of a financial regulatory regime and puts forward 25 rules that Llewellyn argues are the keys to move robust financial systems.

All the lists are a bit overwhelming, but they embody a tremendous amount of wisdom concerning banking crises, and I have only two points on which I differ strongly with the article. I deal with these and then attempt to push beyond the article or at least to shine a lantern down one promising road.

This seems useful because, as solid as Llewellyn's assessment is, it leaves me with the uneasy feeling that it will not lead to reforms that remove catastrophic financial risk from the scene. Politicians and regulators are being asked to do too many things. While they are all worth doing, if we can't identify one or two key actions and put both intellectual and political energy behind getting them done, we will never overcome the doubts, vested interests, and sheer inertia that make any successful economic or financial reform of a public-good character a near miracle. It is crucial to identify a strategic line of attack.

1. Two differences with Llwellyn

1.1. Are we in a transitional phase of deregulation that will be followed by a new steady state with markedly less instability?

Llewellyn sees much of the financial distress of the past two decades as a transitory consequence of financial deregulation: loss of rents pushing managers to take more risk, mistakes made in a new and more uncertain environment, and the heritage of disequilibrium built up in the earlier controlled environment. I agree with the analysis of the past, but it would be dangerous to assume that all will be smooth once we have come through a one-time adjustment.

In 1987, I wrote a paper (Shafer, 1987) in which I argued that deregulation would give rise to financial markets with a permanently greater tendency for instability. I did not argue that the main thrust of deregulation at the time (removal of interest-rate and quantitative lending limits, dismantling of geographical and product-line compartmentalization of competition, and accommodation of new products) should be stopped or reversed, however. The benefits of innovative and competitive financial markets were too great. But I did argue that supervision and an intervention capacity appropriate to a dynamic financial environment would be crucial. I believe this even more strongly now then I did a dozen years ago. The need for stronger regulatory regimes will not pass.

The greatest strength of liberalized, competitive markets is also the source of vulnerability: they present opportunities and strong incentives for innovation, but uncertainty is high, and unseen risks abound as a consequence. These are the old but neglected lessons of Frank Knight (1921) and Joseph Schumpeter (1943). There is not much, if any, profit in producing and selling financial services in a stable environment without rents created by regulatory distortions. In financial markets, as in other markets, firms continually innovate in search of a temporary edge that will earn profits. The edge is temporary because emulators will come into the market and turn yesterday's "hot product" into a "commodity." It is this process, even more than the static efficiencies of perfectly competitive markets, that has enabled liberal markets to deliver high standards of living to widening circles of people, but this process continually creates uncertainty, along with consumer benefits and profits.

If this uncertainty is allowed to build up, financial distress will likely follow. A good recent example of the unending process of innovation, risk buildup, and financial distress is provided by the problems of long-term capital management (LTCM) and others in the fixed-income and derivatives markets in the late summer and fall of 1998, long after the process of deregulating financial instruments had run its course in the United States. That process had brought with it the adjustment problems that Llewellyn points to. But the end of that process was not a steady state of unchanging financial structure. The 1990s were years of relative macroeconomic and regulatory stability during which sophisticated investors placed more and more funds with managers who were achieving high returns with new investment strategies, and market counterparties took an increasing credit exposure to these funds collateralized by their marketable portfolios. When the funds began to lose value in the summer of 1998, market liquidity evaporated in the face of margin calls. LTCM was saved by a Federal Reserve Board–convened consortium. Despite this rescue, aimed at containing the damage that would have followed a forced liquidation, a number of other hedge funds failed, most of Wall Street lost money, and liquidity in the secondary market for fixed-income securities other than Treasuries was slow to recover. The shock was severe, but it did not have serious macroeconomic repercussions because LTCM's positions were not dumped in the market and the Fed added liquidity, reducing the Fed funds rate by 75 basis points. It was a close-run thing.

I don't expect a repeat of LTCM. Market participants have learned lessons about monitoring and controlling risk, whether or not regulators introduce new disclosure requirements. Besides, the investing style of LTCM had attracted many emulators and was well on its way to becoming a commodity. It was becoming hard to generate high returns. Indeed, this is part of the reason that more risk was taken on. But there will be a repeat of the cycle: innovators find a new way of making money in financial markets, the business mushrooms without all of the risks being understood, a large but not inherently catastrophic shock exposes these risks, and markets implode. Whether the next cycle is a footnote in financial history or the trigger of an economic downturn will depend on whether regulators are imaginative enough to recognize the risk and to either contain it or be ready to respond when trouble arrives.

1.2.   Can regulators be nonprescriptive?

Llewellyn advocates an approach to financial supervision that places less emphasis on detailed and prescriptive rules and more on internal risk-analysis, management, and control systems. There is a lot of appeal in this, and it has gained considerable support in the regulatory community. This is because a nonprescriptive approach to regulation comes to terms with the importance of nonquantitative factors and the changeability of the financial environment. But I do not believe that it will prove possible to take this approach very far, at least in the emerging markets. After all, supervisors are in the business of overriding the judgment and activities of the managers responsible to shareholders for the profitability and survival of the institution. Taking on this responsibility, supervisors must not only protect the public interest in financial stability, but they must also maintain a level playing field and a predictable environment. This would be intrinsically difficult, even if supervisors were politically insulated and without any interest other than optimization of the performance of the financial system. The reality is that regulators are buffeted by political pressures and have a range of personal and institutional interests. We may call for independent regulators, but we must be realistic about how much independence they will be able to exercise in the face of powerful interests. Clear rules, even if not first-best from an efficiency point of view, if widely subscribed to will prove much more effective than general guidelines enforced in an uncertain manner. The rules, of course, should be the object of ongoing public debate and review. Objectivity facilitates this debate, as well as ensuring that all are subject to the same rules. The important thing is to limit the rules to those essential to safeguard the public interest in systemic financial stability and protection of small accounts.

2. A strategic approach to more stable banking systems

Llewellyn's broad and incentive-focused approach to regulation is sound, and his 25 principles are good ones. Most are already in the rhetoric of the bank supervision community. But there are many slips between good intentions and practices in a world of intense political pressures—to allow even bad bank managers to continue managing, to keep lending going to politically influential borrowers, to mask problems in the hope that things will improve, not to impose losses on shareholders, and so on.

The core concern is that funds may be misallocated on a macro scale. Not even 1 or 2 percent of gross domestic product in losses would have serious macroeconomic consequences. The lending crises we are concerned about expose losses of 5 percent, 10 percent, or more of GDP. This requires money managers to make huge misallocation of resources. Usually such large problems develop because misallocations build up over a long period of time and then are exposed. There are three conditions under which this might occur:

- Financial managers as a group may simply be wrong about the future direction of the world in some fundamental respect. This happens. The savings and loan industry in the United States positioned itself on the bet that interest-rate regulations would remain effective and in effect. Scandinavian banks and their borrowers bet that inflation would not be brought under tight control. Thai banks and their customers bet on an unchanged exchange rate. Rational or not, big mistakes are made. These examples have an important element of betting on policy, but that is not the only source of big mistakes. Financial markets can reward for long periods of time strategies that prove ultimately unsound, while they impose ruinous losses on those who bet prematurely on fundamentals reasserting themselves. The valuations put on the Internet sector by U.S. equity markets at the time of writing in late 1999 looks like a current example.
- The incentives of financial managers may not be aligned with these of equity holders. Principal and agent problems arise inherently in financial firms.

Incentive compensation systems only roughly align the interests of management and shareholders. The problems are compounded when the state is the equity holder and management is more politically than economically responsible or in other circumstances of murky corporate governance, including cooperative organizations.

• Financial managers and equity holders may expect to shift losses to taxpayers. This is the much-discussed problem of moral hazard in deposit insurance, lender of last resort, and too-big-to-fail arrangements.

All three of these sources of gross resource misallocations have played a role in various crises. Often more than one of them has been a factor. But the second seems a more serious concern to attack within the banking system than the first, and the third a nearly pervasive element in modern financial crises. What can regulators do to reduce the scope for these potential sources of resource misallocation to culminate to the point where they give rise to systemic financial distress? Most of Llewellyn's actions would help. But one, in my view, could be catalytic. That is the proposal that he ascribes to Calomeris to require substantial long-term subordinated debt on the balance sheets of banks.

Requiring substantial private funds that cannot be withdrawn rapidly to be put at risk as a buffer against loss to taxpayers in the event of intervention is the only sure way to contain moral hazard. It makes no difference whether formal insurance is provided or not; the costs imposed on society by a drain of deposits from banks will force the authorities to step in as a lender of last resort in the event of a widespread loss of confidence. Once a liquidity problem emerges, the promise that even large depositors will be made whole becomes essential to limit the drain, and hence the authorities will step in even after saying they will not. Equity holders will have, at most, limited liability at that point. Thus banks want to operate with as little equity as they can to maximize equity returns on the upside and minimize exposure on the downside. The authorities can create a buffer by setting capital requirements, as the Basle Supervisors have required, albeit imperfectly. But intervention rarely, if ever, takes place before the mark-to-market value of assets has dropped well below liabilities. Additional subordinated debt requirements would allow the authorities to play their lender-of-last-resort role, if necessary, with less risk of absorbing losses at the end of the day. The market value of the claims of subordinated debt holders would reflect their risk of loss. This would directly reduce the third and most important source of resource misallocations.

Subordinated capital requirements would also help to reduce the two other sources of resource allocation indirectly. Once one has classes of capital claimants on a bank who are at risk because the authorities can safely allow them to lose money, one has stakeholders with an interest in addressing corporate governance issues. There is no more effective way of creating conditions favorable to improvement on this front than to create a vested interest. Banks would find it difficult to raise long-term subordinated debt without providing assurances that the bank will be well managed in the form of covenants that would give bondholders rights in the event of serious financial deterioration.

To this point in my case for liberal capital requirements, the form of capital makes little difference; equity or subordinate debt would have the same effect of creating stakeholders at risk. As risks increased, the price of a subordinated debt or equity would fall. This would both send signals and force a management response to replace maturing debt. The one difference, perhaps, is that taxpayers would still have a buffer if there were a tendency toward forbearance as long as a bank had equity capital.

Subordinated debt has another role in addition to equity, however. It is as good an antidote as I can think of to the kind of collective exuberance that sows the seeds of financial distress. Llewellyn makes this point, and it is a critical one. Debt holders do not share in the upside. Thus they bring a tempering influence to bear on valuing firms. Equity holders may respond positively to high-risk high-reward lending strategies even if there is no moral hazard present, but subordinated debt holders should not. It is an ironic corollary that U.S. financial stability would be better assured if Internet companies were required to maintain minimum debt to equity ratios. Some firms with large market caps would have considerable difficulty borrowing from banks or issuing straight debt.

The considerations that I have reviewed leave me with the view that the bedrock of a bank regulatory system is the capital requirement. There is room for debate on asset weightings, but, in the end, the requirement should be objective and ample. Subordinated debt has a role to play, not only for the reason of lower costs that lead good banks to favor it but also because subordinated debt holders will exercise their oversight without being as vulnerable to exuberance in good times as are equity holders.

I don't mean to suggest that this is all that is needed in financial supervision. At least 24 other things are worth doing. But getting stronger capital requirements in place, especially in emerging market banking systems, and monitoring compliance carefully (which, among other things, means having market-based accounting and sound auditing of asset valuations) will go far, and it will create a dynamic in favor of many other desirable actions.

References

Knight, Frank H. (1921) *Risk Uncertainty and Profit*. New York: Houghton Mifflin.

Schumpeter, J.A. (1943) *Capitalism, Socialism and Democracy*. Republished by Unwin Paperbacks, London, 1987.

Shafer, J.R. (1987) "Managing Crises in the Emerging Financial Landscape." *OECD Economic Studies* 9:55–77.

Open economies review 11:S1 117–131 (2000)

International Financial Architecture and the Economic Renaissance in Europe

MAXWELL C. WATSON
International Monetary Fund, Washington, DC

Keywords: euro area, European Union, transition economies, convergence, international financial architecture

JEL Classification Numbers: F15, F33

Abstract

Over the past decade two transformations have changed the landscape of Europe: the European Union and the transition in East European countries. Countries like Estonia, Hungary, and Poland have become "converging" countries more than emerging countries. Their experience offers insight on aspects of policy design that helped proof them against turbulence in international markets. In a world of liberalized markets, the international financial architecture has to be strengthened by solving some problems like herding behavior and contagion, moral hazard, and information on markets. The International Monetary Fund has to play a big role in these innovations and challenges.

Introduction

Two sweeping transformations—monetary union in the West and transition in the East—have changed the landscape of Europe over the past decade. With a gross domestic product (GDP) of 8 trillion euro the economy of the European Union (EU) and the most advanced transition economies[1] is on a par with that of the United States. In the international financial system, monetary union has marked a watershed: some half of global issuance in the first six months of 1999 was in the form of euro-denominated bonds. This capital-market activity also evidenced parallel changes underway in the real economy: the funds raised by European firms were swollen by merger financing, as corporate consolidation accelerated in domestic markets—a harbinger of heightened cross-border competition. But the dynamic of integration extends beyond the euro area, or the EU single market, to the advanced transition economies. The European Union accounts for two-thirds of their trade, against one-third a decade ago, and it provides some two-thirds of their direct investment inflows of some 10 billion euro annually. For banks and businesses, EU enlargement is in many respects a fact.

As we reflect on the architecture of the system—the institutions, rules, and policies that influence international financial flows—these changes in Europe suggest both lessons and questions. Exploring this regional perspective on architecture, I focus on three main themes, arguing that (1) the experience of the advanced transition economies underscores that the new architecture begins at home, in a blending of macroeconomic and structural reforms; (2) this experience and the challenges now facing these economies suggest that strong domestic policies are not enough: they need buttressing by changes in the international financial architecture; and (3) the euro area has a crucial opportunity to help foster an international system that supports stable and sustained growth.

1. Experience in the advanced transition economies

Since 1997, a majority of the most advanced transition economies have achieved GDP growth rates of 4 percent or higher annually, fueled by an inflow of foreign savings. Three of them (Estonia, Hungary, and Poland) are today financing current-account deficits of 5 percent of GDP or more—covered to a high degree by foreign direct investment, including flows related to privatization and asset sales. The Asian and Russian crises affected them less than comparable economies. Indeed, they have become converging more than emerging markets. They benefited from a head start in some areas, compared with other transition economies—for example, early price reforms, sizable private sectors, or proximity to the EU. But some had monetary overhangs, and some heavy debt burdens. Typically, also, the structural problems of their budgets, banks, and enterprises were profound. Their ability to withstand market turbulence has reflected, no question, the strength of their policy frameworks.

For the debate on architecture, their experience offers insights, first, on aspects of policy design that helped proof them against turbulence in international markets:

- The foundation lay in credible macroeconomic policies. By the mid-1990s, tax bases were substantially rebuilt, expenditures reoriented to support a market economy, and fiscal deficits contained to financeable levels. Their monetary frameworks moderated inflation early and have now generally cut it to single-digit levels. External debt was set on a sustainable course, and their economies were opened to foreign direct investment—while in some cases keeping powers to curb short-term inflows. Such policies, promoting stability and confidence, facilitated a build-up of external reserves relative to trade and short-term debt.
- Far from a cookie-cutter approach, specifics of reforms varied strikingly. The authorities privatized banks and firms at different speeds, imposed hard budget constraints with varying abruptness, tried different exchange regimes, and handled external creditors in different ways. Among the strong performers, Poland sought debt reduction, adopted a macroeconomic shock therapy, and was more gradualist with bankruptcy and privatization measures.

Hungary built its success on a strategy that was, on these points, the reverse. The similarity in results was achieved by a variety of means.
* But the strongest cases bear a family resemblance in their pursuit of far-reaching structural reforms. These reforms strengthened the financial sector and reduced quasi-fiscal deficits, thus reducing vulnerability through several channels: (1) in a setting where liberalized capital flows are prone to amplify distortions, these reforms—improvements in governance, bank consolidation, more effective prudential supervision—strengthened the mechanisms for allocating foreign and domestic savings; (2) with markets, at times of crisis, alert to credibility flaws, the main quasi-fiscal sources of policy weakness had been addressed; and (3) when there was a need to raise interest rates to face down market pressures, as in Hungary during the Russian crisis, financial reforms eased the institutional constraints on monetary policy.

Resilience thus proved greatest where—as in Estonia, Hungary, and Poland—quasi-fiscal reforms were most far-reaching, central banks most credible, and banking systems most reformed. It was important also that these countries had moved far in restructuring their social-protection systems so that these no longer depended on enterprises but were targeted by government to groups that were vulnerable to the changes of transition: this was crucial in ensuring the social sustainability of reform. Overall, the underpinning of macroeconomic stabilization with key structural reforms helps to explain the resilience of these economies during the Asian and Russian crises—despite the remaining trade links of Estonia and Poland with Russia. It was a strategy, again, that allowed Hungary to defend a crawling peg regime in a setting of market turbulence. More severe stresses occurred where—as in the Czech Republic—enterprise and financial sector reforms had lagged. A first conclusion must be that proposals for a new architecture should seek to foster policy congruence along these lines.

2.   Challenges on the road to EU accession

This experience has been impressive—but, as circumstances evolve, policy makers are aware that shoals may lie ahead:

* These countries' financial markets are still deepening: a process that will reduce risks associated with thin markets but may increase the momentum of flows when sentiment changes and erode more quickly the effectiveness of restraints on short-term inflows.
* They may face a switchback ride in risk premia and capital inflows: at times when international interest rates are on an uptrend, premia may rise even for emerging economies with an entrenched track record. But at times when EU convergence expectations strengthen, there may be an accelerating decline

in premia, for both inflation and credit risk, and flows into fixed interest rate markets may expand sharply.
* The experience of ERM participants in the 1990s suggests markets may be highly alert to fluctuations in policy resolve. Such fluctuations are inevitable—indeed are visible now, to varying degrees, throughout Central Europe, in forms ranging from fiscal slippage to coalition stresses relating to policy reforms.

In this setting, the advanced transition economies face challenges in developing policy frameworks for the period ahead. I focus on issues that relate to their macroeconomic policy frameworks, illustrating how these would benefit from initiatives in architecture that may help limit turbulence and contagion. Let me begin with the dilemmas surrounding their choice of monetary and exchange regimes—the Achilles heel of so many emerging markets.

While these countries adopted a spectrum of monetary and exchange regimes over the past decade, there is a question whether these are now polarizing. Under the influence of market pressures, the Czech crown has been floated, and the band of the Polish zloty progressively widened. De facto, their regimes appear to be tending to extremes of fixity or flexibility: Estonia's well-established currency board, on the one hand; the inflation targeting regimes in the Czech Republic and Poland, on the other. Are Hungary's crawling peg and narrow band, which successfully weathered the inflows and outflows of the past year, a model for EU/EMU candidates—or an exception that proves the rule? In unforgiving markets, can pegs to the euro help these countries import credibility, as did Belgium or the Netherlands? Can they reckon to ride out pressures through temporary band widening, as did France? Or be confident that viable exit strategies to inflation targeting exist, as in the United Kingdom? Let us consider some of the factors that will influence these outcomes.

For these economies, regime choice is complicated by two tensions that interact—one being most critical in connection with EU convergence, the other shared with all emerging markets.

In terms of nominal convergence with the European Union, and ultimately membership of the euro area, they face an awkward choice between stability in the exchange rate or the price level. A priori, pegs appears a natural anchor for open economies that are converging rapidly with a major currency bloc, particularly when shifting transmission mechanisms complicate monetary management. But with strong productivity growth, these countries' exchange rates will tend to appreciate in real terms (that is, the Balassa-Samuelson effect).[2]

With a fixed peg to the euro, this may result in rates of consumer-price increase that are, say, 1 to 3 percentage points higher than Consumer Product Index (CPI) inflation in the euro area. If they adopt an (upward) crawling peg, annual increases in the price level can likely be contained to 2 percent or less, but there is a question how this continuing nominal depreciation would be viewed in relation to expectations of exchange-rate stability ahead of EMU membership.

To put this tension in perspective, however, three points should be borne in mind:

- Balassa-Samuelson price increases preserve microeconomic equilibrium and are not symptoms of macroeconomic imbalance—although they can be reconciled with very low average inflation to the extent traded goods prices decline.
- The tension between exchange-rate and price stability does not flow from a problem of nominal convergence but from real convergence, as productivity in manufacturing rise toward advanced economy levels.
- The tension is between two routes of warranted real appreciation, whereas the stronger concern within the Union, in the past, related to the disruptive effects of unwarranted real depreciation.

More generally and fundamentally, exchange-rate pegs are open to the critique that they heighten vulnerability to market pressures. With liberalized capital flows, the risk is twofold. First, at some point, pegs may be viewed by markets as a one-way bet and attacked. Second, if that occurs when a peg has been in place for some time, domestic firms may have engaged in unhedged foreign borrowing: devaluation losses on this will add to real (and possibly fiscal) adjustment stresses. For economies integrating with international financial markets, it is clear that pegs are extremely demanding in terms of the policy regimes needed to support them. Conventionally, this relates to fiscal sustainability, the subordination of monetary policy to the anchor, sound debt management, and adequate wage-price flexibility to deal with exposure to asymmetric shocks (assessed in light of the structural match between anchoring and anchor economies). But an emerging consensus would extend this checklist to ex ante tests in the financial area, if a peg is not to prove vulnerable, and the costs of devaluation oppressive: notably, sound prudential supervision, to ensure a fairly resilient and liquid banking system, and thus give up-front assurance of an ability to raise interest rates without provoking a domestic financial crisis. Related, but harder to assess, are corporate leverage and unhedged currency exposure—which may, respectively, inhibit forceful defense of a peg and increase adjustment stresses in the event of devaluation. Finally, political commitment to the peg will clearly be crucial in its impact on private-sector expectations—both its influence over wage and price setting and its resilience to financial-market pressures.

Concerns about the vulnerability of pegs have encouraged interest in regimes of greater fixity: currency boards or early *euroization*. These regimes, however, have drawbacks for complex economies still in rapid transformation. They allow limited room for banking support and eliminate a key safety valve in the event of shocks. Euroization implies a loss of seignorage, and assuming it occurred by negotiation, there are questions about what policy tests existing area members might impose.[3] These options, moreover, quell only capital-flow problems relating to exchange-rate speculation—not those prompted by other distortions. Under these regimes, again, inflation is likely to be higher than in the euro area (although in Estonia the annual inflation rate has currently declined to some $2\frac{1}{2}$ percent). There remains, nonetheless, a general recognition that—even if euroization may not be a politically viable option—currency boards carry a substantial degree of credibility: this reflects, more than their strict institutional aspects, the policy commitment that they epitomize.

An alternative is inflation targeting, where the experience underway in the Czech Republic and Poland will shed light on a range of issues—some technical, some more fundamental:

• Technical readiness entails not just central bank independence but the ability to project inflation and relate it to instrument adjustments—thus, a fairly predictable transmission mechanism.[4]
• Key implementation issues include whether the medium-term goal should be to cut inflation to advanced economy levels despite Balassa-Samuelson effects, whether to target core inflation (notably where many administered prices remain or agriculture is prominent), whether to publish inflation forecasts, and how quickly to bring inflation within a current target range. On these issues, approaches vary between the Czech Republic and Poland, and advanced economy experience does not point to universally accepted answers.
• Two fundamental issues are whether inflation targeting, on the road to EU accession, will prove less prey than pegs to speculative pressures and whether this regime is more tolerant of policy errors or market imperfections—offering a country's fiscal, monetary, and prudential authorities more reasonable room for maneuver than currency pegs. The jury is out on these questions. Many observers would reckon pegs to be exceptionally demanding in the policy underpinning they require, but they would also recognize that inflation-targeting regimes face serious dilemmas at times of capital inflows—between abandoning the inflation target or allowing a real appreciation that could lead to an unsustainable current account deterioration.

Given these uncertainties, some have advocated hybrid regimes. An example would be a regime that primarily targeted inflation in a band of 3 to 5 percent but did so in the framework of a wide (ultimately adjustable) band against the euro. Such regimes, inevitably, pay a price: they trade off some degree of transparency against the dictates of pragmatism. And their dual anchors may conflict. But they might allow authorities to demonstrate that they can guide the economy over the medium-term on a course of reasonable nominal stability.

Ultimately, membership of the euro area will provide a satisfactory solution to these regime choices, but there may well be a period of several years ahead in which the first-round accession economies face difficult dilemmas. The nominal convergence issues are specific to these economies. They will be resolved between applicants and the European Union—and here it is important to recall that meeting the requirements to join the Union (the Copenhagen criteria) is distinct from fully meeting the criteria to join the euro area.[5] The more fundamental problem of vulnerability to capital flows is a concern these countries share with all emerging-market economies—though it is particularly troubling to the extent they are expected to demonstrate exchange rate stability on the road to euro area membership. These problems of vulnerability are a first reason to argue for changes in architecture that might mitigate problems of herding or contagion. It is possible that improvements in the international architecture could help increase the options available to these economies, reducing the pressure to move to corner solutions of currency boards or inflation targeting.

A second area in which these economies face difficulties relating to their macroeconomic policy regimes in a setting of liberalized markets is the design of a fiscal framework. While capital-account liberalization improves access to foreign savings, experience shows that there may be swings in the availability of these savings that complicate greatly the management of fiscal policy over the medium term. There are hazards of both feast and famine.

On the one hand, as convergence expectations mount, there is a possibility that market discipline over the policies of the first-round applicants could be—at least intermittently—rather weak. Bond market investors seeking superior returns already find medium- to long-term domestic-currency instruments in these economies attractive, on the basis that inflation is expected to decline further. In other areas of the world such a setting at times encouraged excessive deficit financing by the private or public sector. There will be a continuing need to scrutinize carefully the factors—real and financial—that underlie sizable current-account deficits. This is true even where the fiscal position is in balance or surplus: the question remains whether inflows to the private sector (short- or long-term) are responding to market distortions or implicit guarantees—which may result in large quasi-fiscal liabilities.

On the other hand, if we see continuing episodes of turbulence, there is a risk that emerging-market economies, out of caution, may be driven at times to curtail their access to foreign savings excessively. Whether they adopt pegs or inflation targeting, the concern to avoid speculative attacks and contagion could, over time, induce them to hold their current-account deficits to an arbitrarily low level, irrespective of the rate of return on investments or other fundamentals—to keep their heads below the parapet in embattled markets. Such concerns could entail running fiscal positions significantly tighter than required for public-debt—or total external-debt—sustainability.[6] Forcing countries to strategies of very high-risk aversion entails significant costs to growth if foreign savings are artificially limited.

These economies already face tough challenges in developing medium-term fiscal frameworks, without an excessive external constraint on policy. Their fiscal plans must reconcile deficit-reduction goals with the need to cut taxes on labor income. Most also still have to absorb remaining restructuring costs: coal, steel, and agriculture reform in Poland are examples, as are financial restructuring and pension reform in the Czech Republic and Estonia. There will be heavy demands, too, for spending on infrastructure and the environment, not least to meet EU accession requirements over time.

To meet these fiscal challenges, forceful medium-term public expenditure frameworks will be needed to guide the restructuring of public-sector activities. Such frameworks can help to build durable credibility in international financial markets—increasing these countries' latitude to draw on foreign savings while containing financial vulnerability. All the more reason for these countries to lock in to medium-term policy frameworks compatible with early EU accession—setting out transparent and sustainable economic strategies. And all the more reason to analyze more deeply the elements of real convergence that will strongly influence the final form of successful macroeconomic frameworks—ranging from the likely behavior of private saving and investment to the order of magnitude of Balassa-Samuelson effects. This is an important research agenda, with very concrete policy applications.

Thus far, the authorities have generally adapted their monetary and exchange systems effectively, pressed forward in addressing structural fiscal problems, and gauged their access to foreign savings with prudence. These economies have, admittedly, experienced occasional market pressures in recent months as their current-account deficits widened—notably where this was accompanied by fiscal slippage. The market has sent up warning flares (recent pressures on the zloty, for example) but has ended by looking through to strong fundamentals and a likelihood of shrinking imbalances in 2000. The track record of these countries thus far, indeed, gives every reason to think that they will meet the next round of challenges effectively, continuing to innovate in policy in varying ways, and that they will move forward to EU membership within a very few years. But the fact remains that the accession process cannot proof them against herding and contagion in capital markets. In developing their monetary and fiscal frameworks they may remain constrained—perhaps unduly so—by a concern to avoid any risks from market turbulence.

In sum, the new architecture may begin at home, in domestic reforms, but it cannot end there. If we think of approaches to improve the working of the international financial system, we cannot look at these leading emerging markets, select a composite of conservative regimes, and close the book. It is true that a balanced budget and a currency board should firewall economies against stress, provided prudential polices are sound and quasi-fiscal deficits contained. But to pursue these prescriptions narrowly, rather than trying to improve the financial-market system and allow wider policy options, appears close to a counsel of despair. Even the most advanced transition economies could benefit from improvements in architecture that mitigate capital market risks—and these are economies in a fairly privileged position, with EU membership an ultimate anchor for policies and expectations. Many emerging markets navigate on more open seas.

3.   Initiatives to strengthen the international financial architecture

This brings us to the core of the architecture debate: in a world of liberalized markets, what changes can be made in the system to improve the chances for growth and stability for these and other economies? The challenge is to identify where the rules of the system need to be adjusted to foster stability in a world dominated by rapidly growing private flows and an increasingly diverse range of instruments. After a period when architecture initiatives proliferated dizzyingly, the task now is to pursue and deepen a number of approaches that, acting in concert, could help to change incentives to some degree.

One way of thinking about the problem and analyzing the instruments to address it is in terms of the distortions that are widely accepted to affect capital markets—prime among which are (1) herding behavior and contagion, (2) information problems, and (3) moral hazard. The current initiatives in architecture can be thought of as addressing these distortions in different ways: reducing them or counterbalancing them—and, perhaps most critically, encouraging countries to implement reforms that will help to buttress their economies against them.

3.1.   Herding behavior and contagion

A first priority is to deepen preemptively countries' defenses against turbulence and swings in market sentiment—the problems of herding and contagion.

A key element in this must be stronger international oversight of the financial sector. This is crucial among the advanced economies to address factors that may contribute to destabilizing swings in capital flows, and it is at least as important among emerging-market countries to minimize distortions and fragilities in their financial systems as they progress with capital-account liberalization. Inherently, it is a cooperative venture of country authorities and the main international institutions. Under a new and shared oversight body, an IMF–World Bank Financial-Sector Assessment Program is now in place, with joint staff teams undertaking a first round of in-depth financial-sector assessments. In parallel, a new methodology has been developed to assess adherence to the Basle Core Principles, and 24 countries have been assessed thus far. The Basle supervisors have also put forward a consultative document on revising the Capital Accord—an agenda crucial to reduce financial vulnerabilities. Finally, the Financial Stability Forum has begun its work on offshore-centers, hedge funds (highly leveraged institutions), and short-term flows: recommendations are expected early next year, including for the disclosure of information by the private sector.

A second element in parrying contagion lies in the development of codes of conduct covering key areas of policy: codes involve standards for public policy making, as well as disclosure principles. The Fund has now prepared codes of good practice on fiscal transparency and of transparency in monetary and financial policies—the latter being endorsed by the Interim Committee in Washington. A growing number of countries are now proceeding with self-assessments under these codes. These codes should help improve policy performance, strengthen institutional resilience, and allow lenders to make more discriminating decisions—assessing public and private borrowers against agreed benchmarks.

The Fund has been preparing experimental assessments of a country's progress in observing international standards and codes. These Reports on Observance of Standards and Codes (ROSCs) provide an independent assessment of a country's practices, focusing primarily on areas where the Fund has a direct operational focus—data dissemination; transparency in fiscal, monetary, and financial policies; and banking supervision. To date, reports covering all or part of these areas have been published for 10 countries. In the next year, particular attention will be given to the role that the World Bank and other bodies can play is undertaking assessments in areas beyond the Fund's expertise.

An urgent task is to integrate this deeper analysis of the financial sector and capital flows fully into the Fund's Article IV surveillance. Stronger stress on the financial sector was a key proposal in the recent external evaluation of the Fund's surveillance: to be effective, this needs to grasp the dynamics with which financial flows respond to countries' macroeconomic and regulatory frameworks, including distortions or implicit guarantees. One element already underway is a deeper analysis of external vulnerability. In the context of this financial-sector surveillance, it will also be possible to assess better the speed and sequencing of capital-account liberalization in member countries. And an appraisal of financial-sector linkages is crucial also to assess the underpinnings of countries' exchange-rate regimes.

An initiative, finally, that draws several of these strands together and tries to directly address risks of contagion ex ante is the Fund's new Contingent Credit Line (CCL). This facility provides up-front assurance of Fund support to buttress sound policies and ward off speculation. Discussions are proceeding with a number of countries to explore their interest in the CCL. The CCL, clearly, is not the only route to achieving this, and Mexico's new arrangement with the Fund can be seen as similarly preemptive in spirit.

3.2. Information problems

A second priority in current initiatives on architecture is to inform markets better about countries' policies—enhancing market discipline and reducing information asymmetries at both a macroeconomic and a microeconomic level.

Virtue begins at home, and the Fund's work is being opened much more fully to the public, with increasing numbers of country reports and program documents appearing on our web site. At the last count, around 45 countries are participating in the pilot program for release of Article IV staff reports. Two-fifths of our members have agreed to release program documents and Board assessments of Article IV consultations. Public Information Notices are being published also on the Board's work program and main policy discussions. For the Fund, these initiatives follow some soul searching because it is harder to ensure frank dialogues in a public setting. But increasingly these risks have been outweighed by the case for getting fuller information to markets, stimulating feedback to policy makers, promoting public ownership of reforms—and, indeed, following the principles of transparency and accountability we urge on others.

In addition, the provision of much higher-quality public information is a key facet of the standards, codes of conduct, and reports I have referred to. Each is designed to enhance not only the policy-making process but the basis on which information can be made available to markets and the wider public. In this, they follow in the path of the Special Data Dissemination Standard—which, in turn, is moving on to a deeper coverage of reserves and debt. The SDDS has been gaining prominence in the official sector—including by the Basle Committee in its review of the Capital Accord—as well as private-sector analyses.

3.3. Moral hazard

A third broad priority is to involve the private sector in forestalling and resolving crises—reducing the risks of moral hazard arising from official responses to financial crises.

A major emphasis is on action before a crisis strikes. In addition to strengthening policies, countries are encouraged to arrange lines of credit preemptively (Argentina provides an example of such a strategy). They are also urged to include clauses in trust deeds for bonds to facilitate orderly renegotiation, should this become necessary. And they will need to adjust their domestic regulatory frameworks in ways that buttress market discipline. These are elements the Fund will evaluate in considering countries' eligibility for the CCL.

Once crisis strikes, there is a renewed emphasis on the principle that private-sector lenders cannot free-ride on official rescues—which would deeply distort the allocation of savings worldwide through a systematic mispricing of risk. This is crucial also because official resources are limited—and will become more so if public money is seen to bail out private creditors. In most cases the Fund relies on its catalytic role to help preserve continuing market access, but where this is not possible, the goal must be to encourage a voluntary and collaborative approach to restructuring. The concern with equitable burden sharing can be traced back over the past two decades to the commercial bank new-money packages and short-term rollovers of the 1980s debt crisis. The shift in financing assurances policy of the late 1980s, equally, preempted an inappropriate use of official resources to pay off bank debt arrears. The debt reduction deals of the Brady era were reviewed to ensure they were no more generous a use of official resources than buybacks at the prevailing market price. A key concern in recent cases has been bonded debt—where the dilemmas are even sharper to the extent concerted solutions are harder to arrange. But with each of these initiatives, the philosophy has been the same. Initially, there has been a process of case-by-case learning, with a concern to strike the right balance between the risk of bailouts and risks to market access for each and all borrowers. The complexity and variety of country cases has highlighted many conceptual and practical issues: these will need to be addressed over the coming months to arrive at a clearer framework in which private-sector involvement can be considered.

The kind of architectural improvements I have discussed may appear modest and in some ways experimental—not an art but a craft. The main features are to promote transparency and financial-sector soundness (areas where progress is being made quite rapidly) and also to develop a balanced relationship between private and public sectors and promote capital-market liberalization in an orderly and well-sequenced manner (areas where progress is proving slower). The actions being taken in these directions have aptly been described as *fixing the plumbing and the wiring*. Their impact, however, should be nontrivial. In the world of financial markets, like the everyday world, it is unfixed plumbing that can bring down the ceiling and unrepaired wiring that burns down the house. The recent return of a degree of calm in markets and recovery in the crises countries must not cause the agenda to languish.

4.   The evolving contribution of the euro area

These systemic reforms, to bear fruit, need a counterpart in expanding world trade and relatively stable financial conditions. The links between major country performance and financial stability, admittedly, are not always obvious or direct. It is puzzling that instability has not diminished at a time of low inflation and interest rates in advanced economies. Possibly, a quest for high yields has encouraged boom and bust cycles. But a likely contributor lies in the constrained policy settings of major blocs in the world economy. In both Europe and Japan, there have been constraints on fiscal policy—and, more seriously, delays in proceeding with the structural reforms that would improve the tradeoff between growth and inflation and enhance the robustness of these economies in the face of shocks.

With the advent of the euro, Europe has gained new opportunities and responsibilities to influence global financial developments. It can do so in the real domain by helping to foster a sustained growth in world trade. It can do so in the financial domain by improving the flow of savings among economies (through liquid and well-regulated markets), as well as providing a pole in the system that can serve as an anchor for the economies of the area—ultimately through euro area membership. To conclude this regional perspective, let me turn to the contribution that policies in the euro area may make to a well-functioning system.

4.1. Economic policies

A first priority for the euro area lies in the stance and mix of its economic policies.

In monetary policy, the European Central Bank (ECB) has benefited from strong continuity and demonstrated its capacity for decisive moves. Over time, its credibility will depend on its track record and continuing progress in building transparency, while its effectiveness cannot be divorced from the wider policy setting. Transparency would be further enhanced by providing a more detailed assessment of the outlook for inflation, to strengthen public understanding of how the ECB conducts monetary policy and also by delineating more sharply its inflation goal. There is also in the future, as for other central banks, the risk of serious dilemmas for policy arising from asset price or exchange-rate trends or the lower bound on nominal interest rates under low inflation. These are, again, areas where a high degree of transparency is required so that the public can interpret the extent to which various factors are influencing changes in stance and the ways these factors link to the ultimate objectives of policy. But such problems may also require a blend of monetary, fiscal, and real sector adjustment—underscoring that, ultimately, the success of monetary policy is not only a question of central banking technique: it depends critically on other instruments of policy being unencumbered.

In fiscal policy, deficit-reduction efforts need to be renewed but flanked with structural reforms. On the one hand, little underlying consolidation has occurred since the Maastricht tests were met in 1997. On the other, from a domestic and international standpoint, three additional priorities require action:

- A major effort to restrain the growth of public expenditure to lower the tax burden on labor income and thus also structural unemployment;
- A revitalization of strategies to address population aging, with a new emphasis on curbing early retirement and boosting labor-force participation, not just on generating interest savings;
- More efforts to free fiscal stabilizers on the downside—which may imply countering procyclical actions at lower levels of government and treating cyclical expenditures flexibly in implementing governments' medium-term ceilings on expenditure.

Sound macroeconomic policies must be supported by reforms in product and labor markets—the latter being the area most seriously lagging in the EU's economic strategy. This, again, is vital from an international as well as a domestic perspective. Raising both potential output and flexibility, such reforms can contribute decisively to the health of the world economy—most critically by helping preserve an open trading environment. Such reforms do not entail abandoning core social protection. The Netherlands, Denmark, Finland, and the United Kingdom of the late 1990s all offer routes to reform that are consultative in style and protect core values. But in each case they have implied tangible reform of social benefits. Indeed, throughout the European Union something of a Copernican revolution is required to recenter benefit administration on returning the jobless to work—not just on income support. Support needs to be contingent on a readiness to seek work or training. This is essential for other reforms to have full effect—including lower taxes and more flexible wage formation. More broadly, structural reforms to enhance the flexibility of the euro area economy in the face of shocks should reduce the need for fluctuations in the exchange rate to serve as a safety valve.

4.2.   A stable capital market

A second challenge for policy makers in the euro area is to foster the development of a deep and relatively stable capital market. The cornerstone, of course, lies in sound economic policies, but two priorities in financial-sector policy need to be kept in view:

- Completion of the single financial market, which in many areas remain to be put fully into place. The European Commission's 1998 report on this subject clarifies the range of regulatory and taxation changes that member states need to implement to achieve this.
- Further progress in explaining transparently the prudential and last-resort lending strategies of the area's financial authorities. The two and a half decades since Herstatt have seen ever closer operational links among Europe's supervisors in devising rules and in handling problems, which will stand the area in good stead. But there is a need to be clearer how some institutional aspects of lender-of-last-resort policies will operate and the broad considerations that will guide them—including a readiness to allow failure. We should regard London and Continental Bankers and Baring Brothers as accidents with a silver lining in this regard.

As debate and experimentation in architecture move forward, Europe will contribute not just through policies but through the experience and priorities it brings to the table. Its role in developing supervisory standards was seminal. It was at the forefront of inflation targeting. European voices have pressed for systemic reforms—including a shift in philosophy toward one that is more rule-based. Europeans, too, have been among the first to warn, with every wave of firefighting, about the risks of moral hazard. Rules, standards, and procedures are indeed at the forefront of the Fund's current efforts, and the involvement of private creditors is now a burning issue. This is to say how much the Fund needs the reflections, challenges, and innovations of its European members working to strengthen financial architecture in the period ahead.

Notes

1. The transition economies sufficiently advanced in reform to have been identified as first-round candidates for EU accession—an approach now being broadened—were the Czech Republic, Estonia, Hungary, Poland, and Slovenia.
2. The Balassa-Samuelson effect is the significant increase in the relative price of nontradables that results from their relatively limited supply, under conditions where productivity in tradables is rising sharply relative to that in nontradables (a feature of economies undergoing a productivity catch-up to advanced economy levels).
3. The President of the European Central Bank, in his 1999 Per Jacobson lecture, stressed that the economic steps of accession should be seen as a continuum: joining the European Union, joining ERM II, and adopting the euro.
4. The sweeping, and unprepared, regime shifts in the United Kingdom, Sweden, and Finland, in their successful moves to inflation targeting, signal that these concerns should not be exaggerated, provided inflation targeting is pursued singlemindedly and with appropriate transparency. These countries exited from fixed exchange-rate regimes in crisis situations, with the credibility of monetary policy initially low, and with no prior preparation of an inflation targeting regime.
5. The Copenhagen criteria include, regarding economic aspects: (1) stability of institutions guaranteeing the rule of law; (2) a functioning market economy, able to meet EU competitive pressures and market forces; and (3) ability to take on the obligations of membership, including adherence to the aims of economic and monetary union the (*acquis communautaire*). Macroeconomically, a core requirement, together with goals of high growth and employment, is convergence toward stability—ultimately, for monetary union, that defined in the Maastricht criteria (with its well-known conditions relating to inflation, interest rates, exchange rates, and fiscal deficits) and, more recently, the Stability and Growth Pact.
6. More generally, containing the external current-account deficit through fiscal tightening alone (rather than looking for microeconomic factors that may be influencing it) is a very shorthand approach to addressing vulnerability. And calibrating current-account targets on *sustainable* direct investment flows overlooks the sometimes sizable loan component of such flows, as well as direct investors' ability to shift quite sharply the location or currency in which their liquid balances are held. Gross as well as net flows matter; so do stocks of liquid assets and liabilities.

Open economies review **11:S1** 133–148 (2000)
© 2000 *Kluwer Academic Publishers. Printed in The Netherlands.*

The Present International Monetary System:
Problems, Complications, and Reforms

DOMINICK SALVATORE
Fordham University, New York

Keywords: early-warning system, emerging-market economies, euro, European Central Bank, European monetary system, European Monetary Union, exchange-rate arrangements, exchange-rate mechanism, global financial integration, International Monetary Fund, international monetary system, international policy coordination, optimum currency area, target zones, transition economies

JEL Classification Number: F3

Abstract

In the last decade serious crises have affected financial markets. Some proposals to avoid international financial crises have been made, but more useful could be measures to strengthen the functioning of the present international monetary system. Another way could be a much greater involvement of the private sector. The misalignment among leading currencies of the world can be a source of crisis difficult to solve. The creation of the European Central Bank (ECB) and of the euro leaves unresolved the serious problem of how a European Monetary Union member will respond to an asymmetric shock.

Introduction

This article examines two major problems and one complication facing the present international monetary system. The problems are the inability to prevent frequent international financial crises and the possibility of large exchange-rate misalignments. The complication arises from the creation of the euro. The policies proposed to avoid or minimize international financial crises have a good chance of succeeding. Those advocated to prevent or minimize exchange-rate misalignments (the establishment of a system of target zones for the world's major currencies or agreeing on much greater and formal international macro-economic policy coordination among the major countries) would either not work or be unfeasible. The complication in the operation of the international monetary system arising from the creation of the euro arises from the need to deal with asymmetric shocks within the Union, the relationship between the ins and outs (Britain, Sweden, Denmark, and Greece), the challenges posed by the future admission of the nations of Central and Eastern Europe, and the excess volatility and misalignments that are likely to arise between the euro and the dollar. The international monetary system of the future is likely to involve improvements in the operation of the present system rather than replacement with an entirely new and different one. In this article, I deliberately use the word *system* instead of *architecture* in the context of the international monetary system because the latter term has been overused and misused (see Saccomanni, this volume).

1. The crisis-prone present international monetary system and how to deal with it

This section examines the causes of international financial crises in emerging markets during the past decade and evaluates the reforms advocated to prevent them or minimize and resolve them when they do occur. The problem of exchange-rate misalignments is examined in the next section.

1.1. The crisis-prone present international monetary system

During the past five years, there have been four serious financial crises in emerging-market economies: in 1994 and 1995 Mexico faced financial and economic collapse, in July 1997 the financial crisis in Southeast Asia started, in the summer of 1998 the Russian financial and economic crisis began, and in January 1999 Brazil plunged into a crisis. The Mexican crisis was more or less resolved by the end of 1996, the crisis in Southeast Asia may have reached the bottom but it may take at least another year or two to be fully resolved, and the crises in Russia and Brazil are still evolving.

As a result of rapid liberalization, investors from developed countries poured huge amounts of capital in emerging-market economies during the past decade to take advantage of much higher returns there and for international portfolio diversification. Higher returns resulted from the much faster growth rates and from the many new and unexploited investment opportunities arising in emerging-market economies. Massive international financial capital flows are generally acknowledged to have led to a more efficient allocation of world savings and investments and enhanced global economic welfare. Some of this capital flow was in the form of direct investments, which were long term and rather stable in nature. An increasing portion, however, was financial in character and subject to quick withdrawal at the first sign of crisis. This was, in fact, what happened and what precipitated each of the four crises that affected emerging-market economies during the past five years. Although the fundamental problem that led to these crises was different, the process was very similar (see Frankel and Rose, 1996; Kaminski, Lizondo, and Reinhart, 1998; and Salvatore, 1997a, and 1999).

In the case of the 1994 and 1995 Mexican crisis, the fundamental problem was an overvalued peso, which led to huge trade deficits and loss of international reserves, until foreign and domestic investors, fearing devaluation, rushed for the exit door at the end of 1994 and made a devaluation of the peso a self-fulfilling prophesy. In the vain attempt to prevent further capital outflows, Mexico increased interest rates dramatically. But this not only failed to stem the capital outflows but also plunged the nation into a deep recession and forced Mexico to float its currency. Only with massive aid negotiated by the United States through the International Monetary Fund and some restructuring of its financial and fiscal sectors did Mexico come out of the recession and resolve the crisis by the end of 1996.

The fundamental cause of the financial crisis that started in Southeast Asia in July 1997 was somewhat similar. Since the early 1990s, banks in South Korea, Thailand, Indonesia, Malaysia, and the Philippines borrowed heavily in dollars and yens on the international capital market at the low interest rates prevailing. The banks then lent these funds in the local currency to domestic firms at much higher rates, thus earning huge profits. Foreign loans were not hedged for foreign-exchange risks by the banks because of the belief that the nation's central bank would not change the par value of their currency (that is, would not devalue) against the dollar. Local firms were willing to borrow at high rates because of the huge profits that they were earning in their rapidly expanding economies.

But as local firms expended into more lines of production and into the production of more sophisticated products, they faced more and more world-class competition from leading foreign multinationals: it was one thing to produce bicycles and televisions and an entirely different thing to compete internationally in automobiles and computer chips. Then in 1994, China devalued its currency by about 30 percent, and the Japanese yen depreciated by about 26 percent with respect to the U.S. dollar. Since the currencies of the Southeast Asia tigers were tied to the dollar and they competed head on with Chinese and Japanese products, the currencies of these nations became greatly overvalued, and this led to huge trade deficits. The story then follows the Mexican pattern. Foreign and domestic investors, fearing devaluation, shifted their liquid funds abroad, making devaluation a self-fulfilling prophecy. Unable to repay their dollar- and yen-denominated foreign loans, local banks become insolvent and stopped making loans to local firms, forcing many of them out of business. In the meantime, in a vain attempt to stem the capital outflow, the central bank increased interest rates sharply, which not only failed to put an end to capital outflows but also pushed these economies into recession. In 1998, all of these nations were in recession, with reductions in real GDP ranging from 2 percent in Malaysia to 15 percent in Indonesia. Only in 1999 did economic conditions in these countries (with the exception of Indonesia) begin to improve, but it may take at least another year of two before they are restored to full economic health.

In summer 1998, Russia plunged into deep financial, economic, and political crisis. The immediate cause of the collapse was huge capital outflows that occurred when foreign and domestic investors realized that Russia was unable or unwilling to restructure its economy and the International Monetary Fund refused to provide additional loans to keep Russia afloat. The economic situation in Russia now is very grave, and there are no signs that the crisis is coming to an end. In Russia there is today almost the complete breakdown of the rule of law, and most of the banking sector is in a state of insolvency. The central government collects only 6 percent of the gross domestic product (GDP) in taxes and is unable to provide for even minimal government services without printing huge amounts of money, which led to an increase in prices (inflation rate) of almost 100 percent during the past 12 months. With Yeltsin's health problem and erratic behavior and the chaotic political situation, the economic crisis may even deepen.

Brazil plunged into crisis on January 13, 1999, when it devalued its currency (the real) by about 8 percent. Once again, this was triggered by huge capital outflows in the face of a sharp drop in international reserves and fear of devaluation. From July to December 1998, Brazil's international reserves declined from $75 billion to $36 billion. In addition, Brazil used $9 billion of the $41.5 billion it received from the International Monetary Fund (IMF) in the fall of 1998 to help Brazil defend the real while putting its fiscal house in order. The fundamental problem in Brazil was the huge and unsustainable budget deficit, which was in excess of 8 percent of GDP in 1998. When foreign and domestic investors realized that Brazil would be unable to increase taxes and reduce expenditures sufficiently to abide by the agreement to cut in half its budget deficit by the end of this year (the condition for receiving the huge loan from the IMF in October 1998), they resumed their massive movement of liquid funds out of the country, thus forcing the devaluation of January 13, 1999. But markets felt that this devaluation was entirely insufficient, and funds continued to flow out at a rapid rate, thus forcing Brazil to let the real float. By the end of March 1999, the real had depreciated by about 35 percent with respect to the dollar. To prevent further outflows of liquid capital, Brazil increased short-term interest rates to the incredible level of 39 percent. But this not only did not succeed in stemming the capital outflow but also plunged Brazil into recession in 1999. Even though economic conditions seem to have improved (interest rates have been reduced to about 18 percent, the real appreciated somewhat from its low point in March, and inflation remained contained), Brazil is still in a precarious situation because it has not yet been able to solve its budget deficit problem.

It is clear from what was said above that a world of liberalized capital markets and huge international liquid capital flows is prone to serious financial crises, especially in emerging markets. The danger is that such crises could spread to the rest of the world, including industrial countries, thus leading to calls for reforms of the entire international monetary system. The challenge is how to prevent or minimize the number and depth of financial crises and how to resolve the crises that do occur without falling into the moral-hazard trap.

1.2. Proposals to avoid international financial crises

Since the immediate cause of each of the recent international financial crises was the sudden withdrawal of liquid funds from emerging markets at the first sign of trouble, it would seem logical to think that restricting those capital flows might eliminate or at least minimize these international financial crises. A proposal advanced by Tobin (1978, 1996) would do this with a small flat transaction tax (which, therefore, would become progressively higher the shorter the duration of the transaction) in order "to put some sand in the wheels of international finance." Chile used a variation of this from 1991 to 1998 by requiring foreign investors to deposit 30 percent of their funds in a noninterest-paying account with the Chilean Central Bank for one year. According to some economists and government officials, this regulation succeeded in reducing speculative inflows and minimizing contagion from the Mexican crisis. Malaysia's restriction on capital flows from 1997 to 1999 also seems to have shielded it from worse contagion from the East Asian crisis.

Some years ago, Dornbusch and Frankel (1987) proposed to reduce international speculative capital flows with dual exchange rates—a less flexible one for trade transactions and a more flexible one for purely financial transactions not related to international trade and investments. By restricting international "hot" money flows through capital-market segmentation or the decoupling of asset markets, Tobin, Dornbusch, and Frankel believed that the international financial system could be made to operate much more smoothly and without any need for close policy coordination among the leading industrial countries—which they regarded as neither feasible nor useful. Critics of these proposals, however, point out that it is next to impossible to separate "nonproductive" or speculative capital flows from "productive" or nonspeculative ones related to international trade and investments. Furthermore, these taxes or other restrictions on international liquid capital flows interfere with the optimal allocation of capital around the world.

More likely to be useful are a number of measures to strengthen the functioning of the present international monetary system based on *increased transparency* in international monetary relations, strengthening banking and financial systems, greater involvement of the private sector, and providing adequate financial resources to emerging markets to prevent them from being affected by financial crises elsewhere (see IMF, 1996; IMF, January, May, June, October, 1998). Increased transparency is essential because markets cannot work efficiently without adequate, reliable, and timely information. To this end, the IMF established the Special Data Dissemination Standards (SDDS) in 1996, which have already been accepted by about one-quarter of the membership. These early-warning financial indicators, such as the budget and current-account deficit, long-term and short-term foreign debts, and international reserves as percentages of GDP could signal which emerging country or countries might be heading for trouble. The hope is that foreign investors would take note of the potential problem and avoid pouring excessive funds into the nation or nations, thus possibly avoiding a crisis. The SDDS has since been supplemented by the Dissemination Standard Bulletin Board (DSBB), which is an electronic site on the Internet that provides information concerning countries' economic and financial data systems with more than 40 subscribers, including Hong Kong and

China. The IMF is also proposing to set up a clearing house to keep track of all the loans and liquid investments made by foreign banks and other financial institutions in emerging markets. Lack of this information has led to excessive loans and other liquid investments in emerging markets in the past, which eventually led to crisis.

Another crucial way of improving the functioning of the present international monetary system is by *strengthening emerging markets' banking and financial systems*. Weakness in these were common to all emerging markets that were involved in financial crises during the past five years. A weak banking and financial system invites a financial crisis and guarantees its severity. The banking and financial system can be strengthened by improving supervision and prudential standards and making sure that banks meet capital requirements, make adequate provisions for bad loans, and publish relevant and timely information on their loan activity. It is also important to deal with insolvent institutions promptly and effectively. Implementing these policies is difficult, especially when a nation's banking and financial system is already in trouble, but a sound financial system is essential for the health and growth of the entire economy. The IMF has been formulating standards or codes of good practice in accounting, auditing, corporate governance, payments and settlements systems, insurance, and banking based on internationally accepted Basle Core Principles, and some of these are already being implemented as part of the IMF surveillance function.

The third way of strengthening the present international monetary system is to get much *greater involvement of the private sector* in sharing the burden of resolving a financial crisis in emerging markets by rolling over and renegotiating loans or providing new money rather than rushing for the exit, as a precondition for IMF official assistance. The logic is that lenders should be compelled to take some responsibility for the crisis by having lent so many short-term funds to an emerging market for such nonproductive purposes. So lenders should be bailed in rather than be allowed to bail out and rush for the exit door. This is exactly what happened on January 28, 1998, when the IMF and rich-countries' government leaned over and strong-armed international banks to reschedule $24 billion of debt with a plan to replace bank loans with sovereign-guaranteed bonds. A similar strategy was taken in Brazil in early 1999. This, however, was relatively easy to do in Korea and Brazil because the problem there was primarily a liquidity crisis rather than a much more serious structural problem, which would have raised serious doubts whether lenders would ever be repaid or even receive service payments. The legal framework to compel creditors to accept a Chapter 11-type arrangement as it exists, for example, in the United States today does not exist on a global scale, and it is not likely to be established soon. A formal change in the wording of bond contracts is a long way off. Lenders would either charge much higher interest rates to compensate them for the higher risk or avoid lending to the emerging-market economies. Yet the notion of moving toward some kind of debt-restructuring system is getting a lot of attention at the IMF, the World Bank, and the Bank for International Settlements (BIS). Of course, it should not be easy for an emerging-market economy in a financial difficulty to unilaterally declare bankruptcy (to avoid the problem of moral hazard), but some way of bailing in lenders is clearly necessary to resolve a financial crisis when one does erupt. In those situations, the IMF should certify when an emerging market is sufficiently in trouble to trigger the restructuring mechanism.

One reform that the IMF devised in the fall of 1998 was to *provide strong financial backing to an emerging market before it faces a financial crisis*, if there is a danger that it might be dragged into one for no fault of its own. For example, it often happens that international investors are unable to make any distinction among emerging markets and withdraw funds from all of them when only one or a few of them face a crisis. Thus, when the crisis erupted in Russia in the summer of 1998, international investors withdrew funds also from Southeast Asia and Latin America even though conditions were very different in these other markets. The IMF inaugurated this reform and activated it in the fall of 1998 by providing a line of credit of $41.5 billion to Brazil to help to shield it from being infected by the Russian crisis and avoid a devaluation of the real, while buying time for Brazil to put its fiscal house in order. But when it became clear at the end of 1998 that Brazil would be unable to resolve its fiscal problem, investors, fearing devaluation, resumed the transfer of huge quantities of liquid funds abroad, thus precipitating the crisis. It is important to recognize, however, that Brazil plunged into a crisis in January 1999 not so much because it was infected by the financial crisis in Russia but rather because it was unable to resolve its internal (fiscal) problem, and it does not necessarily mean that preventive medicine cannot help against contagion in future crises. To have the financial resources to implement its plan to be able to provide large financial assistance to an emerging market and so avoid being engulfed by a financial crisis elsewhere, the IMF also negotiated the doubling (to $47 billion) of the amount that it could borrow under the (New) General Agreement to Borrow and to increase the total resources at its disposal to $295 billion.

In the final analysis, it must be realized, however, that even if all the reforms being considered were to be adopted, they would not eliminate all future financial crises. All we can hope is that these reforms would reduce the frequency and severity of financial crises in the future. In short, some international financial instability and crises may be the inevitable result of liberalized financial markets and the cost that we have to pay in return for the benefits that liberalized financial markets provide to industrial and emerging-market economies alike.

2. The misalignment problem and its cure

During the past decade, most concern and effort have been devoted on how to prevent international financial crises in emerging markets. Serious as these crises have been, however, we should not forget that the present international monetary system faces another problem, which is more fundamental, dangerous, and difficult to solve. This is the possibility of large exchange-rate misalignments among the world's leading currencies (the U.S. dollar, the euro, and the Japanese yen). With the more immediate problem of international financial crises in emerging markets capturing the headlines and the attention of international financial officials, however, the more fundamental and serious problem of misaligned exchange rates seems to have been forgotten or at least neglected during the past decade. In this section, we examine the problem of exchange-rate misalignments and the reforms proposed to eliminate or minimize it.

2.1.   The misalignment problem

A currency misalignment refers to large and persistent departure of the exchange rates from its long-run, competitive equilibrium level. An overvalued currency has the effect of an export tax and an import subsidy on the nation, and, as such, it reduces the international competitiveness of the nation and distorts the pattern of specialization, trade, and payments. As opposed to exchange-rate volatility, a significant exchange-rate misalignment that persists for years cannot possibly be hedged away and can impose significant real costs on the economy in the form of unemployment, idle capacity, bankruptcy, and protectionist legislation (see Salvatore, 1993).

The most notorious example of exchange-rate misalignment is the overvaluation of the U.S. dollar during the l980s. According to the Board of Governors of the U.S. Federal Reserve System, from l980 to its peak in February l985, the dollar appreciated and became overvalued by about 40 percent on a trade-weighted basis against the currency of 10 largest industrial countries. This resulted in the huge trade deficit of the United States and equally large combined trade surplus of Japan and Germany. It also resulted in increasing calls for and actual trade protectionism in the United States. It has been estimated (see Council of Economic Advisors, 1986, 1987) that the l985 U.S. trade deficit was $60 billion to $70 billion greater (about twice as large) than it would have been had the dollar remained at its l980 level and that this deficit cost about 2 million jobs in the United States. Despite the fact that by the end of l988 the international value of the dollar was slightly below its l980 and l981 level (so that all of its overvaluation had been eliminated), large global trade imbalances remained and did not show signs of declining rapidly. Economists have borrowed the term *hysteresis* from the field of physics to characterize the failure of trade balances to return to their original equilibrium once exchange-rate misalignments have been corrected. The other bout of major misalignment of the dollar was during the past five years: the dollar was worth 85 yen in August 1995, 147 yen in August 1998, and 110 yen in August 1999.

Although misaligned exchange rates can be regarded as the immediate cause of prevailing global trade imbalances, they were themselves the result of internal structural disequilibria in the leading nations. It is these structural disequilibria and not exchange-rate misalignments that were and are the fundamental cause of the global imbalances facing the leading industrial countries today. What can be blamed on the current international financial system is its failure to provide smoother and more timely adjustment to such large and persistent global imbalances as the trade deficit of the United States, the trade surplus of Japan, and the large and persistent unemployment in Europe. It seems that trade flows now respond with longer than usual lags (ranging up to two years) to exchange-rate changes (see Salvatore, 1998b, ch. 16) and exchange rates reflect primarily changes in international financial flows rather than in trade flows.

2.2. Proposals to eliminate the problem of misalignment

Two proposals have been advanced to eliminate or at least minimize the problem of exchange-rate misalignments among the world's leading currencies. One is the establishment of target zones, and the other is the introduction of much greater and formal international macroeconomic policy coordination among the major countries.

The proposal to establish target zones to eliminate or minimize exchange-rate misalignments (which would also reduce exchange-rate volatility) was first advanced by Williamson (1986). Under such a system, the leading industrial nations estimate the equilibrium exchange rate and agree on the range of allowed fluctuation. Williamson suggested a band of allowed fluctuation of 10 percent above and below the equilibrium exchange rate. The exchange rate would then be determined by the forces of demand and supply within the allowed band of fluctuation and prevented from moving outside the target zones by official intervention in foreign-exchange markets. The target zones would be soft and would be changed when the underlying equilibrium exchange rate moves outside of or near the boundaries of the target zone.

Critics of target zones believe that target zones embody the worst characteristics of the fixed and flexible exchange-rate systems. As in the case of flexible rates, target zones allow substantial fluctuation and volatility in exchange rates and can be inflationary. As in the case of fixed exchange rates, target zones can only be defended and major exchange-rate misalignments avoided by official interventions in foreign-exchange markets that reduce the monetary autonomy of the nation. In response to this criticism, Miller and Williamson (1987) have extended their blueprint to require substantial policy coordination on the part of the leading industrial nations.

Although not made explicit, the leading industrial nations did agree on "soft" target or "reference zones" for the exchange rate between the dollar and the yen and between the dollar and the German mark in the Louvre Accord of February 1987 (but with the allowed band of fluctuation much smaller than the 10 percent band advocated by Williamson), but this tacit agreement was abandoned in the early 1990s in the face of strong market pressure, which saw a sharp depreciation of the dollar with respect to the mark and the yen. Target zones are now supported by the French and the German (and to some extent the Japanese) governments, but the United States and the Federal Reserve Board, as well as the European Central Bank and Britain, oppose them. As interferences with market forces, target zones would either be ineffective or fail, and there is little chance that they will be established in the near future.

The other proposal for avoiding exchange-rate misalignments is based on extensive policy coordination among the leading countries (see Bryant, 1995; Hamada and Kuwai, 1997; Milner, 1997; and McKinnon, 1984, 1988, 1996). Under McKinnon's proposal (the best and most articulated of the proposed plans), the United States, Japan, and Germany would fix the exchange rate among their currencies at the equilibrium level (determined by purchasing-power parity) and then closely coordinate their monetary policies to keep exchange rates at that level. A tendency for the dollar to depreciate against the yen would signal that the United States should reduce the growth rate of its money supply, while Japan should increase it. The net overall increase in the money supply of these three countries would then be expanded at a rate consistent with the noninflationary expansion of the world economy.

Another proposal advocated by the IMF Interim Committee (1986) is based on the development of objective indicators of economic performance to signal the type of coordinated macroeconomic policies for nations to follow, under the supervision of the Fund, to keep the world economy growing along a sustainable noninflationary path. These objective indicators are the growth of GNP, the rate of inflation, the rate of unemployment, the trade balance, the growth of the money supply, the fiscal balance, exchange rates, interest rates, and international reserves. A rise or fall in these objective indicators in a nation would signal, respectively, the need for restrictive or expansionary policies for the nation. Stability of the index for the world as a whole would be the anchor for noninflationary world expansion.

Policy coordination under the present system has taken place only occasionally and has been very limited in scope. One such episode was in l978 when Germany agreed to serve as "locomotive" to stimulate growth in the world economy. Another episode of limited policy coordination was the Plaza Agreement of September l985, under which the Group of Five (G-5) countries (France, Germany, Japan, the United Kingdom, and the United States) intervened in foreign-exchange markets to induce a gradual depreciation or soft landing of the dollar to eliminate its large overvaluation. Successful international policy coordination can also be credited for greatly limiting the damage from the 1987 world stock market crash and for preventing the 1994 and 1995 Mexican crisis from spreading to or having a lasting damaging effect on other emerging markets. These instances of international macroeconomic policy coordination were sporadic and rather limited in scope, however.

As long as nations have very different inflation-unemployment tradeoffs, effective and substantial macroeconomic policy coordination is practically impossible. During the late 1980s, it was often asserted that the EMS provided evidence that significant macroeconomic policy coordination was possible.

However, the EMS currency crisis of September 1992 and August 1993 caused by Germany's refusal to lower interest rates in the face of widespread recession in the rest of Europe and the United States proved otherwise (see Salvatore, 1996, 1997b, 1998a). Empirical research has also shown that although nations seem to gain from international policy coordination about three-quarters of the time, the welfare gains from coordination, when it occurs, are not very large (see Frankel and Rockett, 1988; McKibbin, 1997). Thus, it would seem that target zones and international macroeconomic policy coordination are neither feasible nor effective in preventing or eliminating large exchange-rate misalignments among the world's major currencies. As discussed in the last part of this article, the solution is to be found elsewhere.

3. Complications from the euro and how to deal with them

One complication in the operation of the international monetary system arises from the creation of the euro and the need to deal with (1) asymmetric shocks that are likely to arise within the European Union, (2) the relationship between the ins and outs within the Union (Britain, Sweden, Denmark, and Greece), (3) the future admission of transition economies of Central and Eastern Europe, and (4) the excess volatility and misalignments that are likely to arise between the euro and the dollar.

The creation of the European Central Bank (ECB) and a single European currency (the euro) leaves unresolved the serious problem of how a EU member will respond to an asymmetric shock. This is important because it is practically inevitable that a large and diverse single-currency area such as the European Union will face periodic asymmetric shocks that will affect various member nations differently and drive their economies out of alignment. In such a case, there is practically nothing that a member nation so adversely affected can do, aside from allowing deflation. The nation cannot change the exchange rate or use monetary policy because of the existence of a single currency, and fiscal discipline will also prevent it from using fiscal policy to deal with the problem. Furthermore, and as we have seen earlier, the EU cannot rely (as the United States can) on adequate labor mobility to overcome the problem.

Some economists (see Melitz, 1997) respond by saying that geographical labor mobility is an extremely costly and slow-working method of dealing with asymmetric shocks and that highly integrated EU capital markets can make up for low labor mobility. But this has not occurred adequately even within individual EU nations. Large regional inequalities remain, and so it is entirely unrealistic to expect it to take place on a sufficient scale among EU nations. Indeed, capital flows may even be perverse and move out of an EU nation facing a negative asymmetric shock. Furthermore, while there may be a great deal of regional fiscal redistribution within each EU member nation, fiscal federalism is grossly inadequate among EU member nations in view of the very merger EU-wide budget. Thus, the serious problem of adjusting to asymmetric shocks in the

EU remains, and this may have negative repercussions outside the Union also. Be that as it may, the next few years may prove to be difficult for Europe because of the immediate increase in EU-wide competition resulting from the Euro and the need for rapid deregulation of the economies made necessary by the rapid globalization and in the face of very large structural unemployment (see Salvatore, 1998a). Improving economic conditions throughout Europe, however, may reduce the pain somewhat.

Another complication is the relationship between the euro, the common currency of the EMU members, and the currencies of those nations that either could not (Greece) or would not participate (the United Kingdom, Denmark, and Sweden) in the EMU from the beginning. One possibility is the establishment of an exchange-rate mechanism (ERM II) between the currencies of the four "outs" and the euro. The problem with this arrangement, of course, is the possibility of currency crises in the Union similar to those of September 1992 and August 1993 and that the outs will use competitive devaluations to confer unfair advantages to their industries against the industries of the ins. Once again, although primarily a specific Union problem, the way this is handled by the Union will have important repercussions for the entire international monetary system.

A further complication from the introduction of the euro is determining the best exchange-rate arrangement between the euro and the currencies of the transition economies of central and eastern Europe prior to their admission into the Union, in view of their need to further restructure their economies along market lines. The central and eastern European transition economies have basically three exchange-rate strategies that they could follow prior to joining the European Union (EU). Each choice has some advantages and disadvantages. One choice would be to adopt a *currency board*, or a permanently fixed exchange rate against the euro. This would provide credibility to the nation but would eliminate the possibility of using monetary policy to deal with asymmetric shocks with respect to the EU. (Even if a transition economy wanted to go all the way and adopt the euro unilaterally, this could not take place before January 2002 because of all the preparations required.) The second choice would be for the transition economy to adopt a *fixed* or *pegged exchange rate* prior to joining the euro. But this would be difficult to defend in view of the large continued capital inflows in these economies. The third choice would be for a transition economy to have *managed exchange rates*, such as a crawling peg. This would allow the nation to deal with large capital inflows, but the resulting appreciation of the nation's exchange rate would make the nation unable to satisfy the Maastricht exchange rate and the inflation criteria for admission into the EU. The best that a transition economy could do would be to adopt a managed float with inflation targeting. This would allow the nation to deal with asymmetric shocks and inflation but not the Maastricht exchange-rate criteria. In a recent IMF policy discussion paper, Paul Masson recommended that the European Union relax the exchange-rate criteria for the more advanced of the transition economies prior to joining the EU, while recommending currency boards for the others.

Finally, an even more serious complication for the smooth operation of the international monetary system in the future is that with most trade conducted within rather than between the three major trading blocks (the EU, the North American Free Trade Agreement, and Asia), there will inevitably be less concern about the exchange rate between the dollar, the euro, and the yen, and so the exchange rates among these currencies are likely to be much more volatile than they are today. Much more serious, however, would be possible large misalignments between the euro and the dollar and the euro and the yen. As pointed out above, this could create a great deal of trade friction between Europe, the United States, and Japan in the future.

4. The international monetary system of the future

Although the details of the international monetary system of the future cannot be predicted, I believe that we can infer its main features and broad outlines from the need to address the serious shortcomings of the present system and in the face of the political and economic constraints that nations face. What seems certain is that in a world of huge international capital flows such as we have today, no fixed exchange-rate system could probably survive without extensive controls on international capital movements. Furthermore, nations are unwilling to give up control over their money supply and to be unable to use monetary policies to achieve domestic goals for the sake of achieving external balance. I think that the history of the past two decades has made this quite clear. At the same time, the leading industrial nations believe that exchange rates have been far too volatile and have overshot by substantial degrees and for long periods of time their equilibrium levels (for example, the U.S. dollar in the mid-1980s and during the past few years) and so a freely flexible exchange-rate system is also not acceptable. Also unlikely is an international monetary system based on much greater international macroeconomic policy coordination among the leading nations than has until now been possible in view of their different inflation-unemployment tradeoff and because of disagreements as to the cause of global imbalances and the effect of macro policies. Finally, an international monetary system based solely on target zones is also not likely to work because it attacks the symptoms rather than the underlying causes of the exchange-rate misalignments and may exhibit the worst features of both fixed and flexible exchange rates.

Where does that leave us? What is the best monetary system for the future? It seems to me that the international monetary system of the future will have to be a hybrid system, not too dissimilar from the present system, under which balance-of-payments adjustment is achieved by allowing the various adjustment mechanisms available to operate by different degrees depending on the nation and the specific circumstances under which each nation operates. Specifically, excessive volatility and gross misalignments can be overcome by the leading nations agreeing on some rough equilibrium exchange rate between their currencies and then each nation intervening in foreign-exchange markets, adjusting the growth of its money supply, and responding to calls for policy coordination based on its circumstances, the domestic targets that it sets for itself, and the relative importance of these domestic targets. International financial crises in emerging markets, on the other hand, are likely to be minimized in the future by the reforms examined in Section 2.2 of this article, which are in the process of being implemented.

One thing is clear, balance-of-payment (as any type of) adjustment is painful. Rather than using only one method of adjustment (such as changes in exchange rates, changes in the money supply, and fiscal and other policy changes) each nation will allow all of the mechanisms of adjustment to operate in various degrees to suit its own specific preferences. Thus, a large nation facing a large external deficit will want to devalue its currency or allow it to depreciate rather than restrict domestic demand. On the other hand, another large nation facing an internal disturbance (such as Japan faced a domestic recession in 1998) would want to place a greater share of the adjustment burden on internal (especially fiscal) policies to stimulate demand rather than on exchange-rate changes. Although somewhat reluctantly, the Japanese government has finally caved in and agreed to do just that. Allowing its currency to depreciate with respect to the dollar would be the wrong policy because Japan already has a huge and persistent trade surplus with the United States. Smaller and more specialized economies may also opt for smaller exchange-rate flexibility and greater reliance on internal expenditure-changing policies than larger open economies to achieve balance-of-payment adjustment.

Rather than a shortcoming, such a hybrid system of managed exchange rates around broadly defined equilibrium exchange rates among the world's leading currencies provides the freedom for each nation to determine how much it will rely on the various mechanisms of adjustment and thus is a crucial advantage of the international financial system being proposed. The broad outline of such a system is already in place today, and while its operation can certainly be strengthened by striving for regular consultations and for as much policy coordination as is feasible under various circumstances among the leading nations, no other system, I believe, would be able to better deal with today's international monetary problems.

In the final analysis, most of the global imbalances faced by the leading industrial nations today are rooted in domestic imbalances, such as lack of more internal stimulus in the European Union and the traditional unwillingness on the part of Japan to rely more on the expansion of internal demand for growth than on exports to the United States and cannot be blamed on the operation of the present international financial system itself. Automaticity in correcting internal imbalances would mean that most of the flexibility and discretion that nations enjoy under the present and proposed systems would be lost. Nations simply cannot have it both ways. They cannot impose automaticity on themselves and at the same time retain the freedom and discretion to choose the unique set of domestic targets that they prefer and the specific combination of various adjustment policies that best suits their particular situation. In the end, reform of the present international monetary system is likely to involve improving the functioning of the present system rather than replacing it or completely changing it.

References

Bryant, R.C. (1995) *International Coordination of National Stabilization Policies*. Washington, DC: Brooking Institution.

Council of Economic Advisors (1986, 1987) *Economic Report of the President*. Washington, DC: Government Printing Office.

Dornbusch, R. and J. Frankel (1987) "The Flexible Exchange Rate System: Experience and Alternatives," Working Paper 2464, National Bureau of Economic Research, Cambridge, MA.

Fisher, S. (1997) *Capital Account Liberalization and the Role of the IMF*. Washington, DC: IMF.

Frankel, J. and K. Rockett (1988) "International Macroeconomic Policy Coordination When Policymakers Do Not Agree on the Model." *American Economic Review* 78:318–340.

Frankel, J. and A.K. Rose (1996) "Currency Crashes in Emerging Markets: An Empirical Treatment." *Journal of International Economics* 41:351–368.

Hamada, K. and M. Kuwai (1997) "Strategic Approaches to International Policy Coordination: Theoretical Developments." In M. Fratianni, D. Salvatore, and J. von Hagen (eds.), *Handbook of Macroeconomic Policies in Open Economies*. Westport, CT: Greenwood Press, ch. 4.

IMF (1984) *Exchange Rate Volatility and World Trade*. Washington, DC: IMF.

IMF (1986) *Interim Committee Report*. Washington, DC: IMF.

IMF (1996) *Standards for the Dissemination by Countries of Economic and Financial Statistics*. Discussion draft prepared by a staff team. Washington, DC: IMF.

IMF (1998) *Towards a Framework for Financial Stability*. Washington, DC: IMF, January.

IMF (1998) *World Economic Outlook*. Washington, DC: IMF, May, June, October.

Kaminsky, G., S. Lizondo, and C.M. Reinhart (1998) *Leading Indicators of Currency Crisis*. Washington, DC: IMF Staff Papers, Spring.

McKibbin, W. (1997) "Empirical Evidence on International Economic Policy Coordination." In M. Fratianni, D. Salvatore, and J. von Hagen (eds.), *Handbook of Macroeconomic Policies in Open Economies*. Westport, CT: Greenwood Press, ch. 5.

McKinnon, R.I. (1984) *An International Standard for Monetary Stabilization*. Washington, DC: Institute for International Economics.

McKinnon, R.I. (1988) "Monetary and Exchange Rate Policies for International Financial Stability: A Proposal." *Journal of Economic Perspectives* (Winter) 2:83–104.

McKinnon, R.I. (1996) *The Rules of the Game: International Money and Exchange Rates*. Cambridge, MA: MIT Press.

Melitz, J. (1997) "The Evidence About the Costs and Benefits of EMU." Background Report for the Swedish Government Commission on EMU. *Swedish Economic Policy Review* 4:17–25.

Miller, M.H. and J. Williamson (1987) *Targets and Indicators: A Blueprint for the International Coordination of Economic Policy*. Washington, DC: Institute for International Economics.

Milner, H.V. (1997) "The Political Economy of International Policy Coordination." In M. Fratianni, D. Salvatore, and J. von Hagen (eds.), *Handbook of Macroeconomic Policies in Open Economies*. Westport, CT: Greenwood Press, ch. 6.

Salvatore, D. (ed.) (1993) *The New Protectionist Threat to World Welfare*. Cambridge: Cambridge University Press.

Salvatore, D. (1996) "The European Monetary System: Crisis and Future." *Open Economies Review* (Supplement 7).

Salvatore, D. (1997a) "Capital Flows, Current Account Deficits, and Financial Crises in Emerging Market Economies." *International Trade Journal* (March).

Salvatore, D. (1997b) "The Common Unresolved Problem with the EMS and EMU." *American Economic Review* (May):224–226.

Salvatore, D. (1998a) "Europe's Structural and Competitiveness Problems and the Euro." *World Economy* (March).

Salvatore, D. (1998b) *International Economics* (6th ed.) Upper Saddle River, NJ: Prentice-Hall.

Salvatore, D. (1999) "Could the Financial Crisis in East Asia Have Been Predicted?" *Journal of Policy Modeling* (May):341–348.

Tobin, J. (1978) "A Proposal for International Monetary Reform." *Eastern Economic Journal* (July-October):153–159.

Tobin, J. (1996) "A Currency Transaction Tax: Why and How?" *Open Economies Review* (Supplement 7). Kluwer Academic Publishers.

Williamson, J. (1986) "Target Zones and the Management of the Dollar." Brookings Papers on Economic Activity 1, Brookings Institution, Washington, DC.

Open economies review **11:S1** 149–175 (2000)
© 2000 *Kluwer Academic Publishers. Printed in The Netherlands.*

On Monetary Analysis of Derivatives

PAOLO SAVONA, AURELIO MACCARIO AND CHIARA OLDANI
LUISS Guido Carli University and Guido Carli Association, Rome

Keywords: derivatives, interest rates, innovation, monetary aggregates, monetary policy, international money

JEL Classification Number: E51, E58, F34

Abstract

Financial derivatives are products whose price is linked with that of an underlying asset. The relationship between these two prices has been studied in depth, and the following conclusions have been reached: (1) the volatility of underlying asset's price decreases after the introduction of derivatives, (2) the price discovery effect improves, (3) the liquidity of the underlying asset's market increases, (4) the bid-ask spread decreases together, and (5) the noise component of prices decreases. Those results are microeconomic and are not coherent with a macroeconomic analysis of derivatives. Derivatives tend to change the effectiveness of monetary policy actions by modifying the instruments that can be used. Derivatives have a monetary nature that has not been yet recognized by central banks and international organizations such as the International Monetary Fund and the Bank for International Settlements. This monetary nature can be evident by testing the relationship between derivatives and the interest rate. The consciousness of the monetary nature of derivatives would impose the quantification of transactions at least by the institutions that hold them, such as banks and other financial operators, and consequently by national authorities.

1. A short overview of derivatives markets

Derivatives are the greatest financial innovation of the late twentieth century. Their rapid growth and the limited transparency of over-the-counter (OTC) markets compared with official exchanges have led to a great discussion of the role they play in modern financial markets.

The Bank for International Settlements' (BIS) triennial survey of foreign-exchange and derivative markets covers traditional foreign-exchange derivatives (outright forward and swaps), more sophisticated foreign-exchange derivatives (options, currency swaps, and others), and interests rate products. Although the survey deals only with OTC markets, it makes comparisons with data on exchange-traded derivatives collected in other BIS publications. The market size is measured through the indicators of notional amounts and gross market value, whereas activity is measured by average daily turnover of notional amounts.

The notional amount outstanding[1] of the exchange in derivatives in OTC markets was $72 trillion at the end of June 1998 (BIS, 1999), compared with $13.2 trillion outstanding in exchange-traded, foreign-exchange, and interest-rate derivatives. OTC markets rose by 52 percent from 1995 to 1998, whereas official markets rose in the same period by 34.2 percent. To put this figure in perspective, in 1998 world gross domestic product (GDP) was $29.2 trillion (IMF, 1999).

At the same reporting date, the gross market value[2] in OTC markets amounted to $2.6 trillion; it represents about 9 percent of world GDP. The gross market value for interest-rate contracts was 2.8 percent of notional amounts and was 4.5 percent for foreign-exchange contracts. These percentages reflect the great leverage allowed by derivative contracts.

Activity keeps on expanding more rapidly in OTC than in official markets. The average daily turnover amount on OTC markets was $1.26 trillion per day in April 1998, with a growth of 66 percent from 1995, whereas official markets' turnover was $1.37 trillion per day, with a growth of 12 percent. The daily turnover can be considered a good proxy for market liquidity. It is important to underline that there is a geographical concentration of derivatives: 32 percent of transactions take place in the United Kingdom (London market) and another 18 percent in the United States.[3]

The derivative breakdown is related to the type of risk. Financial derivatives, which hedge against market risk, are separated from credit derivatives that face credit risk. Credit derivatives are a specific category of instruments traded in financial markets, but they were not considered separately in previous BIS reports.

The type of counterpart involved in the transaction has taken on a new importance: 63 percent of the exchanges are with dealers, and hedge funds also grew in importance between 1995 and 1998 (IMF, 1998a). The type of counterpart is related to the market's structure and its so-called opacity (that is, the lack of information and regulation). In particular, while hedge funds are very similar to banks, they are subject to different law and accounting methods. This makes the analysis more difficult for official organizations and private researchers.

Technology is the arena of confrontation among derivative markets. Though the Chicago Board of Trade (CBOT) and Chicago Mercantile Exchange (CME) continue to be the largest derivative markets in the world, most of the innovation in trading systems has taken place in Europe. The European Exchange (Eurex) and the London International Financial Future Exchange (LIFFE) are the most important centers in Europe. Since the introduction of Eurex, which links the German and Swiss derivative markets, LIFFE has progressively reduced its activity, especially in Bund futures.[4] These markets are characterized by different trading systems: LIFFE is based on the open outcry for the majority of its products, while Eurex is an electronic trading platform, which allows participants to trade via computer terminals. It therefore ensures easier remote access than LIFFE. Compared to markets like LIFFE, Eurex offers many advantages: the trading system is more flexible, since it is more liquid, a large number of participants can submit orders on the book, and the market-makers quote bid and ask prices. Finally, it is transparent because it allows participants to see quotes and prices on the screen, and it is secure and rapid, with a response time that is below one second. In the face of increasing competition from Eurex, LIFFE has recently launched a new electronic trading system, LIFFE CONNECT. This new platform will gradually replace the previous open outcry system (Calise and Paladino, 1999).

For the stock markets, in the near future, European derivative markets will appear not to be concentrated in a single platform. The main competitors will be Eurex (which after the failure of a long-term alliance with the CBOT has recently announced two alliances with the Helsinki market and with the New York Mercantile Exchange (NYMEX)), LIFFE (with its new LIFFE CONNECT), Mercato Italiano Future (MIF), Marché à Term Future (MATIF), and MEFF (Italy, France, and Spain). This last group has created a link with CME and the Singapore International Exchange (SIMEX) for a common platform, named Euroglobex. This market, which now has around 60 percent of public bond trading, could represent the strongest competitor Eurex will face in the near future. It is important to underline that the future evolution of derivative exchanges in Europe will depend mainly on the development of new trading technologies.

Making some hypotheses on the future development of European derivative markets, our conjecture is that Eurex will be the platform for trading in bonds, whereas LIFFE will be the financial center where derivatives on interest rate are negotiated.[5]

This short overview of the size of derivative markets shows their importance for modern economics. In many countries the close link between financial innovation and investment, banking, and industrial activities is now very evident. The importance of derivatives is also crucial in shaping economic policies, particularly from a monetary point of view.

The purpose of this article is to analyze some aspects of financial innovation, starting with the relationship between derivatives and the underlying asset and then studying their monetary features.

We analyze the influence of derivatives on portfolio choices and their use as a forecast of the inflation rate in developed economies.

Finally, we extend our analysis to the money for international uses (international money, IM) and its relationship with derivatives. We consider the new regulations covering the balance of payments recently established by the International Monetary Fund (IMF Committee on Balance of Payment Statistics, 1998) and particularly the way derivatives are accounted as assets or liabilities in the exchanges between countries. In fact, the huge growth of derivatives among industrial countries has forced institutions to renew international accounting standards.

2. The relationship between derivatives and the underlying asset

In economic literature, the relationship between the price of derivatives and the underlying asset's price has been studied in depth. Antoniou, Holmes, and

Priestley (1998) have tested the effect of derivatives on the markets by studying the prices of six stock indexes for three years prior and after the introduction of the future. Contrary to the traditional view of futures trading, current research testifies that the introduction of derivatives has improved the price discovery effect. The volatility of the underlying assets market does not seem to have increased with the introduction of the future, and the information asymmetry appears to have decreased with the presence of this kind of derivative (Chan, Chung, and Johnson, 1995). So far, analyses tend to demonstrate in several ways that derivatives contribute to decreasing the market's volatility.

One should pay close attention to volatility (Bhanot, 1998). It is an indicator of the market's efficiency and risk. Conrad (1999) has shown that after the introduction of options, the volatility of stock prices decreased.[6] Moreover, Damodaran and Lim (1991) and others have shown that the variance of prices of the underlying asset decreased after the introduction of derivatives such as options. The noise component in stock prices decreases thanks to the higher liquidity of markets after the introduction of derivatives (futures and options, overall). Skinner (1989) has tried to explain the nature of the noise component of the option price, mainly because one of the possible reasons of the financial crisis of 1987 could have been this new instrument. There is also evidence that the bid and ask spread decreases in derivative markets, if compared with its level in stock exchanges before the introduction of derivatives.

With the introduction of derivatives there are unquestionably fewer uninformed investors, and the allocation of resources is better in a Paretian way. Tse, Lee, and Booth (1996) have studied the hypothesis that three markets with different trading hours can be considered one market for the transmission of information. Taking LIFFE for Europe, IMM for the United States, and SIMEX for Asia, they have proved that the transmission of information about the underlying asset (euro rate) is better after the introduction of the future; the three markets can be considered as one market during the 24 hours. This is validated by the fact that the volatility is less during the trading hours than in nontrading hours, with the exception of the Asian market due to the underlying asset that is more significant for the European and American markets than for the Asian ones.

To sum up, most economists agree that financial innovation results in the following consequences for the underlying assets and the performance of markets where these are traded:

• The volatility and the variance of prices decrease;
• The price discovery effect improves;
• The liquidity of the underlying market increases; and
• The bid-ask spread and the noise component of prices both decrease.

Many of these results have been obtained in a prevailing microeconomic context and reveal an incoherence with the disquieting instability of exchange markets and with the wide and growing external balance disequilibria observed during recent years. It will be of great importance in the near future to deepen our knowledge of this phenomenon and analyze it from a macroeconomic point of view.

One phenomenon should be stressed immediately. Though market conditions seem to improve through the use of derivatives, they also hugely increase liquidity (that is, money for speculation and creating the environment for instability), producing effects not only on the price of assets but also on interest rates. In fact, the ability of the future price to anticipate the interest rate is strictly related to the price discovery effect and to the high liquidity of derivatives markets. It would be interesting to study which of those effects is more relevant, but the economic literature has not yet found the answer. Fung and Leung (1993) show that the future price of euros traded in the LIFFE and IMM can foresee the behavior of the euro deposit rate. This simple statement is important not only to underline the liquidity of derivatives but also to test the econometric reaction of short-term interest rates to changes in derivatives prices.

Testing the relationship between euro futures prices at LIFFE (PDEU) and the euro deposit rate (IDEU) from 1987 to 1992, with daily data, we had the following results:

$$IDEU = 10.83 + 0.85\,IDEU_{-1} + 0.044\,IDEU_{-2} - 0.109\,PDEU,\,^{7} \tag{1}$$

$$\quad\;(14.64)\;\;(33.57)\qquad\quad(1.87)\qquad\qquad(14.65)$$

where R^2C is 0.99, $D.W.$ is 1.93, $S.E.R.$ is 0.077, and $\overline{IDEU}$ is 7.022.

For the period 1993 up to 1998, the results are as follows:

$$IDEU = 5.51 + 0.68\,IDEU_{-1} + 0.26\,IDEU_{-2} - 0.055\,PDEU, \tag{2}$$

$$\quad\;(9.24)\;\;(27.43)\qquad\quad(10.78)\qquad\quad(9.22)$$

where R^2C is 0.99, $D.W.$ is 2.056, $S.E.R.$ is 0.049, and $\overline{IDEU}$ is 5.075.

These results are in line with those of Fung and Leung: the relationship between derivative prices and the short-term interest rate reveals the information effect of derivatives on the underlying market.[8] Also Hull (1994) confirms this evidence, analyzing the relationship between the price of Treasury bill futures and the interest rate of the underlying asset. Furthermore, Craig, Dravid, and Richardson (1995) have tested the impact of the Nikkei index future price on the level of the overnight rate in Japan. Even though the future is traded at the CME in the United States and there is no coincidence between the U.S. derivative market's trading hours and the Japanese ones, information about the Nikkei stock index comes from the future price, and it is incorporated into the overnight level.

After January 1, 1999, the LIBOR rate was replaced by the euribor rate. This interest rate is based on those of the 11 countries that joined the third phase of European Monetary Union (EMU). The euribor rate is settled in the London market (EURIBOR), whereas the future on euribors is traded in the

MATIF (FUTURE). The price discovery effect between the future and the underlying asset rate is important for many reasons: this new rate is an interbank price for EU-11, and the liquidity degree of its market is increasing very fast. We have tested the relationship between these two prices:

$$Euribor = 24.153 + 1.132\,Euribor_{-1} - 0.41\,Euribor_{-2} - 0.24\,Future,$$

$$\quad\quad\;\;(7.01)\quad\;\;(11.53)\quad\quad\quad\;(5.02)\quad\quad\quad\quad(6.99) \tag{3}$$

where R^2C is 0.991, $D.W.$ is 2.0467, $S.E.R.$ is 0.006816, and $\overline{Euribor}$ is 3.0763.

Results—not completely consistent with those on the euro—show that, although we are dealing with a relatively new market, former analyses on the price discovery effect appear to be still acceptable. Anyway, if these estimates are satisfying from a mere econometric point of view, the result cannot be judged as economically significant (for example, the constant is eight times the average of the dependent variable). Again, the "youth" of the euribor rate could be the explanation.

So far we have seen some evidence of the relation between short-term interest rates and the price of derivatives on short-term assets. Analyzing a long-term asset the relationship is significant too. Savona and Maccario (1998) have shown that there is a relation between the Treasury bill rate and the futures price of the Treasury note, the most widely traded asset in the U.S. financial market.

Hence, we can say that the relationship between derivative prices and the interest rate cannot be influenced only by the underlying asset maturity, but it is mainly due to the derivative features and their ability to increase the market liquidity.

3. Derivatives analysis from a monetary point of view

In economics there are several definitions of money; some of them are related to the theory elaborated by Milton Friedman. The "instrumental" definition identifies the monetary base through the instruments by which it is made (Friedman and Schwartz, 1963). The "functional" definition specifies that the monetary base is composed of those instruments whose function is that of compulsory reserves at the central bank or free reserves held by banks (Fazio, 1968).

Based on these definitions, it is difficult to distinguish between monetary base and money when a new instrument "appears" on the market; moreover, at an international level, there is no compulsory reserve on bank deposits in foreign currencies for most countries as it is for domestic money, so any classification between the two categories raises many problems.

The "analytical" distinction between monetary base and monetary assets proposed by Fratianni and Savona (1972) was grounded on the liquidity effect: the monetary base is composed of all those instruments that show an inverse relationship with interest rates; money behaves in the opposite way. Hence, the most efficient way to distinguish between money and monetary base is to test econometrically the reaction of the interest-rate level to changes in the supply of different assets.[9]

As we have seen before, derivatives have some properties that affect directly or indirectly the interest rate in money markets (Gerlach and Smets, 1995). Moreover, combinations of derivatives can create "synthetic" assets that are substitutes for already existing financial and monetary instruments (Glennon and Lane, 1996). A portfolio composed of a long bond position and of a short three-month future on the same bond (or another similar to it in terms of return, maturity, and rating of the debtor) is financially equal to a three-month time deposit (Angeloni and Massa, 1994; Miller, 1991). The latter is a component of a broad monetary aggregate (M3 or M4), whereas the "synthetic" portfolio is not considered. The choice between the three-month time deposit and the "synthetic" portfolio can be influenced by the minimum rate of return of the investment strategy and by the costs of transactions (Rossetti, 1999).

The introduction of derivatives in financial markets allows investors to choose the combination of risk and return that optimizes the resources' allocation. For example, futures are more attractive for investors who want to diversify their portfolio: with a small payment (initial margin) you can open a position in derivatives exploiting the leveraged effect. This effect allows the hedger to invest only a part of his portfolio in derivatives; the other part can be invested in bonds with a certain rate of return. This strategy has, as a result, a combination of risk and return that other financial assets cannot guarantee. This way of using derivatives is useful for a speculator too because it can minimize the cost of opening a position on the market.

Current research seems to show that derivatives do not increase the total risk of the financial system but can change the agent that undertakes it. Yet if derivatives are observed in the context of an IMB-DEU analysis (that is, emphasizing the role of their supply in determining interest rates), the whole meaning of this dominant literature appears to be weakened.

Portfolio reallocation can modify the impact of monetary actions: if those agents who are more sensitive to interest-rate fluctuations hedge themselves with derivatives against the rate risk, the final effect can be different from the expected one (Angeloni and Massa, 1994). In particular, wealth and income effects can change because of the way investors react to interest-rate variations in the short run.

3.1. Influence of derivatives on monetary policy

Derivatives are potential instruments for central-bank policy. Their huge market liquidity allows central banks to invest in the derivative market without influencing prices in a distortive way also thanks to the large range of possibilities for hedging against risks (on interest or on exchange rates) (Deutsche Bundesbank, 1994).

Central banks tend to influence short-term money markets when their long-term objective is to control inflation. Compulsory reserves and free reserves of banks are the instruments used to manage the quantity of money in the system. The high liquidity and the price discovery effect of derivatives can modify the transmission of interest-rate changes on the yield curve; in particular, central banks can modify, if they want, the speed of changes on components of the curve (Banca d'Italia, 1995b, 1995c; Vrolijk, 1997; Rossetti, 1999). Savona and Maccario (1998) show that the offshore interest rate is sensitive to changes in traded futures.

It appears that derivatives have introduced another mechanism of money creation, justifying a reexamination of existing monetary aggregates (Banca d'Italia, 1995a).

This evidence illustrates the need to broaden the concept of money in a wide sense. The economists cited above concluded that the less liquid components of money aggregates (M2 or M3), such as time deposits or certificates of deposit, should be added to those assets not present in the monetary aggregates, acquiring the same degree of liquidity and creating substitutes for speculative money (that is, money in relationship with interest rates) when they are covered by derivatives. Although the authors are aware of the fact that it is nearly impossible to completely quantify all derivatives negotiated in financial markets, they think that an attempt should be made, at least to include those underlying assets of derivatives for which a significant relationship is found. This would allow for better monetary policy management, domestically and internationally, because the authorities could use more efficient instruments to reach the goal of stabilizing money growth to guide interest and exchange rates.

Derivatives are off-balance-sheet items for the banking system (they are not accounted separately from the other financial instruments and are not classified in relation with the type of risk they hedge) (Garber, 1996). The first consequence is that, in determining the ratio of compulsory reserves, they are not considered part of a bank's resources. In fact, banks are the first investor in derivative markets (IMF, 1998b; Bank of England, 1993), but the whole amount of resources invested in derivatives has not been calculated in the traditional banking aggregates, which are included in central banks' monetary targets (Basle Committee on Banking Supervision, 1995). We know there exists a regulation about derivatives' accounting, but the problem is to make it real and executive. Another important effect is on free reserves of the banking system because the bank's liquidity can also be invested in derivatives for a very short period. So with a given amount of monetary base, the money multiplier is higher than without derivatives. Investment in derivatives is usually more profitable than a repo with the central bank: in this way, the Keynesian preference for liquidity is influenced not by central bank behavior on the interest rate but by derivatives markets. To sum up, the free reserves of banks are partly substituted by "synthetic reserves" based on derivatives instruments.

The liquidity effect also influences the public's behavior: firms and other kinds of investors that benefit from huge amounts of liquidity can use short-term derivatives to best manage the maturity mismatching and to get the highest possible return.

Considering the deposits multiplier:

$$DEP = (1/\alpha + \beta + \gamma)\, MB, \tag{4}$$

where α is the banks' propensity for liquidity, β is the compulsory reserves' ratio, γ is the public's propensity for liquidity, DEP is the potential supply of banks' deposit, MB is the monetary base. All three coefficients seem to be influenced by derivatives. If we look at the right side of the equation, we can expect, based on what we stated earlier, that coefficients decrease and the multiplier increases; but if we consider the left side (deposits), we expect that derivatives held by private operators make the banks' deposits decrease so that the final result will be in the hands of the reaction functions of the central bank in creating monetary base. *This confirms the impossibility of deciding the best monetary policy without taking into consideration derivatives.* In particular, we can say that they are underestimated. Because of this effect, the multiplier increases. This is only a hypothesis because balance sheets of banks do not provide sufficient information to reach significant evidence.

If this effect on multipliers occurs, the "potential credit" for the economic system increases, and banks can lend a greater amount of money thanks to the use of these "synthetic reserves" (Tavakoli, 1998). If a "credit target" has been established by the central bank for monetary policy purposes, this could, with high probability, be overwhelmed by the "potential credit." At the same time, the advantage for the central bank is represented by the fact that, given the amount of "credit target," the quantity of monetary base necessary to determine it is, surely, reduced.

Our opinion is that long-term interest rates are almost completely determined by the markets, which are able to manage huge amounts of resources unaffordable for any central bank or monetary authority. These keep on controlling interest-rate levels in money markets (Jegadeesh and Pennacchi, 1996). For example, overnight and two-week deposits rates show a high correlation coefficient (almost one) with the level resulting from auctions on repurchase agreements, managed by central banks.

Derivatives and their price discovery effect help to ascertain if the nature of a shock is real or merely nominal (Hentschel and Smith, 1997). With their high degree of liquidity, derivatives make it more difficult for a central bank to defend an interest-rate policy if the level is not perceived as optimal by the financial markets. Goodhart (1995) and others have proposed to let the rate fluctuate in a fixed range, but often this policy is not perceived as credible. Our opinion is that a central bank can effectively manage a strong interest- and exchange-rate policy only if it enjoys a solid reputation, which allows it to be trusted by the markets. If, for example, the central bank wants to decrease the long-term interest rates by increasing the short-term level, it could reach the goal only if the markets' expectations on the real rate of return on capital are consistent with the central bank's behavior (Savona, 1978).

The level of the rate has to be coherent not only with expectations of the markets but also with other economic indicators (income, savings propensity, unemployment, and international debt) and their influence on these expectations. If international financial markets do not accept the level of the interest rate that central banks want to impose, the losses will be, with a high probability, much greater than the anticipated benefits from the pegging-rate policy. This is also true for the flexible exchange rate as shown by the recent crises in Brazil, Russia, and Asia.

3.2. Potential derivatives uses in monetary policy

Central banks can use derivatives as a substitute for the secondary short-term market; examples are the central banks of Holland and Switzerland, where such a market on Treasury bonds is not developed. The possibility of operating with another instrument is crucial for the optimization of monetary targets. Derivative securities issued by the trading desk of the central bank may tighten connections between policy intentions for the short-term rate and current long-term interest rates. When the level of the short-term interest rate is driven near zero, the channel of information loses its meaning because there is little room left for the spot rate to act as a signal (Tinsley, 1998). This is the situation that should be faced by the European Central Bank (ECB). Some economists (Savona and La Malfa, 1969; and others), following Keynes (1930), have suggested that the central bank can operate directly on long bond rates by purchasing or selling bonds.

By contrast, policy use of derivatives can alter market agents' perceptions of economic fundamentals. Given that the central bank has a monopoly on the supply of the domestic currency, it has the capacity to directly purchase or write options against any proportion of the outstanding Treasury debt (Tinsley, 1998; BIS, 1994a, 1994b). On the contrary, in case of crises the central bank has to balance its open position in derivatives with only a small percentage of the nominal value of the contracts (usually 2 to 3 percent) (Gorton and Rosen, 1995; BIS, 1996a, 1996b).

Derivatives are also instruments that central banks can use to defend their monetary targets (Carlson, McIntire, and Thomson, 1995). Thanks to the small initial payment that market agents have to pay to open a position (usually 2 to 3 percent of the nominal value of the contract), they need a small sterilization. Thus, they do not influence the creation of monetary base at a domestic level. In this context, the most useful kind of derivative is forward contracts and swaps on interest or exchange rates, due to the long maturity of these contracts.

As an instrument for monetary policy, derivatives can be written through the banking system or through other central banks: in the first case the quantity of domestic monetary base changes, whereas in the second case there is no creation of new money.

Derivatives can be both an instrument and an obstacle for the central bank's policy. Von Hagen and Fender (1998) maintain that with derivatives, the financial markets are almost perfect, and a central bank cannot use, either short or long run, the surprise effect on the public. The only way the central bank can influence the public is with monetary base, but we have seen before that it is not an optimal strategy. This is a sign of the high efficiency of the modern financial system: all indicators must be coherent with each other.

Derivatives can also be useful for the defense of the exchange rate in case of crisis: central banks can take open positions in the OTC market with a small initial payment and influence the level of the rate. Rarely, however, does a central bank let the financial market know that it is using derivatives (Hooyman, 1993). The reason is simple: the central bank is an institutional hedger, but in defending the rate it becomes an investor that wants to influence the market expectations and the price level. If the credibility of the central bank is not strong and operators believe that this behavior is inconsistent with the real conditions, the strategy does not work. An example of this statement is the case of the central bank of Thailand, which in the summer of 1996 tried to defend the baht by buying futures with two weeks of maturity. Once these contracts reached maturity, the market operators understood that the baht had to be devaluated and the central bank could not avoid it.

In case of fixed exchange rates, domestic monetary policies lose a large part of their freedom: national central banks have to pay attention to the pressures on the rate, which has to be coherent with other economic indicators. When a speculative attack begins (and experience has shown that speculators base their attacks against a currency on derivatives), losses can be enormous. If the exchange rate is flexible, the central bank is not compelled to defend it, but the effects of exchange-rate movements impact directly on the monetary base. With flexible rates, the central bank surrenders a part of its freedom because an uncontrolled creation of money acts against the stability of the system and a stable economic growth.

Derivatives tend to strengthen the exchange-rate fluctuations: thanks to their high liquidity level and 24-hour trading all over the world, all changes of the rate are instantly incorporated in the spot rate through derivatives, especially futures and options.

The central bank has some benefits from financial innovation, especially in case of currency crises. If the exchange rate is fixed during a speculative attack on a currency, monetary authorities can increase the interest rate to defend the exchange-rate level. Investors know it and accept it for a short period. This monetary behavior is well accepted when the exchange rate is credible and the speculative attack is based only on rumors. If currency devaluation is necessary (as it was for Asia or Brazil), derivatives cannot help monetary authorities. In these cases, the monetarist hypothesis of "stabilizing speculation" occurs.

If derivatives and all the operators use a dynamic investment strategy,[10] the effects on the interest rate could be smaller than without derivatives (Garber and Spencer, 1994). This is mainly due to the short-term strategy that needs frequent modifications to control its exposure to the interest or exchange rate.

Without derivatives, changes in the interest rate are necessary for a certain period and for a defined amount. With derivatives both changes are smaller. This is another sign of the efficiency that innovations provide for the financial market.

The central bank can influence the money market by modifying the portfolio composition through interest-rate changes (money view) and through the supply of credit (credit view). According to the money view, the central bank can employ the convenience of having money instead of financial assets. If the substitutability between assets and money is not perfect, the central bank can alter the portfolio composition. With the introduction of derivatives, investors have more information about financial assets, and the price discovery effect is improved; the noise component of the asset price decreases, and all these effects can modify the ability of the central bank to alter the composition of portfolios. The efficiency of the financial market limits the central bank's ability to influence investors' choices. The most important effects develop in the long run because changes in this substitutability can affect the relationship between money and income, or wealth.

According to the credit view, the central bank controls the substitutability between credit and financial assets: if it is not perfect, this can be due to information asymmetry and to barriers in financial markets. With derivatives, the asymmetry is going to achieve a value near zero, whereas barriers are related to national laws and to economic convenience. Derivatives have an indirect effect on barriers because investors can get the best combination of costs and profits in derivatives markets, avoiding a direct investment in the domestic underlying market.

If the central bank alters the interest rate, the investor can hedge this variation by buying, for example, an interest-rate swap (IRS). If all investors do that, the central bank cannot influence it any longer, at least in the short run. Also, banking credit is conditioned by the rating of the debtor and by its core business. Derivatives allow investors with no rating and without collateral to enter the capital market and get the best opportunity for themselves. They are also useful in shifting the risk to other agents that want it. Within the banking system, the specific instruments are called credit derivatives.[11] With derivatives, a huge international capital flow and mobility occurs, affecting the financial markets. Therefore, the possibilities decrease for the central bank to influence the substitutability between credit, assets, and money.

3.3. Forecasting inflation using derivatives

The ability to foresee the rate of inflation is crucial for monetary policy. Normally, central banks use backward-looking and forward-looking methods that can be helpful in deciding their policy. Backward-looking methods are mainly statistical and are useful in studying this economic variable and its trend. Forward-looking methods are more empirical and, obviously, not perfect. The most common methods used to foresee the inflation rate are related to monetary growth and to the development of trade and income. All these methods are useful, but they are not precise in periods when the inflation rate shows a high volatility.

Rosengren (1987) says that "Many economists think that there is a close link between the growth of money and inflation; others think that the link is between the commercial growth and inflation."[12] A third source of inflation forecast consists of using Treasury bill future prices. In particular, this method was more accurate than others during the period of the oil shock. The prices of other derivatives, such as options, are not supposed to be a good forecaster for the inflation rate because they usually show a greater volatility when compared with those of the futures markets (Rossetti, 1999; Hull, 1994).

The ability of the Treasury bill future price to forecast variations in the inflation rate is important in emphasizing the information content of this financial asset. We have not tested whether the money growth method or the commercial method has done better than the future forecast, nor are we interested in describing inflation as a monetary or nonmonetary phenomenon. Our aim is to show the strong efficiency of the forward-looking method in forecasting inflation, using derivatives.

The following equations compose this forecasting method:

- Equality of after-tax rate on Treasury bills

$$(1 - t)i_t = r_t + p_t^e \tag{5}$$

- Forecasts of changes in inflation rate assuming $r_t = r_{t+1}$

$$(1 - t)(i_{t+1} - i_t) = p_{t+1}^e - p_t^e \tag{6}$$

- Errors from inflation forecasts[13]

$$e_t = \left(p_{t+1}^e - p_t^e\right) - (p_{t+1} - p_t), \tag{7}$$

where t is the marginal tax rate, i_t is the interest rate on a three-month Treasury bill, r_t is the real interest rate after taxes, p_t^e is the inflationary expectations, p_t is the quarterly inflation at an annual rate, and e_t is the forecast error.

Taxes are a very important tool in forecasting the inflation rate. The tax rate on income is related to all the revenues of the investor, and it is not the tax on capital gains. With a marginal tax rate of zero, the forecasting error is smaller than with 40 percent (the maximum level considered in the model). This is related to the distortions that taxation creates in the financial system and in the allocation of resources. In the United State the marginal tax rate is lower than in Europe, so the smaller tax rate is assumed to be the more accurate description of what the real situation will be.

The advantages of this method are that the future prices are determined every day and easy to know. The error in this forecast is smaller than with other forward-looking methods. Based on the equations stated by Rosengren, we have updated the same relationship from April 1995 to September 1998. The results are shown in Tables 4 and 5 in Appendix B. As in Rosengren's analysis, with a zero marginal tax rate the mean of errors is smaller than with a 40 percent tax rate. Also, errors are bigger in periods when financial markets were subject to political troubles. The possibility of foreseeing the inflation rate is strictly related to the relationship between derivatives' prices and the short-term interest rate. We have already said it is possible that information related to futures' prices can influence and anticipate the overnight-rate level.

We have also tested the relationship between derivatives prices and inflation rate in the European Monetary Union, taking five countries (France, Germany, Italy, the Netherlands, and Spain) that represent 85 to 90 percent of the European gross national product (GNP) and their quarterly inflation rate from 1995 up to the end of 1998. Then, we have tested the forecasting ability of the three-month LIBOR on the inflation rate. Results are shown in Table 6 in Appendix B. The main difference between the former forecast, based on the U.S. inflation rate and this one, depends on the tax rate. In Europe, the marginal tax rate is about 35 to 40 percent; so the higher level of the tax rate used in our model, the better the forecast. It is evident that this fiscal component is incorporated in prices so distortions occur, contrary to U.S. markets, for very low marginal tax rates. Substantially, in the long run, the European tax rate is not supposed to decrease below 30 percent (Murray and Jagannathan, 1998).

Differences in results can also be explained considering that in the U.S. chances for paying lower taxes are greater than in Europe. Furthermore, data on European inflation are compiled from an average, so they cannot fit the real situation precisely. Anyway, we think that the extension of the Rosengren analysis to Europe produces results in line with those we expected.

4. Derivatives and international money

At an international level, the consequences of financial innovation have been analyzed by, among others, Savona and Maccario (1998). They built on the International Monetary Base (IMB) analysis made by Fratianni and Savona (1972) and tried to adapt it to the new financial context.

The International Monetary Base is composed of all currencies that are well accepted throughout the world: the U.S. dollar, the euro, the Japanese yen, and all other currencies that satisfy the requirements of the Kenen matrix (Fratianni, Hauskrecht, and Maccario, 1998). A more correct definition of the IMB includes financial instruments that relate to the international financial markets.[14]

According to the authors, international money (IM) is given by

$$IM = m \times IMB, \tag{8}$$

while the world money (the whole amount of monetary assets in the world) is given by

$$WM = \sum DM + DDER + IM + IDER, \tag{9}$$

where *IM* is international money, *m* is the IM multiplier, *IMB* is the International Monetary Base, *WM* is world money, *DM* is money for domestic uses, *DDER* is derivatives for domestic uses, and *IDER* is derivatives for international uses.

The problem is the exact quantification of DDER and most of all of IDER. Garber (1998) has studied international capital flows swollen by the introduction of derivatives. He maintains that interest-rate products, such as swaps between industrial countries, compose a great part of the amount of cross-border transactions. These transactions are crucial for the analysis of risk in case of currency crises. The quantity of capital involved in a single country is the base to calculate the potential losses. There are "good" capital instruments, such as equities and commodities, and investments that "disappear" during crises, such as short-term options and futures. This kind of analysis is applicable also to the balance of payments.

Typically, balance-of-payment accounting data are used to measure how long capital will remain in a country and to distinguish "good" money from "hot" money. For example, foreign direct investment has been considered a more stable form of investment (good money) than portfolio investment or the foreign acquisition of bank claims (foreign acquisition of short-term fixed-interest products is generally regarded as a speculative flow). Balance-of-payment accounts are also used to measure the foreign-exchange position of a country's consolidated balance and, in times of crisis, to determine the potential outflow of foreign exchange through speculation or through covered investment by holders of domestic liquid assets. The problem is that balance-of-payment accounting data use on-balance-sheet categorizations, and they are based on value accounting principles to book and classify asset values. Garber (1998) says "they ignore almost completely the existence of derivatives and their role in re-allocating who bears market risk."[15] Derivatives are the ideal instruments to avoid surveillance and prudential regulations because accounting principles for banks continue to be slow in adjusting to financial innovation (IASC, 1998). International standards on which the balance of payments is based are obsolete, and interpretation of disequilibria based only on balance-sheet data creates a dangerous potential for misinterpreting the implications of major events in capital markets.

A significant step forward was made recently (1998) by the IMF Committee on Balance-of-Payment Statistics, which has introduced new rules to make the balance of payments coherent with financial innovation. The new rules state that derivatives are part of national capital resources and must be counted in the balance as financial assets and liabilities. Derivatives are divided in two groups: forward type (future, swap, and forward) and option type. This classification is functional for the market risk but not for the credit risk. Thanks to this statement, the IMF Committee has introduced another item where credit derivatives are written.

More precisely, the Committee has established that

The statistical treatment of financial derivatives involves four steps:

- Recognizing that the exchange of claims and obligations at the inception of a derivative contract is a true financial transaction that creates asset and liability positions that have, at inception, a zero value in the case of forward instruments, and a value equal to the premium in the case of options;
- Treating any changes in the value of derivatives as holding gains or losses;
- Recording transactions in secondary markets of marketable derivatives, such as options, as financial transactions; and
- Recording any payments at settlement as transactions in financial-derivative assets or liabilities, as appropriate (that is, no income arises from settlement of financial derivatives).

The substantial innovation is that, with these new standards, derivatives can be seen with their own potentiality and separate from other (different) financial instruments. Financial derivatives have been removed from the former general item contained in the current account and have been introduced into a new category of the financial account. moreover, apart from information concerning their stock, the IMF committee, realizing the impossibility of a precise and complete quantification of financial derivatives, has inserted a new item in the annex to the balance of payments called "Supplementary Information." Here you can find derivatives' breakdown by category of instruments (forward and option type), class of risk (underlying asset), and counterpart (government, banks, and others). Financial derivatives are valued "at their market price on the recording date. Changes in prices between balance-sheet recording dates are classified as revaluation gains or losses." It is also possible to value derivatives with other methods if market-value data are unavailable. Although the solution of all the problems of quantification raised by the use of derivatives is still in the future, this IMF document shows that the willingness to make derivatives an "on-balance-sheet" item begins to develop.

Before the introduction of this classification, derivatives were not listed separately in the national balance of payments; the problem does not deal with the instruments that can be used to finance short-term debt but with the information contained in the balance of payments. An international transaction involves two or more countries, and the final value cannot be accurately determined at the beginning. Equity and commodities are often hedged with derivatives such as forward and swaps but also futures and options. Derivatives have a feedback effect on the underlying asset: equity hedged with option can be "bad" in case of crises because the option cannot be exercised. In this way, the underlying asset does not have a "normal" reaction in the market. Its price, can be influenced by the derivative's price and the final effect is uncertain. This has been evident during the last currency crises in Brazil, Russia, Asia, and Mexico.

The failure of several large banks can lead to the breakdown of the payment system and the collapse of the credit markets for firms. This phenomenon is better known as *systemic risk*, and there is a relationship with derivatives: if all banks are taking similar positions, the failure may be widespread (Gorton and Rosen, 1995). Certainly, there is a relationship between international unregulated transactions and systemic risk in modern economies. The systemic risk is strictly related to the credit and liquidity risk. Derivatives can have two opposite effects on them:

- The introduction of derivatives improves the market's efficiency and liquidity; in this way the credit and liquidity risks are going to decrease. With credit derivatives, it is possible to shift and hedge only the credit risk, which is no longer associated with the rating of the debtor but with the financial system as a whole.
- Banks are the first investors in derivatives, and the credit risk at a global level does not change but only shifts. In periods of market stress the variance of price increases and losses in the derivatives markets can be huge. In this case, it is crucial to look at the institution that takes the risk.

It is important to say that with derivatives investors have more possibilities to differentiate the resources' allocation. This makes the credit risk decrease for every single hedger. Looking at the world money (WM) equation, we can say that a source of systemic risk can be the international derivatives (IDER) and domestic derivatives (DDER) components traded by institutions without an efficient hedging system, (Edwards, 1995). There are many different hedging systems, and often it is not possible to know if they work. The information that financial institutions must provide is not sufficient to analyze their exposure and quantify the potential losses during a period of markets' stress.

During the 1990s the BIS imposed on banks a minimum capital ratio and some information about derivatives. This capital ratio is related to the risk of assets or liabilities with a constant relationship: for example, government and public firms from OECD countries are not as risky as non-OECD ones. This is true of financial markets in a normal situation. For example, Mexico is an OECD country and the BIS imposes on its liabilities the same risk ratio as for the United States, but Mexican Treasury bills are not as safe as U.S. or German ones. This is the greatest incoherence, and the IMF and many countries are going to intervene once again on the question.

5. Concluding remarks

Derivatives represent the greatest financial innovation of the last 20 years. They have contributed to enlarging financial markets and have given market agents new opportunities to diversify their portfolios, to hedge themselves against undesired risks, and to choose the combination of costs and profits that best fits their preferences. Furthermore, they could be a potential new instrument for central banks to make their policies more effective, as we have shown in the central part of this work. Dominant literature has pointed out these advantages, underlining derivatives' role in boosting market efficiency with the price discovery effect and with the decrease in market volatility.

Nevertheless, it seems to us that most economists and institutions have not paid enough attention to the numerous questions raised by the introduction of derivatives at the macro level. Our aim, in writing this article, has been to stimulate a debate on the way to reduce the great potential systemic instability that derivatives could generate.

Though derivatives are the most traded instruments in domestic and international financial markets, they are officially ignored in the fixing of updated and appropriate monetary targets. The IMF made a significant step forward with the definition of a new scheme for the structure of the balance of payments, taking into account financial innovation. Yet at a domestic level, monetary authorities face great difficulties in conciliating disequilibria in the financial account of the balance of payments with the results of the foreign net position of private agents. It is very likely that this lack of information is caused by ignorance of the exact amount of derivatives traded all over the world and a lack of the theoretical approach.

However, consciousness on the monetary nature of derivatives is progressively developing. Here, we have provided evidence of this monetary feature, with our analyses and estimates. If these results were confirmed, then it would be very difficult to claim that the greatest contribution of derivatives is that of reducing volatility from a micro to a macro level. The financial crises of the last few years and the fluctuations in foreign exchanges do not seem to be a sign of an acquired greater stability in international markets.

Our conclusion is that the literature should be reexamined and analyzed in light of the monetary characteristics of derivatives. International coordinated policies should not simply operate on the effects (by introducing new controls on monetary assets and on financial transactions). Rather, international organizations should make a great effort to quantify the correct amount of derivatives to succeed in inserting them in monetary targets or, at least, in the balance sheets of financial institutions that hold them. Surely, this would be one of the most significant contributions to the definition of the new architecture of the international financial system.

Appendix A: Glossary

gross market value. Real value of all open position on the market. It is usually a small percentage of the nominal value of the contract and is the accumulation of all gains and losses. It tends to reflect market volatility and is a good indicator of current exposures to counterpart credit risk.

gross transfer of price risk. Price risk is measured with the nominal value of contracts, but its real dimension (the effective losses from where risks can rise) is represented by the gross market value.

notional/nominal amount outstanding. Sum of all nominal value of derivative contracts open at that time. Since there is no payment of principal for many of the contracts, notional amounts in these cases are poor indicators of exposures to counterpart credit risk.

turnover data. Absolute gross value of all deals concluded (but not closed) during the month. It is measured in term of the nominal or notional amount of the contracts. Turnover data provide a measure for market activity and can also provide a proxy for market liquidity.

Appendix B: Statistical Annex

Table 1. Foreign-exchange market turnover (daily averages in billions of U.S. dollars).

Category	April 1989	April 1992	April 1995	April 1998
Spot transactions	350	400	520	600
Forward and swap	240	420	670	900
Total turnover	590	820	1.190	1.500

Source: BIS (1999).

Table 2. OTC derivative-market turnover (daily averages in billions of U.S. dollars).

Category	April 1995	April 1998
Forex turnover	688	961
Forward and swap	643	864
Currency swap	4	10
Options	41	87
Other	1	0
Interest-rate turnover	151	265
FRAs	66	74
Swaps	63	155
Options	21	36
Other	2	0
Total derivatives turnover	880	1.265

Source: BIS (1999).

Table 3. Global turnover in OTC derivative markets (daily averages in billions of U.S. dollars).

	Total		Foreign Exchange		Interest Rates	
	April 1995	April 1998	April 1995	April 1998	April 1995	April 1998
Total reported gross turnover	1,368	1,99	1,114	1,576	254	415
Adjustment for local double-counting	−206	−306	−161	−235	−45	−71
Total reported turnover net of local double-counting	1,162	1,684	953	1,341	209	344
Adjustment for cross-border double-counting	−323	−457	−265	−380	−58	−78
Total reported net-net turnover	839	1,226	688	961	151	265
With reporting dealers	529	764	427	615	102	150
With other financial institutions	181	267	149	178	32	89
With nonfinancial institutions	129	195	111	168	17	27
Estimated gaps in reporting	41	39	32	29	9	10
Estimated global turnover	880	1,265	720	990	160	275

Source: BIS (1999).

Table 4. Inflation forecast based on derivative prices (monthly data).

Period	Monthly Inflation Rate	Variation in Monthly Inflation	T Bill Monthly Medium Price	Inflation Rate Foresee with 0% Tax Rate	Inflation Rate Foresee with 40% Tax Rate	Error with 0% Tax Rate	Error with 40% Tax Rate
1995:							
April	151.9	0.00197	92.31300	0.00042	0.00025	0.00155	0.00172
May	152.2	0.00197	92.27087	0.00395	0.00237	−0.00198	−0.00040
June	152.5	0.00000	92.66636	0.00150	0.00090	−0.00150	−0.00090
July	152.5	0.00262	92.51619	0.00033	0.00020	0.00229	0.00242
August	152.9	0.00196	92.54957	0.00278	0.00167	−0.00082	0.00029
September	153.2	0.00326	92.82762	0.00423	0.00254	−0.00097	0.00072
October	153.7	−0.00065	93.25045	0.00103	0.00062	−0.00168	−0.00127
November	153.6	−0.00065	93.14773	0.00025	0.00015	−0.00090	−0.00080
December	153.5	0.00586	93.12286	0.00498	0.00299	0.00088	0.00287

(*Continued on next page.*)

Table 4. (*Continued*).

1996:							
January	154.4	0.00324	93.62130	0.00481	0.00288	−0.00157	0.00036
February	154.9	0.00516	94.10190	0.00149	0.00089	0.00367	0.00427
March	155.7	0.00385	94.25048	0.00147	0.00088	0.00238	0.00297
April	156.3	0.00192	94.39773	0.00067	0.00040	0.00125	000152
May	156.6	0.00064	94.33087	0.00096	0.00058	−0.00032	0.00006
June	156.7	0.00191	94.42700	0.00005	0.00003	0.00186	0.00188
July	157	0.00191	94.43174	0.00147	0.00088	0.00044	0.00103
August	157.3	0.00318	94.57864	0.00139	0.00084	0.00179	0.00234
September	157.8	0.00317	94.71810	0.00042	0.00025	0.00275	0.00292
October	158.3	0.00190	94.76000	0.00060	0.00036	0.00130	0.00154
November	158.6	0.00000	94.82000	0.00090	0.00054	−0.00090	−0.00054
December	158.6	0.00315	94.90955	0.00116	0.00069	0.00199	0.00246
1997:							
January	159.1	0.00314	95.02522	0.00220	0.00132	0.00094	0.00182
February	159.6	0.00251	95.24550	0.00106	0.00064	0.00145	0.00187
March	160	0.00125	95.35190	0.00048	0.00029	0.00077	0.00096
April	160.2	−0.00062	95.30364	0.00044	0.00026	−0.00106	−0.00088
May	160.1	0.00125	95.26000	0.00390	0.00234	−0.00265	−0.00109
June	160.3	0.00125	95.65000	0.00043	0.00026	0.00082	0.00099
July	160.5	0.00187	95.69348	0.00043	0.00026	0.00144	0.00161
August	160.8	0.00249	95.65000	0.00159	0.00095	0.00090	0.00154
September	161.2	0.00248	95.80864	0.00213	0.00128	0.00035	0.00120
October	161.6	−0.00062	95.59609	0.00021	0.00013	−0.00083	−0.00075
November	161.5	−0.00124	95.61750	0.00008	0.00005	−0.00132	−0.00129
December	161.3	0.00186	95.61000	0.00000	0.00000	0.00186	0.00186
1998:							
January	161.6	0.00186	95.61000	0.00000	0.00000	0.00186	0.00186
February	161.9	0.00185	95.61000	0.00070	0.00042	0.00115	0.00143
March	162.2	0.00185	95.68000	0.00000	0.00000	0.00185	0.00185
April	162.5	0.00185	95.68000	0.00000	0.00000	0.00185	0.00185
May	162.8	0.00123	95.68000	0.00587	0.00352	−0.00464	−0.00229
June	163	0.00123	96.26727	0.00183	0.00110	−0.00060	0.00013
July	163.2	0.00123	96.45000	0.00000	0.00000	0.00123	0.00123
August	163.4	0.00122	96.45000	0.00000	0.00000	0.00122	0.00122
September	163.6		96.45000				
Mean		0.00181		0.00137	0.00082	0.00044	0.00099
Standard deviation		0.00149		0.00155	0.00093	0.00169	0.00142
Variance		0.00000		0.00000	0.00000	0.00000	0.00000

Source: Our estimates.

Table 5. Inflation forecasts based on derivatives prices (quarterly data).

Period	Quarterly Inflation Rate	Inflation Rate Foresee with 0% Tax Rate	Inflation Rate Foresee with 40% Tax Rate	Error with 0% Tax Rate	Error with 40% Tax Rate
1995:					
II	0.00438	0.00214	0.00129	0.00224	0.00309
III	0.00480	0.00543	0.00326	−0.00063	0.00154
IV	0.00911	0.00818	0.00491	0.00093	0.00420
1996:					
I	0.00989	0.00394	0.00236	0.00595	0.00753
II	0.00532	0.00191	0.00115	0.00341	0.00417
III	0.00720	0.00254	0.00152	0.00466	0.00568
IV	0.00673	0.00378	0.00227	0.00295	0.00446
1997:					
I	0.00397	0.00197	0.00118	0.00200	0.00279
II	0.00395	0.00313	0.00188	0.00082	0.00207
III	0.00394	0.00110	0.00066	0.00284	0.00328
IV	0.00268	0.00025	0.00015	0.00243	0.00253
1998:					
I	0.00535	0.00242	0.00145	0.00293	0.00390
II	0.00389	0.00574	0.00345	−0.00185	0.00044
III					
Mean		0.00327	0.00196	0.00221	0.00351
Variance		0.00000	0.00000	0.00000	0.00000
Standard deviation		0.00215	0.00129	0.00206	0.00182

Source: Our estimates.

Table 6. Inflation forecast based on derivatives for five European countries (France, German, Italy, Holland, and Spain) (quarterly data).

Period	Inflation Rate	Future Quarterly Price on Euro Libor 3 Months	Gross Rate of Return of the Future on Euro Libor 3 Months	Absolute Value of the Rate of Return of the Future on Euro Libro 3 Months	Absolute Value in the Variation of the Inflation Rate	Forecast with 0% Tax Rate	Error in the Forecast with 0% Tax Rate	Error in the Forecast with 40% Tax Rate
1995:								
I	0.02887	93.38347	0.0661653	0.003399	0.00161	0.003399	0.001789	0.000429
II	0.03048	93.72336	0.0627664	0.005140	0.00038	0.005140	0.004760	0.002704
III	0.03086	94.23735	0.0576265	0.003261	0.00033	0.003261	0.002931	0.001627
IV	0.03053	94.56348	0.0543652	0.007875	0.00238	0.007875	0.005495	0.002345
1996:								
I	0.02815	95.351	0.04649	0.002768	0.00042	0.002768	0.002348	0.001241
II	0.02773	95.62785	0.0437215	0.000131	0.00368	0.000131	0.003549	0.003602
III	0.02405	95.64091	0.0435909	0.002356	0.00168	0.002356	0.000676	0.000266
IV	0.02237	95.87652	0.0412348	0.000029	0.00137	0.000029	0.001341	0.001352
1997:								
I	0.021	95.87359	0.0412641	0.000499	0.00437	0.000499	0.003871	0.004071
II	0.01663	95.82369	0.0417631	0.001773	0.00241	0.001773	0.000637	0.001346
III	0.01904	95.64636	0.0435364	0.002209	0.00011	0.002209	0.002099	0.001215
IV	0.01915	95.42545	0.0457455	0.002828	0.00512	0.002828	0.002292	0.003423

(Continued on next page.)

Table 6. (Continued).

Period	Inflation Rate	Future Quarterly Price on Euro Libor 3 Months	Gross Rate of Return of the Future on Euro Libor 3 Months	Absolute Value of the Rate of Return of the Future on Euro Libro 3 Months	Absolute Value in the Variation of the Inflation Rate	Forecast with 0% Tax Rate	Error in the Forecast with 0% Tax Rate	Error in the Forecast with 40% Tax Rate
1998:								
I	0.01403	95.70828	0.0429172	0.000480	0.00216	0.000480	0.001680	0.001872
II	0.01619	95.7563	0.042437	0.001179	0.00336	0.001179	0.002181	0.002653
III	0.01283	95.87417	0.0412583	0.005233		0.005233		
IV		96.39752	0.0360248					
Mean							0.002546	0.002010
Variance							0.000002	0.000001
Standard deviation							0.00143754	0.001163

Source: Our estimates.

Notes

1. See Appendix A for a short explanation of technical words.
2. The gross market value of a portfolio of derivatives (created by the BIS) is a useful indicator to measure current credit exposure. It is the sum of the absolute market values of the component contracts. For example, a portfolio that has one contract worth $5 and one contract worth -$2 (a loss value) has a gross market value of $7.
3. The main difference between the previous BIS reports about derivatives and the latest is that the 1999 report is based on 43 countries' data, whereas in the 1995 there were only 26 reporting countries.
4. In September 1998, despite the equal volume of futures and options trading, average daily volumes were higher on Eurex than those on LIFFE.
5. The European benchmark for Treasury bonds will be the future on the German Bund, while the future on Euribor will be the benchmark for interest rates, replacing the former equivalent contract on LIBOR.
6. This market indicator is a very efficient proxy of the impact of financial innovation on modern financial systems.
7. The t-stat is shown in parentheses.
8. The difference in the magnitude of the constant terms of linear regressions could be justified in that interest rates on the euro (the underlying asset of the future contract here examined) reflect the general decrease of rates observed in international markets in the last few years.
9. It should be pointed out that the negative correlation between the interest rate and monetary base holds for unchanged inflation expectations by economic agents; thus it is an unanticipated increase in the monetary base that affects the nominal and the real interest rate. Without this qualification, the relationship changes. If prevalent expectations are rational, the market will react to greater creation of monetary base by raising the interest rates to incorporate higher inflation expectations.
10. A dynamic investment strategy is a portfolio that is balanced between derivatives and spot assets to keep a constant ratio (delta). If the spot or derivative price changes, the proportion invested must be modified. To have an efficient strategy, it must be done every day at every price change.
11. With these financial instruments, banks can shift the credit risk to other agents with a specific contract and condition of payment and insurance.
12. Based on a direct relationship between money growth and inflation, central banks use the M1 indicator. If they base their forecasts on a relationship between commercial growth and inflation, monetary authorities use previous levels of consumer price index (CPI).
13. Expected changes in inflation minus the actual change in inflation.
14. More precisely, Fratianni and Savona define the international monetary base as "the complex of instruments that can be used by central banks (or institutions with equivalent functions), by commercial banks, and by the public to satisfy the requirements in reserves, independent of the nature of such necessity."
15. For example, the acquisition of a large block of equity is classified as foreign direct investment, but a foreign buyer may acquire the block simply to hedge a short position in equity established through a derivative position.

Reference

Angeloni, I. and M. Massa (1994) "Mercati Derivati e Politica Monetaria." *Comunicazione presentata alla XXXV riunione annuale della Società italiana degli Economisti*. Milano: Università Bocconi.
Antoniou, A., P. Holmes, and R. Priestley (1998) "The Effects of Stock Index Futures Trading on Stock Index Volatility: An Analysis of the Asymmetric Response of Volatility to News." *Journal of Futures Markets* 18(2):151–156.

Banca d'Italia (1995a) "I Prodotti Derivati: Profili di Pubblico Interesse." Centro Studi Finanziari, 3° ciclo di Lezioni "Emilio Moar," Università Cattolica del Sacro Cuore, Milan.

Banca d'Italia (1995b) "Lo sviluppo dei prodotti derivati nella realtà italiana. Aspetti di mercato, prudenziali e gestionali." *Tematiche Istituzionali*. Rome: Banca d'Italia.

Banca d'Italia (1995c) "Vigilanza Prudenziale sull'attività Delle Banche in Strumenti Derivati." *Banca d'Italia Bollettino economico* 24:13–23.

Bank of England (1993) "Derivatives: Where Next for Supervisors?" *Quarterly Bulletin* (London) 33:535–538.

Basle Committee on Banking Supervision (1995) "Treatment of Potential Exposure for Off-Balance-Sheet Items." Basle.

Bhanot, Karan (1998) "Stochastic Volatility Functions Implicit in Eurodollar Futures Options." *Journal of Futures Markets* 18(6):605–627.

BIS (1994a) Compendium of annexes to the report on "Macroeconomic and Monetary Policy Issues Raised by the Growth of Derivatives Markets." Basle.

BIS (1994b) "Macroeconomic and Monetary Policy Issues Raised by the Growth of Derivatives Markets." Basle.

BIS (1996a) "Central Bank Survey of Foreign Exchange and Derivatives Market Activity." Basle.

BIS (1996b) "Rischio di Regolamento nelle Operazioni in Cambi." Basle.

BIS (1999) "Central Bank Survey of Foreign Exchange and Derivatives Market Activity." Basle, May.

Calise, G. and G. Paladino (1999) "Driving Forces in the Location of Financial Centres." IMI Working Paper, San Paolo.

Carlson, J.B., J.M. McIntire, and J.B. Thomsom (1995) "Federal Funds Futures as an Indicator of Future Monetary Policy: A Primer." *Federal Reserve Bank of Cleveland Review* 20–30.

Chan, K., Y.P. Chung, and H. Johnson (1995) "The Intraday Behaviour of Bid-Ask Spreads for NYSE Stock and CBOE Options." *Journal of Financial and Quantitative Analysis* 30(3) (September):329–346.

Conrad, J. (1999) "The Price Effect of Option Introduction." *Journal of Finance* 44(2) (June):487–498.

Craig, A., A. Dravid, and M. Richardson (1995) "Markets Efficiency Around the Clock: Some Supporting Evidence Using Foreign-based Derivatives." *Journal of Financial Economics* 39:161–180.

Damodaran, A. and J. Lim (1991) "The Effects of Option Listing on the Underlying Stock's Return Processes." *Journal of Banking and Finance* 15:647–664.

Deutsche Bundesbank (1994) "The Monetary Policy Implications of the Increasing Use of Derivatives Financial Instruments." *Monthly Report* (Frankfurt) (November).

Edwards, F.R. (1995) "Off-Exchange Derivatives Markets and Financial Fragility." *Journal of Financial Services Research* 9:259–290.

Fazio, A. (1968) *Base Monetaria, Credito E Depositi Bancari*. Quaderno di ricerca Ente per gli Studi monetari, bancari e finanziari Luigi Einaudi 2.

Fratianni, M., A. Hauskrecht, and A. Maccario (1998), "Dominant Currencies and the Future of the Euro." *Open Economies Review* 9 (Supplement):467–492.

Fratianni, M. and P. Savona (1972) "The International Monetary Base and the Eurodollar Market: A Reply to the Comments of Heller and Drexler." *Kredit und Kapital*, No. 1, Berlin.

Friedman, M. and A. Jacobson Schwartz (1963) *A Monetary History of the United States 1867–1960*. Princeton: Princeton University Press.

Fung, H.G. and W. Leung (1993) "The Pricing Relationship of Eurodollar Futures and Eurodollar Deposit Rates." *Journal of Futures Markets* 13(2):115–126.

Garber, P. (1996) "Managing Risk to Financial Markets from Volatile Capital Flows: The Role of Prudential Regulation." *International Journal of Finance and Economics* 1:183–195.

Garber, P. (1998) *Derivatives in International Capital Flow*. NBER Working Paper 6623.

Garber, P. and M.G. Spencer (1994) "Foreign Exchange Hedging with Synthetic Options and the Interest Rate Defense of a Fixed Exchange Rate Regime." Working Paper 151, IMF Research Department, Washington, DC.

Gerlach, S. and F. Smets (1995) "The Monetary Transmission Mechanism: Evidence from the G-7 Countries." Working Paper 26, BIS, Basle.

Glennon, D. and J. Lane (1996) "Financial Innovation, New Assets and the Behaviour of Money Demand." *Journal of Banking and Finance* 20:207–225.

Goodhart, C.A.E. (1995) "Financial Globalisation, Derivatives, Volatility and the Challenge for the Policies of Central Banks." LSE Special Paper 74, London School of Economics, London.

Gorton, G. and R. Rosen (1995) "Banks and Derivatives." Working Paper 12, Federal Reserve Bank of Philadelphia, Philadelphia.

Hentschel, L. and C.W. Smith Jr. (1997) "Derivatives Regulation: Implications for Central Banks." *Journal of Monetary Economics* 40:305–346.

Hooyman, C.J. (1993) "The Use of Foreign Exchange Swaps by Central Banks: A Survey." Working Paper 64, IMF, Washington, DC.

Hull, J. (1994) *Introduzione ai Mercata dei Futures e Delle Opzioni*. Milan: Il Sole 24 Ore Libri.

IASC (1998) "Financial Instruments: Recognition and Measurement." Exposure Draft E62, London.

IMF (1998a) "Hedge Funds and Financial Market Dynamics." Occasional Paper 166, Washington, DC, May.

IMF (1998b) "International Capital Markets: Developments, Prospects and Key Policy Issues." Washington, DC.

IMF (1999) "International Capital Markets." Washington, DC.

IMF Committee on Balance of Payment Statistics (1998) "Financial Derivatives." Washington, DC.

Jegadeesh, N. and G.G. Pennacchi (1996) "The Behaviour of Interest Rate Implied by the Term Structure of Eurodollar Futures." *Federal Reserve Bank of Cleveland, Journal of Money, Credit and Banking* 28(3).

Kenen, P.B. (1996) "Analysing and Managing Exchange-Rate Crises." *Open Economies Review* 7:469–492.

Keynes, J.M. (1930) *A Treatise on Money* (2 vols.).

Miller, M. (1991) *Financial Innovation and Market Volatility*. Chicago: Blackwell.

Murray, F. and R. Jagannathan (1998) "Why Do Stock Prices Drop by Less Than the Value of the Dividend? Evidence from a Country Without Taxes." *Journal of Financial Economics* 47(2):161–188.

Rosengren, E.S. (1987) "Forecasting Changes in Inflation Using the Treasury Bill Futures Market." *Federal Reserve Bank of Boston New England Economic Review* (March-April):41–48.

Rossetti, A. (1999) *I Derivati Come Strumento di Intervento della Banca Centrale*. Università degli Studi di Viterbo, Viterbo.

Savona, P. (1978) "Il ruolo della moneta nella politiche di gestione della domanda globale: note allo studio dell'OCSE." *Giornale degli Economisti e Annali di Economia* 11–12, Milano.

Savona, P. and U. La Malfa (1969) "Some Notes on Expectations and the Demand for Bonds." *Metroeconomica* 21(3):733–743, Bologna.

Savona P. and A. Maccario (1998) "On the Relation Between Money and Derivatives and Its Application to the International Monetary Market." *Open Economies Review* 9 (Supplement):637–664.

Skinner, D.J. (1989) "Options Markets and Stock Return Volatility." *Journal of Financial Economics* 23:61–78.

Tavakoli, J.M. (1998) *Financial Engineering: Credit Derivatives*. New York: Wiley.

Tinsley, P.A. (1998) *Short Rate Expectations, Terms Premiums and Central Bank Use of Derivatives to Reduce Policy Uncertainty*. Washington, DC: Federal Reserve Board.

Tse, Y., T.H. Lee, and G.G. Booth (1996) "The International Transmission of Information in Eurodollar Futures Markets: A Continuously Trading Market Hypothesis." *Journal of International Money and Finance* 15(3):447–465.

Von Hagen, J. and I. Fender (1998) "Central Bank Policy in a More Perfect Financial System." *Open Economies Review* 9 (Supplement):493–532.

Vrolijk, C. (1997) "Derivatives Effects on Monetary Policy Transmission." Working Paper 121, International Monetary Fund, Washington, DC.

Open economies review **11:S1** 177–181 (2000)
© 2000 *Kluwer Academic Publishers. Printed in The Netherlands.*

Comment on Savona, Maccario, and Oldani's "On Monetary Analysis of Derivatives"

PETER M. OPPENHEIMER
Christ Church, Oxford

Commentators and discussants tend either to focus on disagreements with principal authors or else to pursue their own unrelated thoughts. So let me stress at the outset that I strongly endorse the authors' central conclusion concerning tension between the findings of microeconomic research on derivatives and their possible macroeconomic impact. Microeconomic research, as reported by Paolo Savona, Aurelio Maccario, and Chiara Oldani (henceforth SMO), appears to show that derivatives reduce volatility and enhance efficiency of financial markets, but macroeconomically derivatives create a potential for more severe financial-market disruption. I return to this contrast in my concluding paragraphs.

The main focus of SMO's paper, however, is not financial-market regulation but the other component of central-bank responsibility—namely, monetary policy. Observe in passing that in the European Union the European Central Bank (ECB) is confined exclusively to the latter domain, leaving the former in the hands of national central banks and also, by implication, leaving monetary policy wholly unaffected by considerations of financial-system stability. Not the least interesting question about the future of the ECB and the euro is how far this sharp separation of powers can be maintained.

Be that as it may, the authors are concerned (as I understand it) first with the appropriate measure of monetary aggregate or money supply to serve as an indicator or possible intermediate target in the presence of derivatives and second with the conduct of monetary policy (operations on the monetary base and so on) designed to achieve whatever target is set. Before proceeding, I have to confess that I found SMO's survey of empirical literature on derivatives unduly allusive. They assume in their readers a familiarity with the literature that I do not possess. Of course, that is my fault, but not, I suspect, uniquely mine, and I hope that in developing their research on the subject SMO will devote more effort to guiding the uninitiated through the technical complexities underlying the empirical investigations.

Regarding the conduct of monetary policy via derivatives markets, I am skeptical. The lack of transparency in derivative markets will tempt central banks to misuse their policy-making powers. SMO themselves refer to the Bank of Thailand's unhappy efforts to fend off devaluation of the baht in 1997. Three decades earlier the Bank of England had a similarly unfortunate experience with interventions in the sterling forward-exchange market. As a rule of thumb, the more such subterfuges appear necessary, the less likely are they (or the policy goal driving them) to be appropriate. One could go further and say that since positions in derivative markets are inherently speculative, central banks have no business adopting them either directly or indirectly. Investors in Long-Term Capital Management (LTCM), the so-called hedge fund ignominiously bailed out by the Federal Reserve in 1998, reportedly included central banks, the Bank of Italy among them. The governors of such banks should have been required to resign.

As regards indicators and targets of policy, I have a modest suggestion. Faced with a structural change or large-scale set of innovations in the financial system (as exemplified by derivatives in recent decades), policy makers should try to focus directly on ultimate target variables and avoid reliance on intermediate ones whose relationship to final objectives may not be dependable. In other words, targeting inflation is preferable to targeting either monetary aggregates or exchange rates. The past decade has indeed seen a shift from the latter to the former. This is a clear improvement. Furthermore, if data from the derivative markets enable inflation forecasting to be improved, as SMO claim, so much the better.

The explosion of derivative activity was not needed to bring about the move to inflation targeting, however. Other innovations and other (earlier) structural changes had already given the necessary impetus. There were at least two such changes. One was the rapid spread of credit cards for transactions (and precautionary) purposes. This implies a shift in money-demand functions, intensifying previous trends toward a higher velocity of circulation of narrow money. The other change was the world inflation episode of the 1970s and 1980s and the process of adaptation to it. Formerly non-interest-bearing or low-interest financial instruments were gradually rendered more remunerative, and portfolio demand for them, which had initially suffered, revived correspondingly. Demand for broad money first shrank and then recovered.

Arguably, however, the most interesting parallel between derivatives and other financial innovations is to be drawn from a more distant era—namely, the nineteenth century, which witnessed the rise of commercial banking in its more or less modern form. (It took 70 or 80 years then to realize change on a scale nowadays accomplished in 10 or 20 years.) The second quarter of that century produced in Britain the celebrated monetary debate between the currency school and the banking school. The currency school emphasized the importance of linking the note issue to gold for preservation of price and currency stability (the gold standard). The banking school rejected this proposition, at any rate in its simple form, on the grounds that bank deposits accounted for a large and growing fraction of the money stock and that price-level stability was therefore an endogenously generated result of maintaining a well-run banking system rather than an exogenous result of central-bank restraints on the note issue.[1]

The verdict of history on this debate was fascinatingly inconclusive. Few would deny that nineteenth-century price stability owed something to the gold standard (enshrined in Britain's case in the Bank Charter Act of 1844). But three points need making on the other side.

First, long-run price stability in England antedated the introduction of the gold standard (in the early eighteenth century by Isaac Newton, no less) by more than a century. And stable price expectations undoubtedly furnished a powerful systemic anchor for the gold standard itself. Second, as Robert Triffin showed in his researches on long-run monetary history, national money supplies of gold-standard countries in the nineteenth century expanded much more than monetary gold stocks and relied rather on a growing centralization of such stocks in the hands of central banks, together with a fractional-reserve system.

Third, the gold standard in Britain might not have survived through the nineteenth century had the Bank of England not learned to manage or subdue the banking crises that occurred at intervals during the middle decades of the century. In other words, one cannot disregard the possibility that macroeconomic stability depended in part, as the banking school maintained, on microeconomic stability of the financial sector.

At this point we are brought back to the present day, with its intense debates on last-resort lending, moral hazard, and the form and extent of prudential capital requirements. There is a massive contrast between Bank of England regulation in the late nineteenth century and today's struggle to maintain stability in world financial markets. Nineteenth-century globalization notwithstanding, the Bank of England presided over an increasingly oligopolistic banking system, in which the British commercial banking network gradually coalesced into the Big Five, while the handful of merchant banks that financed world trade and oversaw foreign bond issues in London depended for their status on membership of the London Accepting Houses Committee, sanctioned by the Bank of England. If moral hazard ever became an issue, it was dealt with by the Bank of England governor's eyebrow.[2]

To put the point as provocatively as I can, much of today's problem of financial stability, whether associated with derivatives or not, arises from the excessively competitive structure of contemporary financial systems. Competitive pressures impel financial institutions toward excessive risk taking or, to vary the terminology, toward overlending and overinvesting. The impetus is hard to resist because of the combination of (1) unavoidable uncertainty regarding risk and return on capital assets, hence scope for self-deception and for unwarranted optimism, and (2) the cost and inconvenience of proper market research, which encourages herd behavior in preference to independent assessment, further enhancing the judgmental weakness identified under (1). These two are the factors at work in the early phases of a speculative bubble. They may be dampened by minimum capital requirements and other forces of legal regulation. But they will not be eliminated.

In the earlier phases of a bubble, optimism is likely to prove self-justifying, just as, in bubble-free periods, normal returns and stable underlying price patterns may be successfully extrapolated. With respect to such circumstances it is not surprising that microeconomics should show derivatives as contributing to diminished volatility and a denser structure of internally consistent asset prices. Such findings, however, tell one absolutely nothing about how badly institutions or individual investors will be exposed and what sort of wider domino effects will be threatened when the bubble bursts or the economy is subjected to some exogenous and unforeseen shock. In this respect derivatives are no different from other devices supposedly designed to hedge or diminish risk. A celebrated example in the 1970s was the syndicated rollover bank credit used to channel petrodollars to Latin American and other borrowing countries. Interest rates, adjusted every six months in line with the cost of bank funds (LIBOR), allowed banks, as they thought, to fund long-term credit with short-term deposits. So long as interest rates remained low and rather stable, the scheme looked sound enough. But then came the massive and unenvisaged rise in interest rates after 1979, whereupon the scheme turned out to be basically a device for transforming interest-rate risk into risk of default or outright repudiation. The result was the prolonged less developed countries debt crisis of the 1980s.

An analogous distinction between fair-weather findings and the impact of dislocation applies to the insulation theorem of floating exchange rates (referred to in Robert Z. Aliber's paper, this volume, as well as by SMO). The proposition that floating exchange rates enable countries to maintain autonomous national inflation rates holds in steady state. By allowing the Swiss franc to appreciate at a steady rate of 3 percent a year, Switzerland can maintain a 2 percent annual inflation rate so long as the rest of the world's inflation is at a steady 5 percent. But if the rest of the world, in a fit of expansion, abruptly raises its inflation rate to 8 or 10 percent a year, Switzerland is unlikely to achieve a smooth and instantaneous adjustment to appreciation of 6 or 8 percent a year. Much more probable is a Dornbusch-style overappreciation in the short run, threatening Swiss enterprises with bankruptcy and thus putting the Swiss National Bank under pressure to reverse the overappreciation by accelerating its own rate of money growth and hence also the Swiss rate of inflation.

The spread of derivatives is an important element in the increased fluidity and integration of the world's financial markets. SMO are right to pose questions about the proper response of monetary authorities to this particular element. Whether the formulation and pursuit of monetary policy targets ought to be affected in a more radical manner than hitherto is not yet proven, but neither can the possibility be excluded.

Notes

1. Notice that both schools could claim the eighteenth-century (Humean) Model of the gold standard as their intellectual ancestor. In Hume's Model the national money stock consisted exclusively of gold and was endogenously determined (by the full-employment level of output at given

world prices). The currency school stressed the gold base, and the banking school stressed the endogeneity with respect to economic activity at a given price level.
2. The desirability of limiting competition in financial markets was a prominent feature in the nineteenth-century writings of Walter Bagehot. For an important twentieth-century restatement, see Hirsch (1977).

Reference

Hirsch, F. (1977) "The Bagehot Problem." *The Manchester School*. Manchester University, Dept. of Economics.

Open economies review **11:S1** 183–193 (2000)

The New International Financial Architecture: Progress and Challenges

ANTONIO CASAS-GONZÁLEZ
Banco Central de Venezuela, Caracas

Keywords: international financial architecture

JEL Classification Number: F33

Abstract

Recent economic crises have affected different countries in the last decade. Crises shook not only countries that were directly affected but also other more developed countries. Part of the risk of crises derives from the considerable negative effects imposed on economies by the volatility and reversibility of short-term capital flow. International financial reforms should consider (1) regulation and supervision, (2) statistical standards, (3) the goods and services trade, (4) liquidity and lender of last resort, (5) unified action, (6) private-sector involvement, and (7) other contingency measures. The Venezuelan experience suggests some other domestic reforms, but reforming the international financial system, in the direction of globalization, has to be the principle goal of international organizations.

1. Recent economic crises

It is well known that the world economy has evolved unevenly over the past decade, with ups and downs and even negative growth for groups of countries. Just when it was widely believed that the world economy was on a path of sustainable growth—a product largely due to the developing economies' openness model—the Southeast Asian and Russian crises were unleashed in 1997 and, more recently, the Brazilian crisis. All of these crises had systemic effects of great significance and have demonstrated characteristics that are very similar to those that accompanied the Mexican problem in 1994 and 1995. Accompanying those problems, other emerging countries (Colombia, Chile, Ecuador) found themselves in distress, although not to the extent of a threat to the world economy.

These crises shook not only the countries that were directly affected but also other more developed countries. This shows that the financial problems of our times are not only of a domestic or regional nature but are also transmitted to countries that are geographically distant. This is primarily due to the interconnection of the markets and the speed of communications. It also shows that even developed countries are at risk of contagion.

For this reason, the capacity and effectiveness of international organizations to deal with crises have been called into doubt. Many observers have questioned the advisability of making greater resources available to such institutions and oppose allowing them to effect disbursements more quickly to handle situations that may be present. Others go so far as to warn about the inability of these multilateral agencies to deal with the problems and call for their dissolution or profound restructuring.

The truth is that even countries that were considered successful, such as the Asian tigers, became vulnerable to crises, leaving the developing world without clear examples to follow. The crises of our age have made evident the tremendous lack of information regarding the true condition of the world's economies. And while it is true that the main lesson learned from the crisis era is that it is necessary to apply sound economic policies, it is also true that good policies are not sufficient to keep countries from being affected. Moreover, policies must be credible to the markets, and, even so, there is no guarantee that contagion will be avoided. If markets do not discriminate among the characteristics of the economies of the various countries, then all countries are exposed to problems.

2. The transmission of crises through short-term capital flows

At the risk of stating the obvious and to make it easier to identify solutions, it must be stressed that part of the danger derives from the considerable negative effects imposed on economies by the volatility and reversibility of short-term capital flows. The negative effects of these short-term capital flows can exceed their benefits, at least during some periods. That is why the destruction of confidence and productive capacity in terms of investment, employment, and output are so important. Indonesia is a case in point illustrating a net loss of development. This danger is evident by the exponential increase in the flows of this type of capital, which are basically comprised of portfolio flows and channeled through institutional investors using derivatives (futures, swaps, options, forwards, and others), although short-term bank loans should be considered as well.

We will not go into a detailed description of the advantages to be obtained through deepening financial liberalization. It is necessary, however, to note that such desired liberalization and deepening occurs in the context of asymmetrical information, which is costly and difficult to evaluate. Moreover, some relevant aspects of that information, such as the evolution of fiscal accounts and future decisions regarding fiscal, monetary, and exchange policies, are based on financial analysts' assumptions and guesses. To this problem of lack of transparency, we must add institutional immaturity and the weakness of mechanisms to regulate and supervise financial systems.

In this era of uncertainty and incomplete information, a type of imitation effect is easily fostered. It results in sudden capital outflows when portfolio decisions of investors who are considered leaders are blindly followed. When this happens, the seriousness of the authorities in the host country regarding the implementation of stable and consistent macroeconomic policies is disregarded. This is reinforced when interest rates are not congruent with risk expectations, other than that their increase may, in the end, affect the banking system and all of the real economy as a self-fulfilling prophesy. There is only one step from this point to the transmission of the problem to other economies with similar characteristics and risk indicators. After that, the contagion effect is produced. At the end of the process, the scenario of systemic crisis is created by the profit-taking and risk-mitigation strategy implicit in portfolio diversification. This is the prescription of the previously mentioned Mexican, Asian, Russian, and Brazilian crises and, more recently, the Ecuadorian crisis. My own country, Venezuela, did not escape this sequence during the banking crisis of 1994 and 1995.

The current problems go hand in hand with globalization. This requires a similarly international reaction in many of its aspects and brings us to the need to support reform, adopting at the same time domestic policies that favor stability and long-term investment in our countries.

3.   Suggested reforms

International financial reform therefore suggests the introduction of a series of measures coordinated by the global community. Some important ones are summarized below.

3.1.   Regulation and supervision

The job performed by financial intermediaries needs to be strengthened through more rigorous regulation and supervision, including the strict observance of the principles put forth by the Basle Committee. This incorporates the unification and transparency of financial statements presentation, capital adequacy, and risk-weighted assets, as well as the development of updated systems for managing risks at private institutions, which presupposes the strengthening of deposits guarantee and protection funds.

The rigorousness of the Basle Accords regarding banking regulation and supervision depends on closing the gaps as to the application of standards by countries that receive capital inflows. Failure to fulfill these requirements should lead to sanctions by the Bank for International Settlements (BIS) in the form of an announcement of such irregularity to the international community or of a higher cost of financial assistance in those cases where funds are required.

The development of risk-management systems should not be limited to emerging-market institutions that receive funds. Part of the political opposition observed locally against financial assistance packages during the Mexican and Asian crises were linked to the fact that they were considered rescue operations to guarantee purely speculative portfolio investment returns, protecting those investors from the risk inherent in any investment and in detriment to the country's net international financial position. In this way, according to that view, economic and political peace in the creditor countries was bought at the expense of heavier indebtedness by the countries receiving capital, without the associated productive investment.

Overcoming this perception is possible if the authorities in the issuing and the receiving countries share the responsibilities of regulation and supervision. In this regard, it is worth considering the introduction of some type of reserve requirement in the home countries for institutional investors. The level of reserves required would be tied to their exposure to risk, which could in turn be related portfolio concentration. To avoid significantly increasing the cost of capital, these reserves could be placed in interest-bearing accounts. This measure would obviously contribute to discouraging excessive flows of portfolio capital toward emerging markets, minimizing the risk of conflict in capital-exporting countries.

3.2. Statistical standards

The design of statistical standards should be encouraged to (1) properly reflect the economic and financial condition of a country at the macro level, in addition to those developed for companies, and (2) promote more intense efforts to design and implement codes of conduct regarding fiscal, financial, monetary, trade, and social policy. The evaluation of "early warning indicators" to call timely attention to potential problems should be part of this effort so that the crisis-awareness and -prevention work being carried out will make sense. This could take place in the context of the macroeconomic evaluation tied to the International Monetary Fund's (IMF's) Article IV Consultation. Among other indicators, we could mention the relationship of the current account deficit to gross domestic policy (GDP), international reserves to short-term external debt, M2 to international reserves, net short-term capital flows to GDP, terms of exchange and relationships of interest-rate arbitrage, fiscal deficit to GDP, and so on.

While the benefit of standards is obvious, there are a few concerns that should be taken into account in their application and possible monitoring in the future. From a country's perspective, the IMF's assessment derived from surveillance based on the application of standards can have an impact on the relationship between the country's authorities and the Fund. Many of the national authorities view the Fund as an advisor that has been given a very special trust. In particular, the Fund deals with issues that can be of a confidential nature. It will be difficult to determine a way for the advisory role to be juxtaposed with the process of preparing and publishing assessments based on standards. There could be an issue of conflict of interest. Another issue related to these assessments based on common standards is how the market will perceive them. This is a delicate situation that warrants substantive care to avoid misinterpretation of reports and the identification of the Fund as a rating agency.

Another important element from a country's perspective is the need to recognize that the establishment of standards presupposes the existence of an adequate institutional capacity. This means that if the right conditions are not present, an organization such as the IMF should also play a role with technical assistance. At the same time, this obviously has implications relating to the establishment and assessment of the standards. Very intimately related to these points is the need to develop participation in this process by the national authorities. This element is of central importance in developing a commitment to apply standards that might be established by a national authority. A gradual and interactive approach is necessary in this area.

In addition, a detailed assessment of the human resources necessary to carry out the development of standards is needed. The process of monitoring their application will also need to be evaluated. It might be rather costly, but, taking into account a proposed gradual approach to the subject, it might be possible to develop in-house expertise in time to carry out these efforts efficiently.

3.3. Goods and services trade

International financial stability should not be based exclusively on the search for stability of capital flows but also should seek the flow of goods and services trade. In the case of many small and medium-sized countries whose main source of foreign exchange is trade—even more so if they are single-commodity exporters or quasi-single—stability of international trade is key. Very little if any real progress will be made unless equal attention is paid to trade flows, since their disruption will have immediate repercussions on international monetary and financial stability. The work of the World Trade Organization (WTO) in terms of seeking trade stability is key to a new international order, and its relationship, coordination, and complementation with multilateral financial organizations like the IMF is obligatory in achieving world stability.

3.4. Liquidity and the lender of last resort

A central element of international financial reform is related to the need to provide sufficient and timely liquidity during crises associated with massive capital outflows. The experiences in handling economic crises over the past few years reveal that the IMF suffers from certain limitations regarding its ability to act through its own system for providing resources to contain an emergency. This is so not only because of the amount of resources involved but also because of the political consensus that the agreements require (that is, the conditionality) before disbursements begin.

A growing international concern is certainly evident regarding the need for a lender of last resort, and the possibility of creating a new agency dedicated to this function is under discussion. Nonetheless, some modifications in the legal architecture that governs the financial agencies of the Bretton Woods system (IMF and World Bank) could be established, even on a regional scale (the Inter American Development Bank, in the case of Latin America), or institutions from the various regions (the Latin American Reserve Fund, for example) could be incorporated to encourage rapid arrangement of financial packages. In these cases, and depending on the urgency, conditionality could be replaced by supervisory measures such as those used in "shadow programs," accompanied by higher interest rates.

The observation regarding conditionality is similarly linked to conceptual and theoretical problems linked with the classification of the crisis. The IMF's financial-assistance programs were formulated to provide resources during balance-of-payment crisis situations originating in excessive domestic spending. Nonetheless, we have seen that economies with stable paths in their fiscal results or, in general, with fundamentals consistent with the goal of domestic-external equilibrium, may suffer capital outflows in circumstances in which the evolution of domestic spending and financing do not suggest potential risks of changes in the exchange-rate regime. In these cases, the requirement of conditionality could slow the rescue operation, allowing the crisis to grow (contagion effect).

Of course, the figure of a lender of last resort brings with it problems of adapting the use of regulation and oversight measures to the new international financial architecture. This adaptation indicates that the prospect of immediate assistance could increase the opportunity for governments to loosen regulation and supervision of their financial systems, distorting or deliberately ignoring warning signs in exchange for short-term political objectives. Consequently, in trying to build an urgent financial assistance framework, the use of interest rates or the threat of withholding loans could discourage situations of "moral hazard" by the local authorities while the pertinent conditionality was being designed.

3.5. Unified action

All of these efforts would benefit from a more proactive, outgoing, and organized attitude by the developing countries. This effort might very well be channeled through the Group of 24 (G-24) (the Group of 24 comprises eight members each from Africa, Asia, and Latin America, currently Algeria, Argentina, Brazil, Colombia, the Democratic Republic of Congo, Cote d'Ivoire, Egypt, Ethiopia, Gabon, Ghana, Guatemala, India, Islamic Republic of Iran, Lebanon, Mexico, Nigeria, Pakistan, Peru, Phillippines, Sri Lanka, Syrian Arab Republic, Trinidad and Tobago, and Venezuela, and China as a "special invitee"), which, while reflecting the concerns of the developing countries as a whole, also recognizes the individual needs of each region or subgroup of countries. A new financial architecture that works efficiently must be built on the basis of active participation by all countries. It is not possible to assume the role of simple recipients of proposals from the industrialized countries. It is necessary to be properly organized to be able to influence decision making regarding the new international financial architecture where all the countries are equally represented and seeking the benefits of globalization. The capabilities exist. It is only necessary to put them at the service of world stability and growth, where the developing countries project themselves and express their interests in a united way.

The interaction between the Group of Seven (Canada, France, Germany, Italy, Japan, the United Kingdom, and the United States) (G-7) and G-24 to discuss subjects of mutual interest should be deepened. My country is proud of the responsibility that the G-24 granted Venezuela to promote the technical relationship with the G-7 countries. But we believe this approach should also take place at the political level. Otherwise there would not be clarity in the achievements that can be made. For this purpose, the efforts of the developing nations should be organized and not exclusive, in contrast to groups such as the Group of 15 (G-15: Algeria, Argentina, Brazil, Chile, Egypt, India, Indonesia, Jamaica, Malaysia, Maxico, Nigeria, Peru, Senegal, Venezuela, and Zimbabwe) and the Group of 22 (G-22: Argentina, Australia, Brazil, Canada, China, France, Germany, Hong Kong SAR, India, Indonesia, Italy, Japan, Korea, Malaysia, Maxico, Poland, Russia, Singapore, South Africa, Thailand, the United Kingdom, and the United States), which have served to divide developing countries rather than unite them. The idea, as we suggested within the G-24, is to form regional groups whose members are able to discuss their needs and suggest actions.

3.6. Private-sector involvement

The need to take concrete actions to involve the private sector in the resolution and prevention of crises is equally important and requires each party to assume its cost. In addition, it is necessary to study new and more effective formulas to temper the reactions of the market players, especially those that participate in security markets, all this with the goal of limiting the adverse effects on other economies. This recommendation, is also aimed at the cooperation of the private sector with the public sector, based on supporting economic reform programs that strengthen countries' credibility and on accepting proposals that minimize moral-hazard risks by distributing the cost of a crisis (bailing in).

An example of this type of proposal seems to be developing in the case of the eventual financial assistance for Ecuador. According to press information, the multilateral agency would condition its assistance on burden sharing by private investors through their "orderly financial insurance," in addition to the usual fiscal and banking reforms. In this way, the cooperative agreement between the public and private sectors would allow Ecuador to meet interest service on its Brady bonds and would limit the moral hazard that develops when countries and investors act irresponsibly, expecting the IMF to bail them out.

While private-sector involvement is needed to prevent or resolve crises, implementation will have to be handled very delicately. Even as this subject is being discussed, markets can react. This would affect the accessibility to capital by emerging and transitioning economies and, possibly, influence spreads to the detriment of already fragile economies in many of these markets and debtor countries. Although it is important to define, as quickly as possible, if and how the private sector would play a role in financial crises, it is just as important to exercise caution so that the approach that does not make matters worse.

One consideration is the element of risk assumed by an investor or creditor when participating in sovereign financing. Markets have changed considerably over the last 10 years. Before, direct banking finance through syndicated loans was the norm. Today, most of the resources come through capital markets via bond placements. This means that bond holders must be involved in restructuring, among other things, along with other public and private creditors. The use of standard clauses on sovereign bond issues might be a step in the right direction. Initiatives taken by triple-A rated sovereigns, as well as those that issue paper in their domestic markets, might be instrumental in fostering acceptability without necessarily affecting other financial characteristics related to risk of the issuers.

A collective framework for negotiations among debtors and lenders, through ad-hoc creditors committees in the case of bond placements, appears at this moment to be an alternative. The fundamental issue in a restructuring is the generation of liquidity and the elimination of insolvency. In the case of sovereigns, the basic issues are the fundamental policies that are needed to generate the proper adjustment process and thereby foster the capacity of the country to pay in the short-term and on a sustainable basis for the medium and longer term. This capacity to pay centers in the strengthening of the fiscal accounts, as well as the external sector.

Although one must recognize significant efforts that have already begun to monitor private debts—particularly regarding short-term private debt—the design of private contingent credit lines, improvements in debt assessment, and management in many countries (through Article IV Consultations, as well as the World Bank) contribute to this process.

For debtors, these issues are of great concern because they can help to minimize the difficulty of restructuring at a time of crises. In most, if not all cases, when crises arise, private funds leave debtor countries at a time when those funds are most needed. They are usually difficult to determine on a short-term basis, but they have benefited from and enjoyed the good times. Maintaining certain levels of financing throughout the resolution of a crises can certainly speed up the recovery time when coupled with strengthening fundamentals. Another aspect is the significant role that can be played in avoiding acceleration or other legal procedures caused by default. Time is of the essence for analyzing the situation, determining a course of action, and ensuring that creditor countries go down the right path.

Efforts will be effective only if all parts are represented and proposals and contributions are considered seriously. In this regard, developing countries have experience in dealing with difficulties and know well the specific implications and constraints of their economies, especially regarding institutional capacities and the structure and development of their markets. Efforts to understand positions of creditors, debtors, and multilateral organizations have to be placed in the center of all discussions if we really want to prevent future crises effectively. This will give the discussions a sense of practicality, always needed to be successful. In this regard, the private sector, as one of the players, is called to open its spectrum in terms of how to benefit from international stability rather than only to smooth out the specific transactional relationship with their creditors.

3.7.   Other contingency measures

Regarding sovereign initiatives, some countries that were directly affected by these crises and others that could potentially have their economic stability compromised by the occurrence of new financial crises have adopted some contingency measures. Such is the case in Argentina with the Contingent Lines of Credit established in December 1996 with 14 private banks for $6.2 billion in government bonds, denominated in dollars and up to $500 million in Argentine mortgage bills also dollar-denominated. The goal of these credit lines is to provide emergency liquidity as an alternative to the lender-of-last-resort function played by the traditional central bank.

In Mexico's case, in response to the 1994 and 1995 crisis and to the uncertainty provoked by the lack of information transparency on investors, the Mexican authorities established an Office of Relations with the Investment Community. In 1996, this office began to publish quarterly statistical reports for the investment community, apart from teleconferences with analysts and investors linked to the preparation of these reports. These efforts have helped market participants to differentiate Mexico from other Latin American countries, minimizing the contagion effect on Mexico.

Another example that can be cited, in this case referring to Venezuela, is the creation of a Macroeconomic Stabilization Fund, whose objective is to decrease the volatility of public expenditure associated with oil exports.

4.   The Venezuelan case

The proposals for reforming the international financial architecture in the face of challenges posed by globalization and the prospect of crises spreading through contagion are oriented along several lines. All of them, however, share the common element of advocating sound domestic policies to help each country cope with turbulence.

In Venezuela's case, after 40 years of protectionist policies and the predominance of all types of controls and regulations of its principal markets, we began a program of opening its economy in the 1990s. This program continues to this day.

To a great extent, the result of this effort in economic matters has been the shield with which the country has protected itself from the effects of the crisis in Southeast Asia in 1997, in Russia in 1998, and in Brazil in 1999.

The Venezuelan experience in this last international crisis suggests three courses for domestic policies:

* Maintain fiscal and monetary discipline. It is important to honor announced commitments without wavering.
* To the extent possible, avoid subjecting the economy to large swings in fiscal spending fed by foreign-sourced revenues. The establishment of a stabilization fund for a county's mayor commodity appears advisable for this purpose.
* Isolate financial institutions from a dependence on external liabilities, which can amplify the contagion's effect on the domestic economy. At the same time, maintain the quality of financial institutions' operations.

These three recommendations relate to minimizing or avoiding negative externalities for private economic agents—that is, the effects of the contagion. Once the macroeconomy has been defended against these adverse effects coming from the rest of the world, on which private economic agents exert no control, responsibility for their performance rests on each and every one of them. In other words, since a crisis in developing countries tends to affect all resident business and financial institutions, the problem to address is the impulse to infect the aggregate economy. In industrialized countries, the crises are usually restricted to individual institutions or industries (such as the savings and loan banks in the United States) and not the entire economy.

In any case, once each country should make its contribution—perhaps through policies such as the ones suggested here or some other recommendation tailored to the particularities of each economy—we should remind ourselves that international instability originates in systemic problems of a global nature, meaning that the solution must also be global.

5. Conclusion

Developing countries are faced with the challenge of maintaining and deepening their structural reform efforts and finding appropriate economic policies combined with political stability and the search for basic social equilibrium. Developed countries, meanwhile, are called to foster a stable environment and to stimulate trade and financial flows toward the centers of development.

This is possible only if the international community as a whole works jointly, understanding that the globalization process should benefit all and not just a few. The idea should be to maximize earnings and minimize the costs for all involved parties. Otherwise, the world's economic evolution could lead to stages of undesired—and to a large degree already rare—protectionism. This could happen if becomes widely believed that the process of globalization could lead to much greater costs than benefits, with the risks of economic isolation that could arise from these decisions.

The previous observation was clearly stated by Michel Camdessus, managing director of the International Monetary Fund, when he said that international monetary and financial stability are a "global public good." If the international monetary and financial system does not work well, we all suffer. But if it works properly, we will all have an opportunity to benefit.

Open economies review **11:S1** 195–203 (2000)

Some Challenges for Reformers and Architects

ALEXANDER K. SWOBODA
Senior Policy Advisor, International Monetary Fund, Washington, DC

Keywords: exchange-rate regime, economic policy, misalignment, international monetary system, new architecture

JEL Classification Numbers: F32, F33, F34

Abstract

In these brief concluding remarks, I confine myself to a few reflections on some of the themes that have been broached today, without much reference to individual authors or comments, as it would be impossible to summarize everything that has been said at this conference about the new architecture of the international monetary system.

Introduction

By way of introduction, a few words about use of the term *architecture* in the present context is relevant. It is an unfortunate usage that inappropriately glorifies what is certainly not the deliberate design of a brand-new system. I suspect that the term was borrowed from the security field where, after the end of the cold war, one talked about a new security architecture for Europe and the world. The transplant to international finance is not a happy one. One does not design a new architecture of the international monetary and financial system from scratch, nor does one strengthen an architecture. One can look at the architecture, one can admire it as I would in this building and in Florence, and one can compare it to one's ideal. What we can do is some plumbing and at most some remodeling of our existing financial building. Although it is important that academics and even policy makers should try to delineate and be guided by a vision of the features they would ideally like the system to possess, to think that you can design a new international monetary system *ex nihilo* is naive. Historically, even Bretton Woods was not quite an exception even if it was a heroic effort. After all, Bretton Woods did build on an existing system, and the system as it was envisaged by its founders started to function only after the return of the major currencies to convertibility in 1958 (and then not quite in the way in which it was planned).

One implication is that we should not have the illusion that we can build a crisis-proof system. And even if we could, we wouldn't want to have it: the Soviet

Union to some extent built for many years a crisis-proof economic system, and I do not think it is the kind of system we would wish on ourselves. The best thing we can do is to try and lessen the probability of crises and especially lessen their costs when they do occur.

With these semantic remarks out of the way, I would like to comments on four issues: What is new about the system and its architecture? What challenges does the new world economy raise? What are the implications for the system and its future? What, more specifically, are the implications for the IMF?

1. What is new and not so new?

When considering the new architecture of the international system, it is worth asking, What is new, and, just as important, is it really new? The first item on everybody's list of novelties is capital mobility and the international integration of capital markets. There are two remarks I would like to make in this context. First, the recent increase in capital mobility and the problems this has created are often attributed to deliberate, almost exogenous deregulation of financial markets in both advanced- and emerging-market economies. While deregulation certainly has had an important role to play, the basic force driving capital-market integration has been technology. The revolution in information technology and in telecommunications has resulted in a dramatic fall in transactions costs and in the cost of financial innovation, simultaneously eroding the effectiveness of regulation and increasing its welfare and competitive costs to countries attempting to resist the trend through a tightening of controls. Thus, the deregulation has been as much, and probably more, a response to capital-market integration as a cause of increased capital mobility. In many instances, the deregulation represents an attempt to reregulate the system in the generic sense of that expression. Second, while it is true that the degree of capital-market integration has been increasing steadily since the end of World War II, by some measures we are only now reaching the level of integration we had at the end of ninetienth century and the beginning of the twentieth century. And we should not forget that problems with capital flows and the challenges they pose to inconsistent macroeconomic policies are nothing new. After all, if the Bretton Woods system broke down between 1971 and 1973, it was in part because the policies of the European region and Japan (or more precisely of the surplus countries, on the one hand, and of the major deficit country, the United States, on the other hand) were inconsistent with the maintenance of major parities. Their inconsistency was revealed in 1971 by massive capital outflows from the United States.

One feature of financial-market integration is certainly new, at least in a post–World War II perspective. This is that the so-called emerging market and transition economies have been, and are, increasingly drawn not only into world markets for goods and services but also, for the past 10 years or so, into increasingly globalized capital markets. The concomitant financial opening of previously relatively closed economies raises major issues that are at the core of the debates of this conference. One is that private capital flows have come to play the major role in the financing and adjustment of the current account of an increasing number of developing countries. The boom-bust character of capital flows is related to this development and is one of the main issues that the efforts at strengthening the international monetary system are attempting to address.

I mention only two further, and related, fundamental changes in the international system here. The first is the creation of the euro; the second is the end of the cold war. The euro is to some extent a reflection of the change in the political and security system from a bipolar one to a more complex relationship between a superpower and a number of major powers. In the economic sphere, the euro is the manifestation of the erosion of the hegemony of the United States and of the dollar. Although the dollar does remain the dominant currency, its role is now being challenged.

2. What challenges for economic policy?

This new international monetary and financial system, together with the spate of crises it experienced in the 1990s, raises a number of challenges for would-be architects and reformers. Let me comment briefly on these challenges, the first two of which have been at the center of the debate here and elsewhere.

The first issue is the *exchange-rate regime*. One of the questions raised here is the likelihood that we will have continued volatility and misalignments between major currencies: the U.S. dollar, the Japanese yen, until recently the German mark, and now the euro. My answer, and I would guess that of most people, is that we are quite likely to continue to see the type of volatility we have seen in the past 20 years or so. With colleagues at the International Monetary Fund (IMF) we have looked at the volatility of major currencies over the period 1978 to 1998, including that of a synthetic euro. What one finds is that there is no particular trend in the volatility, whether monthly or quarterly, of exchange rates over that period. That is, if one divides the period into equal halves, thirds, quarters, or fifths, one cannot find a significant difference in the variance over time of monthly or quarterly changes in the exchange rates of (among others) the dollar, the yen, the mark, or the euro. You can identify periods that are less volatile and periods that exhibit more volatility, but if you take periods of arbitrary length, you cannot find significant differences.

A second concern is of misalignments of the exchange rates of major currencies. This is a more difficult matter as not all of us would agree all the time on whether some exchange rate is misaligned or not. For instance, Dominick Salvatore has referred to the misalignment of the yen, relative to the dollar, in the past year and a half. I am not sure I would call this a misalignment; I would probably call it volatility and might add that it was excessive.

This brings us to the question of whether we do something about it and if we could whether we would want to. The answer to the first question is that, yes, we could do something about it: we could "just" fix the exchange rate between the euro, the dollar, and the yen. But we also have to realize that the consequences are that at least two of the three central banks would become subservient to the third. I don't think any of them is likely to accept that, certainly not the European Central Bank and certainly not the Federal Reserve Board. It could be argued that there is a stronger case for the Japanese to peg to the dollar or to a basket composed of the dollar and the euro, as the yen exhibits the strongest volatility of the three major currencies.

Even if strictly fixed exchange rates between the dollar, the euro, and the yen are ruled out, one may still try to implement a more modest scheme, such as target zones among these currencies. I don't think target zones are either workable or a good idea. Basically, if you really want to go that route, you might just as well have a pegging arrangement with a well-defined band with clear rules that are less demanding of discretionary policy coordination.

This does not mean that we should not worry at all about misalignments. The question is, Can we and should we do something about them? My answer is this: if we can identify and do something to moderate the worst misalignments, we should. The first issue is identifying them; the second, deciding what to do. I do believe that some of the work that the Fund has done on trying to identify discrepancies between a particular concept of a long-run equilibrium exchange rate and its current value today constitutes a promising approach to designing a warning system signaling that there is, or may be, something wrong. This allows you to start discussing what could be wrong. Identification of a potential large misalignment and discussion of possible corrective measures would properly take place within the IMF surveillance process and could give rise to informal concertations among the Group of Three (G-3) (Germany, Japan, and the United States). Very occasionally, that might call for intervention to send the signal to the market that it is going on the wrong bubble if one is really convinced that there is a bubble. This is as far as I would go at this stage. If you want to go further, you would have to go much further in terms of coordination and rules, and I don't see the political will for that today. Attempting intermediate solutions such as target zones would, in my opinion, be counterproductive and lead to outcomes that are worse than the problem they pretend to correct.

So much for the exchange-rate regime between the three major currencies. What about the exchange-rate regime for other currencies?

The new conventional wisdom has it that there are only two exchange-rate regimes that can work: strictly fixed rates (very hard pegs of the currency board or monetary union variety, if you wish) or pure floats. I happen to be one of the early contributors to that view in the sense that both singly and with my colleague Hans Genberg I have argued since at least the middle 1980s that capital mobility means that you absolutely must run macroeconomic policy, and more specifically monetary policy, in a way consistent with the exchange-rate regime you choose and that fixed but adjustable pegs are an unsustainable oxymoron. Either you say "we fix," and you take the appropriate measures (and that means your monetary policy becomes totally devoted to the maintenance of the peg you've chosen and, hence, on the monetary policy of the country or zone that you are pegging to), or you run an independent monetary policy and then you have to let the exchange-rate float. You cannot reach two targets (say, the exchange rate and the domestic interest rate) with the same instrument. The argument should, however, not be pushed too far as there has recently been a tendency to do. For instance, it does not imply that any intermediate regime cannot work and cannot serve a useful purpose; there are intermediate regimes that are not internally inconsistent. Thus, fixed rates or active, gradually decreasing, crawling pegs have played a very useful role in stabilizing from high inflation. In addition, there is scope for a number of countries that are not (yet) well integrated into capital markets to have a rather active exchange-rate policy. There is also much sense for smaller countries with a dominating trading and financial partner to peg their currency to that partner's currency. In short, although one has witnessed, and probably will increasingly witness, a move toward the extremes of the exchange-rate regime spectrum, this does not mean that two simple extreme sizes fit all.

Those emerging-market economies that are becoming more and more closely integrated in world capital markets will be pushed toward the extremes of rigid pegs or substantial flexibility in their exchange rate. For those that do move to increased flexibility, three issues are worth singling out here. First, the anchor that has been provided by the fixed exchange rate will have to be replaced by something else—inflation targeting, for instance. There should be no illusion that this is an easy task, especially where the institutional framework for carrying out monetary policy is not well developed. Second, such countries will not be able to afford the luxury of exercising the same degree of benign neglect toward their exchange rate as the largest advanced countries. With their foreign (and in some instances a substantial part of their domestic) transactions and their balance sheets in good part denominated in foreign currency, the exchange rate is too important a variable for them not to let its trend influence monetary policy or to try to moderate its volatility when it becomes excessive. Third, however, if they are going to have what is basically a more flexible exchange-rate regime, they should let the exchange rate actually fluctuate. Not letting the rate fluctuate is tantamount to giving implicit guarantees, creating moral hazard and problems that are well known from recent crises. Moreover, if they don't let the exchange rate fluctuate, the institutions needed for a well functioning foreign-exchange market will not develop.

The second challenge to would-be architects is the *boom-bust character of capital flows to developing countries*. Bob Aliber told us that these are not novelties—and he is absolutely correct. He also drew our attention that some of the build-ups of capital flows and abrupt reversals have occurred among advanced countries, the case of the United States in the 1980s being the prominent recent example. Of course, as he recognizes, one of the problems in the two major postwar episodes of capital flows from the industrial countries to the developing countries—one leading up to the Mexican payment crisis in 1982 and the other to the Asian crisis in 1977—is that here we have countries whose international business and part of their domestic business is denominated mainly in foreign currencies. This makes it much harder for the emerging-market economies subject to capital-flow reversals to deal with them. This, incidentally, may be the silver lining in the cloud that is overhanging the United States. After all, if you look at what the position of the United States is in today, if there is a hard landing, it bears some similarity to that of, say, Mexico, except that its foreign debt is denominated in its own currency. I will come back briefly to the volatility of capital flows when I address measures currently being taken.

At a more basic level, the challenges we face today are really the result of *two related fundamental challenges*. The first is to reconcile the freedom of markets with the stability of the financial and monetary system. The second, and here my wording is almost the same as that used by Michele Fratianni, is to reconcile the globalization of markets with the fragmentation of policies made at a national level. These are the two challenges that have driven, or should be driving, the agenda for strengthening the international monetary and financial system.

3.   The agenda for reform

The search to achieve stability of markets and to moderate the boom-bust character of capital flows have dominated the architecture agenda and have resulted in the recommendations and policies that were summarized by Fabrizio Saccomanni. The first item on the agenda has been the improvement of *transparency and information* (and I think we all agree that it is a good idea), even though if information is costly, less than an infinite amount of information should be provided. We have, however, probably not reached the level at which the costs outweigh the benefits. But we must remind ourselves that what is important is not only to have transparency in information but also to use the information properly. For instance, going back to the Thai crisis, a great deal of information about impending trouble was available. It was not just the IMF that was worried and sending staff to Bangkok to argue with the Bank of Thailand and the authorities. If you read some of the brokers' reports on the emerging markets, they were quite alarming about what was happening in Thailand from the late summer of 1996. Then why was the information not used to moderate capital inflows earlier? I don't believe it was moral hazard created by international financial institutions but a set of perverse incentives in both borrowing and lending countries and a bubble mentality.

The second point on the architecture agenda is *strengthening financial systems*. The difficult question is how to get countries to actually strengthen their financial systems. This is where the standards that Saccomanni mentioned come in. If you can design good, generally accepted, standards and codes of conduct, markets could be relied on to some extent to provide incentives for strengthening financial systems by rewarding those countries that adhere to those agreed and monitored standards and codes of conduct.

There is, third, *supervision and regulation* of financial systems—and here David T. Llewellyn had some very interesting things to say. As in the case of exchange-rate regimes, there are two polar cases of regulatory regimes. The first is one of universal caveat emptor. You don't regulate at all, but you don't provide any safety net either, except possibly for some lender-of-last-resort functions for central banks. You trust markets to discipline lenders and borrowers. Although that system system's logical consistency lends it intellectual appeal and could in principle work, it would still be subject to occasional crises and would experience some problems familiar from the free-banking era. These would rapidly lead to state intervention. In other words, such a system is not believable or politically realistic in a world that believes in too big to fail. Agents would soon believe that implicit guarantees will be granted, and moral hazard could well be generated on a grand scale.

On the other side of the spectrum, you could have a tightly and fully regulated system. But such a system would buy stability at the expense of efficiency as it would stifle innovation and, unless universally adopted, would tend to be done by international competition in lax regulation. The question therefore is, Where can you reasonably go in between these two extremes? And that is where I think the emphasis that David put on thinking in terms of complete regulatory regimes, of the tradeoffs that are involved between the various components of such a regime, and of the importance of finding incentive compatible regulation or regulatory regimes is precisely on the mark. Perhaps we should have Jeffrey Shafer talk to the International Financial Stability Forum to tell them to concentrate on one or two important reforms and, with Llewellyn as an advisor, we may make some progress by concentrating on a few crucial features of regulatory regimes.

Involving the private sector in the prevention and resolution of financial crises is the last item on the official reform agenda. *Involving the private sector* is another detestable buzz word—as if the private sector was not involved. Bailing in rather than bailing out the private sector is a popular image. The only trouble with it is that nobody quite knows what it means or, at least, it means so many different things to different people that it is not terribly useful. That being said, there are two aspects of that particular debate that may be worth mentioning here. First, the basic purpose is to try to avoid the rush for the exit typical of a crisis and the sharp capital-flow reversals that have proved so costly of output in recent crisis episodes. This is one area where progress is likely to be slow and involve a series of measures such as the removal of distortions that bias capital inflows toward the short term or toward unbalanced foreign-currency positions rather than some dramatic measures as internationally mandated standstills or stays. Second, it should be made clear that the introduction of measures to reduce the cost of default by encouraging better workout procedures when restructuring is unavoidable are not a way of imposing a penalty on lenders but a way of reducing the cost of such workouts for both lenders and borrowers. Thus the introduction of collective-action clauses into bond contracts and the creation of debtor-creditor committees is to be seen as a way of improving the efficiency of the international financial system and not as a measure to force burden sharing on the private sector. What is clear, however, is that there must be some way in which you can avoid having the international community or the IMF systematically having to put together very large packages of emergency assistance whenever a crisis occurs.

4. The role of the IMF

Let me conclude with a few remarks about the role of the IMF. Bob Aliber asked the question Has the IMF lost its way? And his answer was yes, it has lost its way. I would argue that it has not quite lost its way. True, the road ahead is a little bit fuzzy, and the Fund is searching for a new way. In this respect, a number of recent proposals on the IMF merit consideration.

A first important question concerns the governance of the Fund. A recent report prepared by di Gregorio, Eichengreen, Ito, and Wyplosz (1999) for Geneva's International Center for Monetary and Banking Studies has proposed that the IMF should be more like an independent central bank, accountable to an identifiable political body rather than being governed, as it is now, through the Executive Board, where the executive directors represent their governments and their constituencies. The specific solution proposed by the Geneva group is a little bit of a pie-in-the-sky idea, but the question of how you can give the Fund a more independent voice, but with political accountability, is well worth thinking about.

Second, there is the Council on Foreign Relations proposal that, as far as IMF is concerned, has essentially two components. The first is to suggest that for its ordinary operations and programs, the IMF should enforce relatively strict access to its resources. This is one way of saying "Let's go back to regular country programs, which is an important part of the Fund's mission." This may not please Bob Aliber, who seemed to be saying that the IMF doesn't think about systemic issues and that's the only thing it should be thinking about. Part of the role of the IMF, as laid out in the first of its Articles of Agreement, is to give comfort to its member countries and help by providing temporary financing of payment imbalances to enable adjustment to take place without severe consequences for the country and untoward repercussions on other members of the system. I think this remains a very important role of the Fund. In that context, I would agree with many commentators that Fund conditionality should not go into too great structural and microeconomic detail but that it cannot avoid dealing with the strength of the financial system of countries. The state of the financial system is too intimately tied with that of the economy and with the impact of macroeconomic policies be left outside of the IMF's mandate.

I would, however, personally fully agree that the IMF should not become a long-term lending agency and should not venture into a number of fields where it has no comparative advantage.

The second part of the Council on Foreign Relations' recommendation is that the IMF should set up a large emergency fund, which would be drawn on only in situations of systemic crises and contagion and only in such circumstances. To me, this is again pie in the sky at least for the near future and for two reasons at least. First, I do not see evidence of the political will or willingness to commit the very large sums of money that would be required. Second, distinguishing between what is a systemic crisis and what is not is extremely difficult to do ex ante, just as it is difficult to distinguish between a liquidity and a solvency crisis. That means that you cannot expect rescue packages for individual large countries to remain small when a crisis is deemed to be local rather than systemic—for there will always be those that argue that the crisis threatens the system. This raises severe moral-hazard problems and runs the risk of biasing capital flows toward the large "systemically important" and hence too-large-to-fail countries.

A last point on the IMF. As I have emphasized earlier, one of the fundamental challenges of the day is to reconcile the globalization of markets with the fragmentation of policies and politics made at the national level. This is one reason why we do need international financial institutions. If we didn't have them, we should invent them. They do have more than ever a useful, if changing, role to play.

Reference

Gregorio, José de, Barry Eichengreen, Takatoshi Ito, and Charles Wyplosz (1999) "An independent and Accountable IMF." Geneva Reports on the World Economy 1 (International Center for Monetary and Banking Studies).

Open economies review **11:S1** 205–234 (2000)

New Financial Architectures and Legal Infrastructures: Toward a Corrected and Compensated International Monetary System

ALBERTO PREDIERI
University "La Sapienza," Rome

Keywords: nonsystem, polyarchic systems, financial architecture, legal infrastructure

JEL Classification Number: K33

Abstract

The international monetary system features a powerful subsystem of nations with an organized polyarchic economy—in other words, a market economy adjusted and balanced by government authorities to protect the market against forces operating within it but failing to abide by the rules (as in the defense of fair competition), in which excessive asymmetry runs the risk of toppling the system. The central bank is the body guaranteeing both stability and the system. However, globalization prevents the central banks from controlling the massive flows of derivatives. In the absence of a supranational authority, the only remedy realistically feasible today lies in the network of informal agreements among the leading economic powers—the G-7, G-8, and G-20 countries. These countries, on the one hand, intervene on a case-by-case (or crisis-by-crisis) basis and, on the other, strive to bring chaotic corrective and compensatory measures into a market dominated by "turbocapitalism" to ward off future crises. Their actions thus strengthen legal infrastructures and the information flows that ensure transparency and involve financially sound nations, weak nations, international organizations, assorted classes of operators, and major private institutions.

Introduction

I am indebted to David Llewellyn's article (this volume) for the reference to infrastructure (formerly referable to Babylon or to Adam Smith and to Immanuel Kant) (Kant, 1798), whether as a metaphor or a widening of the field of semantics, from which I have taken my cue since I am a strong upholder of the theory that it is the nation's duty to supply infrastructures. By this I mean that combination of capital goods (in other words, results that can be and are used from a previously accomplished work) (Braudel, 1985, p. 52) that are not used directly in the productive system but that provide a series of services to producers of goods and services as well as to consumers.[1] Such infrastructures, with respect to the market and the production system, bear positive externalities (for instance, lighthouses, beacons, roads, and so forth) enjoyed by those who do not take part in the production or distribution of such goods and reduce negative externalities. These services are considered indispensable for the functioning of the economic system in a specific historical moment. The droughts and floods that the monarchies of waterworks (Wittfogel, 1957) had to face in a world that had only just attained the agriculture of the higher neolithic age required infrastructural remedies in defense of socioeconomic aggregates, just as in this day and age monetary and bank crises require them in defense of the *politeia* of an organized polyarchic economy in its version of financial capitalism.

The father of economics identified an invisible hand but also the insuppressible function of a nation to vouch for property and to produce regulations that allow various aspects of society to prosper—trading, the distribution of work, to politics, public allocations, national decision making and sovereignty, ethics, and justice (Eschilo, verse 604). Smith undertakes the building of infrastructures as his third task, which, after defense and internal safeguard against unfairness and oppression, he assigns to the nation (Smith, 1776, bk. 5, ch. 1; Hume, 1995). "The third and last duty of a sovereign is to create and uphold those public institutions and public works which—while seeming to be of great advantage to the whole of society—are of such a nature whereby the profit could never repay the expenses to any individual or to a small number of individuals, and that consequently can never be borne by a single individual or a small group of individuals." The use of the metaphor seems appropriate if we put together the necessity of providing infrastructures with the opinions of Adam Smith, who asked for government intervention to avoid altering the optimum proportion between paper money and full gold standard circulation. Furthermore, he thought that the nation should establish the maximum interest rate to prevent an overly high rate from causing that the largest part of the money loaned should go (Smith, bk. 2, ch. 4) "to squanderers and speculators who would be the only ones willing to pay it. Cautious persons who are willing to give for the use of money no more than a part of what they will presumably obtain from its use would not venture into competition. A large part of the nation's capital would thus be removed from the hands of those who would presumably use it in a profitable and advantageous way, and would fall into the hands of those who would probably waste it or destroy it." Adam Smith also stressed that the speedy growth of the wealth of nations in the vital sector of agriculture was due more to the establishment and the contract system and less to the abundance and fertility of the land.[2]

1.　The architecture and the system

In our first conference, last year, there was much discussion of Professor. Hamada's (1999, *Open Economics Review* 9 (Supplement 1):417–445) assertion about the nonsystem in his paper on "The Choice of International Monetary Regimes in a Context of Repeated Games." Robert Triffin (1986) defined the nonsystem as "maze," "disorder," or, more blatantly, scandal. A different opinion is expressed by Dominick Salvatore (1992, esp. p. 20), as well as the Task

Force created by the U.S. Council of Foreign Relations, mentioned by Michele Fratianni (this volume), which deals with reform of the international financial system (Institute for International Economics, 1999). Salvatore (to remain among the participants in our proceedings) describes a monetary system's operation and underlines its problems, such as rules, habits, instruments, and organization by which international payments are made distinguishing the systems according to interest rates, alternatively according to the different forms whereby international reserve activities are held.

I do not intend to enter into a discussion of Hamada's political economy ideas or of tactics theory (Gilpin, 1987). I merely repeat the measured words of the governor of the Bank of Italy, Antonio Fazio (1998, p. 5): "the system is not governed, it has no anchor." For those who don't deny the existence of the system, there is a subsystem in the system (according to Salvatore) in the architecture of the markets and practices used by governments, firms, and individuals when performing economic and financial activities according to the IMF definition. This definition is in part the object of international agreements and in part the object of the World Trade Organization (WTO) expectations. It appears held together by a combination of homogeneous principles whose consolidation is somehow guaranteed by the procedures of the organizations for conflict resolution (Mengozzi, 1999, p. 3).[3]

At this point conceptual and semantic arguments come out. Fabrizio Saccomanni (this volume) at our meeting said that the "international monetary system (IMS) is a macroeconomic concept that encompasses the foreign-exchange regulations, the capital movement system, all 'the rules of the game' for the adjustment of international payment imbalances. The international financial architecture (IFA) is, in contrast, a microeconomic concept and should not be considered synonymous with the IMS. The IFA is one element of the IMS" (Saccomanni, this volume). Operators of this system work with their subsystems, which are, in the European and Western case, reconnectable to the type of economy of a market heterocorrected by the nation by means of the subsystem or instrument of the central bank. But subsystems aren't homogeneous to the system, which knows a market economy that has only clues of heterocorrection and heterocompensation and in which monetary movements can't be known for what concerns derivatives.

The great distinction is the role that the central bank could play in its function as a decision-making body guaranteeing price stability directly and indirectly according to the law books of economics.

The international financial architecture is an element of the system. A game of reciprocal interference opens up, and how it is carried out can improve the functioning of architectural infrastructures.

2. The market as a system

In polyarchic economies, the objective is to increase competition, decrease imperfections, forbid dangerous businesses, and reduce externalities. They must be heterocompensated by public resources to reduce differences that are prejudicial for coexistence and to increase the excessively low incomes of certain subjects who are at a disadvantage due to external diseconomy or factual situations, with an often long-lasting effect. The market is the means of establishing prices, but government allocation, gifts, and self-production are elements of the nation's economy in its corrective and compensating functions. The market is in the system, but it isn't the whole system. Society needs to look for economic and social efficiency, which the market can ensure when it is a matter of producing and distributing goods, but the market doesn't go any further.

If the market is chaotic action that is in part balanced by the market itself with its stability and creativity, then by passing from chaos to the constitutive order of a new order in times of failure and crisis *ex post* it is balanced by the nation, with the arrangement of the structures necessary for setting down rules and applying them, to heal crises and try to avoid them.

Compensation works in society to modify diseconomic or distorting market results, most of the time by taking measures *after* the market. Instead, correction works *in* the market within its procedures—in particular the procedure for establishing prices. As we have often repeated, the market is regulated because without heteronomously regulations and without public institutions there would be no markets or property rights,[4] just as no programming can take into consideration the market or the relations between the market and a polyarchy.

3.   Polyarchic system and stability

In polyarchic economic systems, the central bank controls fundamental economic functions. Currency is ruled by a constitutional machine that maintains stability by alternating public power and maneuvres of the market and that seems shaped by the nation and the *politeia* and therefore essential to its organization. When the government or public power is an element or factor of the economy, institutional inefficiencies are macroeconomic inefficiencies, even though the government no longer claims to be the ethical bearer of its absolute values but recognizes values, principles, and basic rights above, beyond, and preceding it and its duty to defend them and lends its instruments to their service. It becomes the only justified guarantee of the efficiency but coauthor of the inefficiency. Crises are caused by perverse synergies and by nonperceivable factors where nonetheless the lack of regulating power is always present though not always determining; Llewellyn's (this volume) contribution is pertinent.

Stability appears the aim and essential value of the *politeia* in the organized economy of the market and the nation. Goals change as we talk about the international monetary system. Historically, it can be oriented to instability, as long as it can be in a market economy. Stability is a choice: in certain times instability has been the rule and stability has been disliked because of social goals. Stability is the essential function in governing the market, which is not the replacement of strategies for market strategies but a supplementary measure, for "the modern model of unbalance considers that measures of political economics are necessary to compensate the failings of the market and rigidity in prices" (Henin, 1986, p. 20). This cannot work "if the currency on which their stability is based does not inspire trust," as John Maynard Keynes (1975, p. 7) says. He went on to say that "unemployment, precariousness of the workers' life, disappointment of legitimate hopes, sudden loss of savings, excessive earnings of certain individuals, speculators, profiteers, all of this derives mainly from monetary instability."

Stability means that the system should not itself produce a shock or enlarge the ones produced outside and combines with flexibility (the ability to operate in all circumstances and to adapt to market conditions) and resilience (the ability to continue operating faced with external shocks). The task of guaranteeing stability is a fundamental government function. Stability, though not forming a subjective right and though appearing foreign to the Bill of Rights (this is confirmed by the German constitutional court in the ruling of March 31 1998),[5] operates at the constitutional level at least for a constitutional body inserted in the plan of government, such as the central bank. Stability is embedded in the social contract, which little by little will be translated into legislation in a number of constitutional countries, following the German example. It will become a regulation for the European Union, with ultraconstitutional validity for member states. The aim is reasserted as having value in the Declaration of the Group of Seven (G-7) (Canada, France, Germany, Italy, Japan, the United Kingdom, and the United States) in October 1998 (point 20). However, there is divergence among the positions of the different leaders who have such an obligation constitutionally and those who do not: both will converge in the European Union policies of the G-7 or Group of 20 (G-20) (the G-7 and 11 major emerging economies—Argentina, Australia, Brazil, China, India, Mexico, Russia, Saudi Arabia, South Africa, Korea, and Turkey—plus two institutional representations—the European Union and the IMF/World Bank).

4. Stability in the economic system as a primary goal

The government's power and duty to maintain price stability are a basis for self-regulation and a part of economic stability (it could not be otherwise, since domestic and foreign prices are correlated to *trade off* between their stabilities). Likewise, there is a social compensation power and duty regarding the negative effects that the market, even though corrected, can cause (a firm can observe the rules of competition but still pollute) and regarding asymmetry in incomes. Stability in the framework of correction is dependent on the hypertext of the social contract (the same as compensation). *Hypertext* is used not in the computer science meaning but in the meaning of literary critics when they say that the hypertext of Joyce's *Ulysses* is the *Odyssey* or that of Italo Calvino's *Cavaliere Inesistente* is Ludovico Ariosto's *Orlando Furioso*. Consequently, as

is openly stated in the reconstruction of the system made by the German constitutional court in the ruling of October 12 1993,[6] stability becomes the regular
assumption of freedom, at least economic freedom, and therefore the primary
aim of the state or European Union metastate, binding all national and European
Union agencies.

Price stability is an objective that must be attained within the framework of
economic stability. In general, it is based on domestic and foreign price stability,
which is therefore also financial. This stability is a constitutional value for the
nations that recognize it in their constitution, which all the nation's agencies, not
merely its central bank, must uphold. In other words, it takes on a role similar
to the one held by proprietorship in nineteenth-century law, with a collective,
general guarantee managed dynamically by public authorities, in place of the
individual, subjective, static one that was recognized and protected though not
managed by public authorities. The German Model—established by ordinary
German law in 1924, taken up again after World War II, and adopted by the
European Union—has been confirmed by Article 88 of the German constitution.
It inaugurated an important innovation in Western constitutionalism. It is the
clear introduction of a new stabilizing *constitutional objective* that ensures stability and that assigns policy authority to the central bank. These policies modify
the model of the democratic state, since they entrust the task of decision making
to a subject that is outside of it. In practice, the economic constitution intro-
duces a system of balances that supports the traditional one, with a model that
assigns a function of political decision making that is important for the *politeia*
to an agency that is alien to the linear system flowing from electoral body to
parliament to government. It is independent of the system and simultaneously
is the guardian of the economic constitution.

Consequently, when there was a transfer of powers from the central bank
of the member countries of the European Union to the Central European Bank
and to the European system of central banks, stability remained the objective
of the national agencies that did not lose their powers following the transfer
of those remaining powers. Thus, for instance, the Ministry of the Treasury
continues to exercise its powers. When ministers or directors perform their
duties with greater or lesser discretion according to the circumstances or when
they participate in the G-7 meetings, they remain bound by their duty to pursue
stability.

Likewise, the Italian central bank has lost the powers of a central bank regarding stability but has maintained the powers that ensure prudential stability,
which are different from the powers pertaining to monetary policy. Prudential
supervision is structured "by different kinds of risk: credit risk, market risk, regulation risk, legal risk, and so on" (Padoa-Schioppa, 1996, p. 63). It involves a
limited discretionary power and by its subjection to the law of the controlling
body differs substantially from the discretionary power of a political decision
maker such as the Central European Bank. As with the terms *macroeconomic*
and *microeconomic*, there are coincidences and differences between these

notions and the macrolegal ones. In my opinion, the microlegal area directly involves legal situations of the subjects, which are justice, rights, and duties. Macrolegal concerns involve relations between public constitutional bodies, the dynamic reconstruction of methods and systems of checks and balances, and the coherence of the legal and constitutional systems. The new architecture is microlegal because it proposes rules related to duties undertaken in relation to intercurrent agreements.

Macrojuridical refers to the behaviors of offices, bodies, and operators that are not prejudicial or beneficial to the rights of private parties but that are guided by rules and evaluations of lawfulness and legitimacy. Therefore, macroeconomic control may largely coincide with a macrojuridical area, while microprecautionary may, similarly, coincide with the microjuridical. The macrojuridical and the microjuridical interweave with reference to the instrument used (contract), the exercise of financial activities (behavior), and the qualification of the operator (subjectivity) (Carbone, 1998). To complicate matters, we must add the complex intersection among the present functions of the state, which in the first session of our conference I tried to individualize with the words *lose, transfer, negotiate,* and *network*. These signify for our country a particular series of problems. Control was already in the hands of the central bank, but some functions (especially concerning monetary policy) were transferred to the European Union. Precautionary microstability functions were left to our central bank, maintaining a function of corporate stability.[7] In particular, the reference to transferring emphasizes other interventions suggested by the emerging new duties of the state.[8]

5. The culture of stability

Stability and the culture of stability are extremely important as elements of the social contract. They are shaped by the *politeia* system and the culture in the sense of taking on theoretical reconstructions of events. The facts about the essence of economics and cycles make up the basis on which to make decisions about directions to be taken. By interpreting facts in a way that interprets the rules of this culture, the economist must have cross-disciplinary knowledge if he is talking about systems or balance, even though his balance is not the same as that of the sociologists. Culture is also culture in a sociological sense—a general way of feeling of a particular society at a particular moment. Stability and balance become the information (and beliefs) of that fundamental and pervasive culture. Culture should be understood in its widest possible meaning. It must be taken as a guarantee of the basic regulations of freedom for the members, who need the stability that the government must provide to ensure orderly cohabitation, which is the premise for the assertion of constitutionally guaranteed rights. These rights consent the realization of the social contract hypertext that I mentioned above.

We might go as far as to state that the decisions that guarantee a firm basis for cohabitation *ne cives ad arma veniant*. The jurisdictional function guarantees stability of relations in the legal system creating them and avoids its collapse by not allowing members to take the law into their own hands. The guarantee function of price stability ensures the economic stability indispensable to the preservation of cohabitation organized by the legal system, avoiding its collapse by making the best of the market, avoiding civil war, and producing essential services such as the collective asset of price stability. For this reason the fundamental market in the *politeia* system must be corrected to the extent that if, due to its incentives, prices increase, the central bank should make corrective measures. In a market of financial capitalism, correction is operated by financial measures and not by productive measures. A mixed economy proceeds by means of the authority of the central bank and not that of public enterprise or that of the government or enterprise of the industrial nation that Galbraith wrote about (thinking of the United States, not the Italian or more generally European public enterprise). The public authority's support measures—not chance, exceptional measures, or a government becoming entrepreneur or banker out of despair—are those of a government that is constitutionally institutional in the steps it takes as expected *a priori*, whether in a supplementary or merely sanctionary form. They will make rules and use legal power to have them observed, and they will basically be the same whether dealing with the central bank or a public enterprise, keeping in mind that the central bank, to attain its objectives, operates as an enterprise in the open market with the instruments of private management, even though it is a public body operating for constitutionally provided public purposes.

6.   Globalization, international financial markets, and derivatives

The market that is without a guarantee of price stability is without control on the part of the central bank. It is opposed to the market economy model. Correction and compensation needs, which overcome the unbalances (from asymmetries), prevent development as we get into the international area. Stability correlated to an organized economy isn't related to the international monetary system. Referring to Fabrizio Saccomanni's work, it means the contrary. Stability is a constitutional duty for the European System of Central Banks (Consolidated Treaty, Article 105). The Council "manages the ECU exchange rates and according to BCE and the Commission, deliberates in qualified majority, to adopt or change the ECU central rates" (Article 111 of the Treaty). It is still a Council task to formulate "the general principles of exchange policy." In other words, community law pursues its own price-stability policy, which is a limitation of its discretion. If an instability system is preferred, traumatic crises are not necessarily desired. Diversity between the international and domestic areas corresponds to different countries' policy management. In the domestic area there is discretion bearishness and a prudential monitoring, while in the international side the need for a wide discretion is strong.

The contrast of the two models can be horizontal—between countries with the monetary- and financial-market model corrected by the central bank and countries that do not follow it. Or it can be vertical—between areas where hete-rocorrection is operated and those where it is not. This is a symptom, one might say, of a system that waives the logic of any top level and is left with a network logic that "has neither head nor tail, with a plurality of connections that increase possible interaction among the network components. There is no central exec-utive authority controlling the system from the top" (Pagels, 1989, p. 50). That might have the functions of differential correction and compensation, which the nation can exercise in an organized polyarchic economy. Besides the state and the metastate, there is only the archipelago—the world of interplay. The abili-ties and deficiencies of systems and operators in evaluating the consequences of actions accurately and far-sightedly are sifted with different values—from defending one's property to achieving power. That's the world of international economic relations, opposed to the organized polyarchic economy working for stability.

In this chaotic and faulty international system, globalization did not seem to extend to a planetary level. The metaphor of market principles would have led globalization to request "more extensive liberalization in order to increase the productivity of a world market which is put into action by competition and not exploited and made instrumental by government control" so as to "gradually reduce the control of the perverse logic of friend-enemy ... substituting it rather with emulation and with peaceable cooperation" (Zanfarino, 1998, p. 21).[9] It has made its appearance as a different entity—neither command nor market. This new form of hypercapitalism (Colcker, 1998) or of turbocapitalism (Luttwak, 1998) does not juxtapose one against the other because globalization refuses traditional juxtaposition by innovating and networking everything. A number of times, particularly in ancient times, nations have divided the world into "us" and "them"—an evil chaos or open space for conquest. From the *Two Cities* by St. Augustine one route would lead us to the *aut aut* of the house of Islam[10] and the territory of war (or also, with a different formula, the territory of justice and that of impiety).

Globalization, in unifying the world, interiorizes chaos, just as order is inside and is not outside. Globalization, neither market nor command (and also neither *status quo* nor reform), seems like a new route that up to now has been unknown in history. Although theorized by some people as optimum spontaneous self-regulation, emphatic demonstrations preach the omnipotence of the laws of the market, refusing corrections by the state (the euro has side-stepped a central bank system by rebelling against Regulation Q). Crises and protests continue to require homogenizing the two worlds, and this is the ordinary mark of a market that exercises differentiated correction and compensation by a higher power. In the present, the country's aim is different from the past. Now the aim is losing power, transferring power, negotiating new power aggregations, and building flexible network systems. As we look for ways to carry out our aim in the international markets, we encounter difficulties.

7. Derivatives, regulation, and risks

The market that the central banks correct has been deeply altered by the explosion of derivatives—"those contracts whose value derives from the price of an
underlying financial activity, or rather from the value of the corresponding financial indicators: stock market index, interest rate, exchange" (Caputo Nassetti,
1997). These include futures (standardized future contracts), forwards, options,
interest-rate swaps, currency swaps,[11] and other instruments that favor greater
availability of funds in financial markets, development of trade, coverage of a
position, or undertaking risks with the objective of making a profit (Carbone,
this volume). These are the increasingly sophisticated instruments of financial
engineering. These instruments, historically, are built on contract models that
normally are used in practice but whose most significant characteristic is that
they go beyond specific national regulations (Carbone, this volume).[12] I omit
any mention of the private international right problems, which are increased
because of the Internet and the electronic commerce. Financial instruments
demonstrate the wide "self-governing power, of contractual reference indicators that may not necessarily fit into a specific national system, of rules and
venues for the resolution of conflicts coherently with the expectations of the
subjects who have drafted the 'contract program' of the economic operation,
and also of the deferment to national regulations selected according to their
compliance with the solutions adopted in the contractual rules and regulations
of the relationship rather than to their connections to it." Conforming to these
standards is Article 4 of Law 218/95, which is inspired to "the mandatory parameters related to the exercise of the laws in force in the so-called European
legal system; it recognizes ample operativeness of the clause derogation to the
Italian jurisdiction in all those cases dealing with controversies about available
rights and the willingness of the parties in this regard results as proven in writing', provided that the derogatory effect is related with the actual exercise of
jurisdiction on the part of the judge appointed by the parties"[12] (Carbone, this
issue, p. 236).

   These instruments make the financial system is more complete because they
divide or group the risks. The instruments are an answer, in part, to the risks
related to financial assets or loans used by dealers to create investment or
indebtedness. They partly meet an insurance requirement that is typical of a
contemporary "society of risks" whose financial markets have become the risk
bazaar and are constantly searching for financial innovation. These instruments,
however, have proven to be ineffective against chain collapses deriving from
the failures of large-scale debtors (Brazil, Mexico, Argentina, and Poland).

   The system becomes more complete because to know the price trend (thanks
to networking, also in real time) of each individual risk and each financial activity
means to possess the best information about the present economic situation on
the international level. Derivatives themselves "not only do not generate new
risks but consent (though do not ensure) a better distribution of the existing

ones. In this as in other aspects they do not belong to the sphere of gambling but to that of insurance—a field of economy and finance without which neither families nor enterprises could prosper" (Padoa Schioppa, 1996, p. 61).[13] Dealers, and especially central banks, thus operate in a market that is made more transparent but are in a position better to perceive how the market reacts to their monetary policies and therefore to correct this policy, if necessary: in these terms, the effectiveness of economic and monetary policies can be considered increased.

In the first session of our conference last year, the governor of the Bank of Italy, Antonio Fazio, in speaking about derivatives ("probably the most 'magical' financial instruments of this century, which have increased their value six times from 1990 to 1997, with a national value—the value whereby are calculated the interests exchanged among opposite parties—of about 60,000 billion dollars, and characterized by a huge 'leverage' that considerably extends the possibilities of gain or loss" (Pollio Salimbeni, 1999, p. 32) said that they are such complex instruments that it is "hard for the dealer himself to estimate the total risk to which he is exposed in particular in the event of price fluctuations in financial activities that, in size and simultaneity, differ from previous experiences" (Fazio, 1998, p. 61).

I do not intend to follow the pessimistic comment of Antonio Pollio Salimbeni (1999, p. 32), to whom "when one no longer has the feeling of risking, it means that one is approaching a crash." However, in the area of derivatives, nations have lost the ability to control the monetary basis that they once had.[14] This loss of the ability to control in the short period is relative to administrative measures taken in the previous period of gold adjustment, which left the market with the task of finding stability. Over two-thirds of the banks' activities with nonresidents have brokers as their counterparts. Interbank activity supplies the forming of international liquidity, which is not subject to the direct control of any monetary authority. With an amount of derivatives large enough to have decisive influence on prices of all financial activities, it can expand to such an extent as to cause financial and inflationary turbulence.

Savona and Maccario (1998) refer to this subject extensively in their report to this conference (Savona, Maccario, and Oldani, this volume). In the previous conference they noted a disturbing reversal: the intermediary objective of monetary policy should be the interest rate (or asset price) and not the amount of currency if instability derives from the financial system (the shock on the function of the demand for currency); the objective should be the amount of currency if instability derives from the real sector. The desirability of the asset price as a middle-term goal is not so clear, since the new financial instruments, by allowing the stabilization of payment flows and the reduction of exposure to interest-rate shocks, also influence the function of the demand for investments and the function of the demand for currency. The consequence is that the net effect on the desirability of the asset price as a middle-term goal, in turn, is not very clear. This situation, in which determining the objective is difficult, lowers the effectiveness of the monetary policy. Faced with market speculation caused by improper use of derivatives, the real effect in the short term of monetary expansion is hard to determine. The ties between currency and inflation are loosened. Otherwise, the nature and operations of financial markets are altered (Von Hagen and Fender, 1998) due to the risk connected with the unstable evolution of exchange and interest rates, subjecting business as well as financial operations to an unbearable insecurity that might slow down the flow of current transactions, which in turn has an influence on the risk market.

"Savona, Maccario and Oldani remark that "a significant step forward was made recently (1998) by the IMF Committee on Balance-of-Payment Statistics, which has introduced new rules to make the balance of payments coherent with financial innovations. The new rules state that derivatives are part of national capital resources and must be counted in the balance as financial assets and liabilities."

The "new" market might appear not as a flow within embankments (which generally follows typical patterns, even though innovation is always present) but rather as imagination, invention, and noncontrol. With wide propagation of movements with the emergence of colossal institutions of the *politeia*, such as institutional investors, "decisions depend the destination of funds estimated around 28,000 billion dollars, which is exactly the amount of a year's world product" (Pollio Salimbeni, 1999, p. 19).

"Compared to 1987 the speed of exchanges in financial activities has multiplied ten times. According to the president of the Federal Reserve, Alan Greenspan, 'the effectiveness of financial markets consists in their ability to convey errors faster than anyone might have imagined a generation ago.' Taking risks 'is a necessary condition to create wealth, but the highest grade of aversion to risk should be supported by rational evaluation on the situation of the market and not by the fear of avoiding the fire of selling'" (Pollio Salimbeni, 1999, p. 24). "The 'financialization' of the economy has made the balance on which the entire mechanism of accumulation is based more fragile. In other words, it has created the conditions to destabilize the value of money. Investments, employment levels, and revenues have become hostages of currency fluctuations and stock market turnovers. Money has become an unpredictable raw material. In the past twenty years the jolts in currency exchange rates have been so strong as to appear totally irrational. The dollar was worth 260 yen in 1985, the following year it was worth 130, in 1990 160, in 1995 80, and a few months later 100. There was nothing in the reality of economics to justify such violent movement: the United States did not suddenly become a declining power, nor as suddenly become productive" (Pollio Salimbeni, 1999, p. 20). The organized market-economy model (in which the central bank is the fundamental, establishing, constitutional organ) contrasts and clashes with the activity of hypercapitalism, which refuses it and with this refusal alternates profits in its favor and crises to its detriment.

8. Derivatives' effects on monetary policy

Control of the national or central bank system, as outlined at the beginning of the derivatives era, was composed of three types: one was microprecautionary, directed at market stability; the second was macroprecautionary, directed at market stability; and the third, macroeconomic, directed at the stability of the entire economy. These still hold even though the market has changed, and control, to a great extent, has disappeared. The first type sees new problems with the "possibility of transferring the risk to different operators from the ones where it originates (as in the cases of swaps and securitization) and the possibility of its growing concentration with a limited number of large-scale institutions to state problems of a new kind" (Padoa Schioppa, 1996, p. 62). The second includes the relationship between derivative market and underlying markets, the relationship between regulated markets and over-the-counter (OTC) markets—the regulating phase. The third assigns the possible influence of derivative circulation on monetary policy, which also assigns the regulation of monetary and financial markets in their interaction. "There is definitely an effect on the transmission mechanism of monetary impulses, since derivative markets are more liquid and relative and they influence the underlying markets rapidly altering interest-rate structure according to expiration. Other effects are identified in the possibility that, by facilitating alternative financing for enterprises—that is, direct financing—the derivatives may reduce the effectiveness of the credit channel, or in the possibility that they influence the demand for currency since they are capable of modifying the characteristics of liquidity of the other financial instruments and thus their replaceability relationship with the currency itself. The monetary policy—commented Padoa Schioppa (1996, p. 71) whom I have been broadly following—does not seem less effective due to the presence of derivatives, since the latter cause redistribution of the rate risk and not cancellation of the risk. Consequently, one could only argue that that the monetary effect retains its value, though influencing different categories of economic subjects."

Needless to say, at the macroeconomic level there can be other retroactions. The presence of derivative instruments may increase "price volatility of the underlying activities; this is a concern that is expressed by observers of financial circles, by dealers in this sector, and it is often shared by the central banks themselves" (Padoa Schioppa, 1996, p. 65).[15] However, the credit channel loses importance in actual fact. "Just as derivative products enhance replaceability between bank credit and securities, in bank assets as well as in corporate financing the credit channel tends to lose importance. For instance, the risk of an investment in securities issued by enterprises can be met, as far as the component of the market trend is concerned, by stock market futures, and, for the specific component of each individual enterprise, by the use of derivatives on the specific securities" (Padoa Schioppa, 1996, p. 69).

9. The juridical problem of international financial markets

The unified objective of nations contrasts with the diversity of the objectives of financial operators, which are private subjects aiming first of all at profit and power maximization (typical of oligopolies), of international public bodies or domestic public law bodies, and of lesser nongovernment organizations, which are bodies of uncertain and maybe temporary or changing placement. An example of this might be the Paris Club, an international organization not established by charter (Abi Saab, 1998). It is a soft organization acting as a match for soft law, located between law and not law. Thus, even an organization may, in part by law and in part not by law, produce an aura of moral suasion and of influence. It is often no less important (or even more so in some cases) than its legal production. Two centuries of central bank experience are telling.

Each one of the subjects will move, within the microlaw, with its legal instruments, keeping in mind that among the operators we have public agencies that work with private instruments in the open market, like the central banks. We have seen that the central banks are institutionally amphibious between the public and the private, as was public enterprise—or as it should have been, at least according to the founders of the Italian system. The logical consequence is that remedies always tend to move in a setting where amphibians are at home, in a continuous mix of private-law activity for public purposes and private-law activity for private purposes but with effects that are prevalently due to the dimension in the public area. Countries will move domestically with normative and precautionary acts that are binding and absolute and will move internationally with agreements and contracts that are in a position to operate fully or in part as binding and absolute acts of an international order. Acts and instruments of general, regional, or sectorial (including the highly important OMC) international organizations, some binding and others not (such as recommendations),[16] can also operate internationally—though with unequal effectiveness. They also can operate with informal agreements, which seem to be recalled on account of their difference in the Treaty on the European Union, Article 19, dealing with "mysterious category of 'formal agreements.' ... It was introduced in spite of all the criticism that had already been expressed at the time of negotiation, and forced the annexation to the Treaty of an ad hoc declaration to specify that these agreements are no more than normal international agreements" (Tizzano, 1997, p. 459).[17] National acts can develop through the rich series of instruments that the law, particularly economic law, offers to employ basic authoritative mechanisms of doing or not doing, of giving or not giving. The acts of international organizations express decisions made by a majority or by consensus.

Private persons will contract with private instruments, including frame contracts and standard contracts, whose effects actually come near to those of regulating acts. A specific example would be the Basle code of laws, which is followed not only by the contracting parties but by subjects who did not participate in the agreement and therefore are not bound by it. The defense of private persons against their counterparts in the event of default or interruption of contractual balance can be approached from several directions. In particular, when trying to select the basic essential or procedural rules (whether before a judge or arbitrator) that correspond more closely to their interests in the event of litigation, they are not exempt from conflict with their country's laws. Inquiring into the best way to enact a typical principle of international relations, even though not exclusive to this, the *rebus sic stantibus* clause guarantees fulfillment of the established balance when this is lacking due to occurrences that are not ascribable to a party. The contractual clauses are perfected. The typical distinction between long-term financing and short-term financing loses significance when in certain long-term international bonds issued by Southeast Asian countries at the end of the 1990s certain clauses were introduced that changed the bonds in the event of a crisis into short-term instruments, since the possibility of immediate reimbursement was scheduled as soon as evaluation of the country's solvency had fallen below a given level.

10. Globalization and the lack of uniformity

We know that globalization has not made the social foundation of the world homogeneous, nor has it unified an economic reality. Nations are still profoundly different, and these differences are not comparable to the ones among European countries or Western countries. There is no world community of systems, of social contracts, of hypertexts. It is not possible to imagine corrections based on a metastate of the European Union kind or of some other type. Corrections should be made not only on a world basis but with instruments that necessarily operate at this level and can be established only with cooperation, which isn't still institutionalized. This means overcoming the requirement of intergovernmental agreement on every decision and allowing the ordinary agencies of authority to make certain decisions, even important and qualifying ones. We should start preparing for change with a network of relations that are the alternative to an order that no longer exists (it hasn't been overwhelmed by external causes, as wars or revolutions, but from within). A new institutional order needs to be designed to be long-lasting and universal. A remedy cannot wait, and the return to an outline of market stability, like the one on which Bretton Woods was founded, doesn't seem possible.

The international community, in this age of globalization more than ever before, must protect itself against those inside the market that alter it and thereby increase the risks of financial crises and instability and against (Saccomanni, this volume) the superpower masters of international trade that have changed, in some instances, the structure and foundations of certain nations. In the oil-producing countries, for example, relations and social contracts are all outside of the country, between the prince and the oil companies from which the country derives huge profits but on which it depends. The new financial feudalities and the new feudal-financial nations have no boundaries. The community itself is bound in a network of mutual relations and must defend its weaker parts from the tyranny of its stronger parts. We know that the geopolitics of power preceding World War II have been substituted by geopolitics of hunger (Brunel and Bodin, 1998) and of chaos (Ramonet, 1998). We know that we are living in a world where the fortunes of the three largest private groups exceeded the gross domestic product of the 48 poorest nations (Ramonet, 1998, 1). Asymmetries are realistically evaluated interests; firm beliefs and ethics are conducive to overcoming dangerous targets.

11.   The G-7: An example of international organization

The best-known and most outstanding example of a network organization that is flexible to the point of almost being a nonorganization, with conspicuous informal real powers, is the G-7 (and soon to be G-20). The G-7 came out of that deinstitutionalization (which I already discussed) that results in economic powers increasing their power and reducing their responsibilities. It is not an international organization that can produce binding international acts or non-binding recommendations. Strictly speaking, it is not even an intergovernmental organization. The G-7 is not a collective joint subject, a decision-making body with legal effects attributable to it. The policy decisions are equal, in fact, for the individual states, but remain acts that are not attributable to one subject or even more generically to a subjective figure but are attributable as programs or self-limitations, as unilateral commitments. For instance in the G-7 document of October 1998, point 8 states: "we undertake to strive to guarantee that the private institutions of our Countries respect these principles, standards, and behavior codes," which corresponds to an obligation to act, going as far as mandatory instructions, for instance, to supervising organs of banks and financial brokers. Point 19 of the same document states: "we agree to immediately take all those measures to keep our commitments. These measures will strengthen the foundations of the international financial system and will consent to help those nations that are hit by crises to come through their difficulties." Equally binding, if not even more so, are the commitments made within the G-7 for payments in favor of the IMF or other similar institutions.

In general, it may be said that these commitments have been made simultaneously but are not conditioned to fulfillment on the part of the others (except for the application of the principle *inadimplenti non est adimplendum*). They are valid according to the regulations of one's individual legal system and justifiable according to these (for instance, in the case of Italy, by violation of the law or by excess of power), but it's not easy to imagine concrete actions. These complex relationships, with their lack of rights to stability and with the risk that the matter will become over looked, are in reality networks and not loose organizations.

We have already mentioned the need to overcome the two worlds and to succeed in expressing globalization as a heterocorrected and heterocompensated market system as requested by countless observers. With inadequate institutions and faced with a dangerous chain of crises, the retroaction was to undertake exceptional tasks of heterocorrection and heterocorrection *in desperation* on the part of those who hold the greatest power—the G-3, G-7, and G-20. At home this organization already exercises heterocorrection, and even—more or less successfully—heterocompensation and cannot avoid in its own interest using, if not the same instruments, similar ones to the ones it uses at home to maintain the system according to a hypertext, in an attempt to widen its basis, consensus, and contributions. These types of actions should be considered individually and not in a program, unless it is one for the construction or development of infrastructures, acquisition of knowledge, supervision or monitoring, control, or management of a penalty or award legal system (in the latter case awarding prizes or incentives), but they can be referred to the classifications mentioned. Therefore, the development of the IMF procedures for the enforcement of transparency or mandatory communication may be classified as heterocorrection, differentiating debtors according to the country's poverty conditions (already ventured in 1984 with the Baker plan first and later the Brady plan), which afterwards was the object of a general principle resolution at the Venice summit and later led to the resolution of September 25, 1999.

The G-7 and G-20 are not international organs. They do not use, nor can they use, binding instruments or even nonbinding instruments: if they make recommendations, these do not pertain to international law. They do not make majority decisions, even though the consensus that seems to have been used in the G-7 Venice summit consequently is the result of laborious compromise though stimulated by urgency. In point of fact, the G-7 has powers of coordination that functionally and structurally are no different, at least in tendency, from the powers that are exercised by interdepartmental committees. The G-7 cannot be assigned functions that may be typical of an individual country because the G-7 is not an international body producing mandatory decrees. Policy making is made by the appropriate agencies of the individual state (Ministry of the Treasury or similar).

Informal activity increases the risks that choices might not be put into effect due to the arising of obstacles on the part of constitutional organs, such as the parliament of the nation itself. The highly political character of international relations has caused serious conflict (for instance, with the North American congress) relative to the IMF. Camdessus, general manager of the IMF, clearly stated that 84 percent of the shareholders have consented to an increase in dues while 16 percent (including the United States) have not given. The United States, as usual, "represents the hardest nut to crack. Reaching an agreement with them is never easy, particularly on account of Congress is resistance, which has its reasons in domestic policy and not always noble objectives" (Calderoni, 1998, 3). Proposals to give operative roles to the IMF in crises, turning it into a bankruptcy court or an official receiver, have been met with the objection that in cases of insolvency it is a creditor (Holmgren, 1998, p. 283).

12. Financial crises and regulation

The succession and frequency of crises have highlighted a number of trouble-some weak points in the system, making it necessary to search for that anchor that Fazio talked about and to look for alternatives. Management is primarily oriented toward the function of *losing*, faced by the crises of the system's self-defense and the failure of the market. Therefore, there is a need for the strong intervention of the principle of subsidiariness, with the advent of *negotiating* and *networking* functions, since it is not possible to *transfer* until the time when networking and negotiating will lead to new institutions, as was the case with WTO. If monetary crises are triggered by short-term capital movements (Aliber, this volume), the bank crises and the crisis chains that influence enterprises and their clients are always and everywhere the result of a mix of economic, financial, and structural weak points. The real causes of the crisis are in any case not imputable merely to macroeconomy problems, as is customary, but rather to serious shortcomings within the banking system. In pointing out the mixed characteristics of the origins of bank crises, Llewellyn underlined the importance of a lack of standards and therefore of appropriate regulations and adequate controls.[18] The Summit in Cologne had the same position. The cru-cial point of Llewellyn's work is that a "regulated regime" must be conceived on a wider scale with respect to regulations enforced from outside on financial institutions. Regulations are only the first of six key components. The others are control, supervision (private and national), incentive structures, intervention and sanctions, market regulation, and company control.

13. A way to strengthen international financial markets

The text of the meeting of the G-7 of October 30, 1998, has been important in identifying objectives for international financial architecture reform and for het-erocorrection. The text publicly tackled a preliminary policy of infrastructures for financial crises with a bland formula that in some points (though not all) was comparable to international recommendations (in the case of the Common Mar-ket and domestic ones) (Predieri, 1992, p. 696), which are not binding, though not devoid of legal effects (Malaguti, 2000). The text of the Summit of G-7 in Cologne of June 1999 approved a report prepared by the finance ministers, titled "Strengthening of International Financial Architecture," which individual-ized the main components of strengthening the international financial system and which is auxiliary to the objective of founding a financial system "that may profit from all the benefits of global markets and capital flows, to minimize cri-sis risks, more effectively protect the weaker classes and promote international monetary stability which is an element of a stable financial system" point 20. The text made the following recommendations:

- *Broaden transparency.* The program points out the basic need to turn in-ternational markets into markets governed by transparency regarding public institutions. Examples include the standards regarding fiscal transparency in the International Monetary Fund (point 6), private institutions (particularly points 7 and 18 to 20a), self-regulation (points 7 to 20), and technical regulations. These should be linked with public institutions that create the same type of regulations.

- *Reinforce financial regulations for industrialized countries by strengthening prohibitions.* The program proposes a system that will provide supervision (point 11a), monitoring (point 14a), supervision (point 15), precautionary rules (point 20h), coordination (point 11b), general principles of the management of social policies (point 16), measures of heterocorrection (point 13), and agreements on terms of insolvency (point 14b). It would involve the private sector in the activity of selfregulation, in particular the issue of national or quasi-national bonds (point 14a), the mechanisms of financing in the event of adverse market conditions (point 14d), the management and solution of crises (point 14d), and the stability of nations and of the system in general (point 20c).
- *Strengthen macroeconomic policies and financial systems in developing markets.* The International Monetary Fund will emerge stronger, with measures that must be indicated and evaluated (point 21) and with an increase in the tasks of its several components, such as the Interim Committee. The statement does not go into detail about the latter, while the French motion spoke of it as a body that was destined to become the actual board of directors, going back to the provisions of the articles of association. Also according to the French proposal, the finance ministers of member countries representing the entire international community, including developing countries, should establish the strategic guidelines of the Fund by means of their resolutions, when voted.
- *Improve heterocorrection of the market.* This includes the prevention and management of crises with an updating of legislation affecting the microlegal area, prevention of crises facilitating shocks, innovative financial agreements (including rollover options), using clauses of joint action in domestic bonded contracts, provisions to facilitate creditors' coordination, reliable bankruptcy proceedings, strong judicial systems, predictability, and impartiality.
- *Promote social policies of etherocompensation to protect the poorest.*
- *Increase autoregulation.* This involves promoting behavior codes applicable to countries, banks, financial intermediaries, and societies that reflect official statistics of economic and financial growth, accountancy methods, society management, accounting controls, policy elaboration, and execution (Saccomanni, this volume).

The program intends to promote the conditions of a market that is capable of self-discipline, mainly through continued and systematic recourse to transparency to supply information. The program promotes requests for monitoring data and information, market self-discipline (point 14), self-management of crises (points 14a and 20d), policy coordination for the exchange mainly of information (point 11b), precautionary standards in financial institutions to establish standards on an international level and to stimulate through international cooperation (point 13) compliance with these regulations, greater strength and range of precautionary vigilance (point 20a) and market discipline (point 20b), and introduction of a system of self-controls (points 14c and 18b) as far as the International Monetary Fund is concerned. A series of measures of market *correction* accompanied by specific measures of *compensation* are designed for "minimizing the human cost of financial crises and encouraging the adoption of policies protecting the more vulnerable persons" (point 20f) and "more effectively protecting the weaker persons and promoting international monetary stability, which is an element of a stable financial system" (point 20), as well as of general heterocompensation of the system.

14. Standard principles and codes of conduct

Going into further detail, the 1998 text contained an indication of purposes (points 3 and 20) (that is, financial stability of our economies) and indicated various means to attain these purposes, involving governments, public organizations, public subjects operating in areas in which nongovernment organizations operate (such as the Club of Paris) (Holmgren, 1998). It follows that, in the event of a crisis or of crisis prevention, the response to different perverse synergies must be equally synergetic.

The G-7 program moves in anticipation of standard principles and codes of conduct that have a public origin. IMF (points 6a and 6b) has the commitment to respect nations (point 6). A code of principles on corporate governance led to the OECD. The World Bank supported general principles of conduct in social policies in the cases of crises that the World Bank will need to solve (point 16). The G-7 made a commitment that "the countries that are part of global capital markets likewise undertake to follow these codes and standards agreed on internationally" (point 9).

The program anticipated that the "IASC (International Accounting Standard Committee) would propound for early 1999 a complete range of accounting standards agreed on internationally. The International Organization of Securities Commissions (IOSCO), the International Association of Insurance Supervisors (IAIS), and the Basle Committee should complete a timely review of these standards" (point 7b). It also stated that "the appropriate committees registered with the BIS, together with new markets, national authorities, and the public and private organizations, should examine the problem of appropriate transparency and of openness standards for the private financial institutions involve in international capital flows: investment banks, hedge funds, and other institutional investors" (point 7c).

These codes and standards, the program suggested, should be followed and their enactment verified. In point 9b it added that "the International Monetary

Fund should verify the enactment of these codes and standards within the scope of regular surveillance according to Article IV; c) that the IMF should publish in a timely and systematic manner, by means of a Report on Transparency, the results of the control on the degree to which each member country meets the codes and standards of transparency and openness; d) we request that the IMF, the World Bank, the OECD, and the international regulation and supervision organizations work together to advise and, where necessary, supply assistance to the Countries in complying wit these codes."

Simultaneously, the G-7 anticipated improvement in the procedures, in particular regarding a widespread "publication of information, except in the event that this would clash with the problem of privacy" (point 18a), widening the field to the consideration "of the possibility of strengthening precautionary measures in industrial countries to encourage sensible analysis and weighing risks and benefits, including the appropriate transparency for all participants in the markets." The "strengthening of precautionary rules and of financial systems in new markets by means of the control of possible measures to increase the flexibility of financial systems and promote the adoption of international and conduct standards, for instance by maximizing market disciplines and other legal measures in an attempt to encourage the countries to adopt and verify international practices and standards" (points 20a and 20b). This improvement in adjustments was supposed to be achieved "in particular by verifying the implications arising from the activity of speculative financial organizations, including hedge funds and offshore institutions. Appropriate means should be identified to encourage offshore centres to observe the standards that have been agreed on internationally" (point 13). Here again the G-7 confirmed the commitment of acting toward having "the countries taking part in global capital markets adopt similar action" (point 13) to obtain similar action.

The G-7 also anticipated control procedures "intended to strengthen surveillance in the financial sector and for international financial institutions, working in close cooperation with international supervision and regulation organizations, to carry out surveillance of national financial sectors and their supervision and regulation systems with all the information accessible to them" (point 10). The G-7 was thereby undertaking to support the establishment of a procedure for the strengthening of surveillance in the financial sector using national and international expertise on regulation and supervision and the continuous surveillance of the Monetary Fund on member countries, according to Article IVb). To this end it would bring together the international institutions and national authorities involved in the stability of the financial sector to better coordinate their activities in the conduct and development of such policies as would add to the stability and reduce the systemic risk in the international financial system. This would allow them to exchange information about the risks of the international financial system in a more methodical way, starting from the assumption that "the opening of capital markets in newly formed economies should take place in a cautious and gradual manner if the countries are to gain benefits from integration of global economy. In particular, financial sectors and the supervision and regulation systems must be solid and adequate to deal with these risks. International financial institutions must have a constructive role in the orderly openness of capitals" (point 15). Consequently, the development of the IMF appeared necessary. This would involve a "large number of reforms to improve IMF effectiveness including transparency, to change loan policies, terms, and conditions for credits" (point 17) and the request that the IMF "develop a formal procedure for systematic evaluation, including the input form outside, on the effectiveness of its transactions, of its programs, its policies and its procedures" (point 18b). The Fund would continue its policies regarding particular surveillance conditions on a case-by-case basis (points 14b and 14c). At the same time, the commitment to require the countries that "participate in the global capital market to give their support to the formation and enactment of this procedure" was ensured (point 12).

Also the private sector was requested to "facilitate the 'collective action clauses' in an attempt to find the most orderly procedures and we intend to consider the use of such clauses when issuing national and quasi-national bonds" (point 14a). The private sector was asked to "develop, thanks to its experience in new markets, financing procedures with conditions that should provide for greater flexibility in payments, or the assurance of new financing in the event of adverse market conditions. The private sector must also be involved in the conduct and solution of crises" (point 14d).

15. Strengthening international organizations: IMF and World Bank

In 1998 the G-7 spoke of "development of new measures to meet the crises by means of investigation of new structures for official financing ... and the examination of new procedures for the coordination of all the international institutions involved and national authorities, and for greater participation of the private sector in the control and resolution of crises, even by means of innovative financing techniques; e) verification of the proposals to strengthen the IMF, in order to improve its programs and procedures to anticipate and resolve crises; as well as verification of the proposals to strengthen interim and development committees of the IMF and the World Bank; f) minimizing the human cost of financial crises and encouraging the adoption of policies to protect the more vulnerable parties" (point 20). At present the IMF still represents the heart of the scheme, although from time to time it has been accused of contributing to the overthrow and waste of spendthrift countries that live above their means, while developing countries see it as the secular arm of capitalism imposing its rules and starving those who have nothing. "This must surely have been the point of view of the Reagan administration until 1982, when it understood that it needed the IMF to save the American banking system, which at the time was threatened by the crisis of the world debt" (Gilpin, 1990, p. 418).

The main debtors are the nations, as always: "Beginning with bankers in the Middle Ages as well as those of the Renaissance, the nations' need for financing offered much more advantageous profits than economic and trading activity. And as early as the eve of World War I the great majority of capital movements corresponded to subscription of long-term loans issued by the governments which in this way financed industrialisation and armies" (Pollio Salimbeni, 1999, p. 30).[19] The strengthening of the financial systems of individual countries has been pursued by the IMF and by the World Bank with the creation "of a committee linking the two institutions ... an experimental program for the evaluation of the financial sector," while the "forum for financial stability has created three groups to examine the implications for the high financial leverage broker market, capital flows, and offshore financial centers" (Sarcinelli, 1999, p. 7).

16. Codes of best practices: An example of private autonomy

It is no easy job to summarize the 1998 and 1999 program. The work to prepare the codes has been carried on together with "the special one for the circulation of data on international reserves and on foreign debt," to which should be added "the Code of good practice for fiscal transparency and the one ... for transparency in monetary and financial policies .... The OECD has published the principles of corporate governance, and before that the BIS defined the basic rules for efficient banking supervision. Banks are against discretional interventions. Nevertheless, the discussion about the introduction of prudential rules is always open.[20] Codes of law are voluntary and should therefore be applied and especially verified. The also have to provide a uniform regulation: "the financial stability itself risks being compromised, instead of strengthened, if microprudential rules are different, concerning the same operations (derivatives, in our case), in different places for different institutions" (Padoa Schioppa, 1996, p. 63). The IMF is endeavoring, by means of technical assistance, to encourage its circulation and has experimentally begun the task of evaluating it" (Sarcinelli, 1999). However, the response cannot be entrusted solely to the authority of private interests and their representatives (with the production of private autonomy deeds along the lines of the *lex mercatoria*, which for certain is a primary source and which, we repeat, we have excluded)[21] or solely to public authority (though structured on a representative basis). In point 8 of the program the following is stated: "we undertake to do our utmost to ensure that private institutions in our countries respect these principles, standards, and codes of conduct." Mention is made of requests "to the World Bank in cooperation with the IMF and other multilateral development banks to work with its members to introduce insolvency systems and new debtor/creditor relations" (point 14b). Agreement requires greater recognition of autonomy and binding technical regulations (Predieri, 1996a, 1996b, p. 251).[22] Rules of conduct are produced by confirming terms and contents, by independent groups, through cross-examination (to mention a fundamental aspect of our democratic legal proceedings) (Predieri, 1964), and by adjustments required by public authorities (which to be effective must be provided with an "executive clause" by the public authority). This model is the one put into legal form by the sections of the Italian constitution governing the relations between the state and various religions; it is the law only if there has been a previous understanding. In point of fact, it is the one that has governed relations between the state and its social partners in overcoming financial and monetary crises and that corresponds to the tendency "to overwhelm opposition between pure self-regulation and regulation to get to the adoption of a mixed prescriptive technique that has the advantages of constitutional discipline. The constitution guarantees the main principles established by each domestic legal system, protects public interests, permits the advantages of self-regulation, and is able to quickly and effectively understand the market's innovative needs" (Regoli, 1993, p. 431).

17.   Limiting the inflow and outflow of foreign capital and starting a heterocompensated policy for undeveloped countries

The request for control measures is continuous, but the IMF excludes controls at exit and favors controls at entry (where they can lead to the extension of debt expiration). The big banks' refusal to participate in the developing countries' recovery is continuous, and they "have foreseen a modest increase of capital flows to developing markets beginning next year" (Merli, 1999, p. 3).[23] In Washington, in an organized seminar, "Stanley Fischer, the second most important man of the IMF, reminded participants that 'There is no political determination from the G-7 or anyone else' to proceed to any bailout with public money to the advantage of private creditors" (Merli, 1999, p. 3).[24]

It has been said that "the only modification to the present international financial 'architecture' is due to the latest credit concession made by the IMF in response to an American request. Can we say that the system seems significantly strengthened by it? The Contingent Credit Line is granted to member countries that pursue strong economic policies as a precautionary line of defense against future balance-of-payments problems that might derive from international financial contagion. In Monetary Fund language, this means that at the time of approval of the CCL, past policies and future projects must be considered so that recourse to Monetary Fund resources is unlikely, economic results obtained by the nation must be evaluated positively, progress has been made in the assimilation of considerable interprivate standards, and the country has constructive relations with private creditors, has taken substantial steps in correcting its vulnerability from abroad, and finally submits a satisfactory economic and financial program to the Monetary Fund. It is more likely that under these conditions a camel will go through the eye of a needle" (Sarcinelli, 1999). What the Bank for International Settlements had stated is taken up again—that "it recognized that in 1997 to 1998 many of the countries seriously infected by the Southeast Asia crisis were already exercising budgetary policies that were considered internationally valid. The general manager of the IMF, Michel Camdessus, who certainly cannot be considered a supporter of active market intervention, has spoken of the 'chronic disease' of the financial system, predicting the institution of a special fund to aid member countries who apply healthy policies domestically 'not to endure the consequences of a temporary loss of confidence on the part of international investors'" (Pollio Salimbeni, 1999, p. 25).

The meeting of September 26, 1999, was important for the undertaking of the burdens of heterocompensation and for the provisions related to the reduction of the debt of poorer nations. It would not be far-fetched to think that after the two texts, heterocorrection and heterocompensation of the international monetary system has been attained and that two similar and balanced trends have been outlined. For the time being, trends at present are to avoid dramatic crises, avoid disasters, and restore efficiency. These goals are indicators of the legitimacy of the system.

Notes

1. On the distinction between the two types of services, see Hill (1997, p. 315), Daniels (1993), Marshall (1988), Kassab (1992), and Ochel and Wegner (1987).
2. Adam Smith emphasizes that for the farmer short-term contracts without guarantee of obtaining at least part of the fruits deriving from investments do not promote but rather restrain or even halt productive growth (see Sylos Labini, 1992, p. 395). Similarly, on the importance given by Adam Smith to "laws and institutions" in the economic order, see Brennan and Buchanan (1985), Brüggemeier (1977) ("the market economy and mixed economy tend to a decentralize many economic decisions, but without the support of the institutional legal apparatus the invisible hand holding such economies would be paralized"), and Friedman (1975). It is amply treated in the contemporary economic analysis by Dardi in Becattini (1990). No differently, continuing to talk about historiographic data, Cattaneo (1983, p. 298) wrote that the farming industry is part of the trading life of nations but does not derive from a bucolic bent. It is caused by the institutions and laws that give access to the land to capital and industry.
3. This in part regulates the agreements of December 1997, which have extended opportunities for financial services to increase their presence in trade with foreign operators and to widen the range of products that can be offered and financial activities that can be exercised. "The commitments of each country have been specifically undertaken and listed in schedules that are signed from time to time and that are subject to the general exception by which national governments maintain full right to limit access under prudential and surveillance regulations to guarantee stability and security of the financial system. Activities linked to the management of the monetary policy of each country are left out of the agreement, as are those of central banks (Article 1, GATS Annex on Financial Services). ... The principle governing a government's regulatory activity for prudential purposes in compliance with WTO agreements is as follows: regulations must be *functional* to reduce market risk and ensure stability, *necessary*, in the sense of being proportionate to its purpose, and *nondiscriminatory* and nonhindering (or not making market access to foreign dealers more difficult" (Malaguti, this volume).
4. Quotations are superfluous. The observation is frequently found in Anglo-Saxon literature. See, among others, Cawson, Morgan, Werber, Holmes, and Stevens (1990, p. 20); Kuttner (1997, p. 328); and Hodgson (1991, p. 251).
5. Az. 2 BvR 1877/99 e BvR 50/98.

6. In Giurisprudenza constituzionale, 1994, II, 677 ss.
7. The first protection of stability dwells in the firm itself within the market, which "being a center for trade and the circulation of information where the choices and situations of the firm are divulged and judged by the public, represents the second protection. The necessary complement of inside controls and market discipline—the third protection of the stability of institutions—is represented by the regulating authorities themselves" (Padoa Schioppa, 1996, p. 62).
8. I could say that my research is more in the macroarea, while Carbone's and Malaguti's studies are related to the microarea. This means that they have a concrete impact, directly interfering with subjective rights. When I refer to the constitutional problems of a monetary or financial policy, I don't mention single aspects.
9. With "an extraordinary opportunity for progress and civilization," confidently says Zanfarino (1998, p. 21).
10. *Dar al-Islàm* is also *dar al-'adl* because justice and Islam are inseparable (Gardet, 1976, p. 26).
11. Defined as "the contract according to which the parties undertake to make mutual payments whose amount is determined on the basis of different reference parameters" (Caputo Nassetti, 1997).
12. Carbone (this issue, pp. 235–246) adds that such regulation has its primary source in rules of international trade, codified in the specific models I have just mentioned. I must add that I do not agree with the authoritative opinion of Sergio Carbone for the reasons already mentioned in Predieri (1999).
13. Hicks (1954) has already written on the subject of future contracts. He correctly understood that "future markets give an important contribution to the attainment of stability in time, imposing convergence between expected prices and real prices; especially sensistive to the determining factors of the prices, as regards brokers who only perform hedging operations and for this reason have have a limited viewpoint and left to themselves would cause structural unbalance between demand and supply."
14. Understood as "the combination of the Central Bank's liquid liabilities: legal tender ..., demand deposits with the Central Bank and the margin available in the advance accounts of the banks with the Central Bank" (Cassese, 1998, p. 157). The author mentions how "the amount of base money is modified by means of rediscount and advance to banks, the purchase and sale of currency and securities on the open market, variations in the account that the Treasury has with the Bank of Italy," so that "by buying or selling foreign currency" the Central Bank "expands or reduces the amount of base money."
15. Padoa Schioppa (1996, p. 65) remarks that in this regard it should be mentioned that the numerous empiric studies carried out to verify the grounds of these fears have not come to irrefutable conclusions.
16. A recommendation is "a statement that is not prescriptive so much as valuational: a statement that qualifies a type of conduct not as mandatory, but rather as good, fair, convenient, or appropriate" (Guastini, 1995, pp. 154) or an exhortative act. It contrasts with "a decision, a binding act by international organizations, even though, actually, a recommendation produces effects, even obligations, that are secondary or side effects" (Conforti, 1987, p. 188). Conforti goes on to say: "the thing that by definition it cannot produce, without becoming a decision, is the effect of binding to the recommeded behavior. In other words, in the presence of a recommendation, the nations or other subjects of international law (such as other international organizations) to which it is addressed remain at any time free to behave more or less as required" (Malintoppi, 1958, esp. ch. 3).
17. For the sake of completeness I am mentioning the theory in Italian law that makes informality of functions (in the event of informal agreements) not free by law from responsibility (expressed with regard to informal deeds of the president of the Republic), while customary procedures exclude responsibility, excepting in instances standardized by custom. In this regard, see Piergigli, (1987) and Rescigno (1980, p. 9).

18. Similar conclusions are drawn by Watson (this volume), who says that the most frequent causes of financial crises are lack of control of deficit and regulation.

19. Pollio Salimbeni (1999) adds: "with the opening of the Japanese financial system in 1983–1984 enforced by the United States, and progressive dismantling of national controls on exchanges in Europe, the single capital market speeds up geographical mobility of money. Investment and disinvestment operations are carried out by brokers without any distinction as to nationality and the currency of their choice. Here is the time jump. ... The difference in the revolution of the eighties is that finance has definitely severed the links of time and space, becoming an 'independent sphere of action" of productive and trade activity to such a degree that the balance of payments, which gives account of all payments and all proceeds of a country with the rest of the world, has become more like the statement of capital movements than the statement of export and import of goods." "Since 1528 the Genovesi main opponent is the Spanish monarchy, with its strong need to find money. In Spain, Genovesi lenders replaced the Germans, in particular the Fugger; they were in big difficulties because of the first bankrupty of Philippe II" (Corradini, 1994, p. 7).

20. It is Blinder's opinion that, between them, there should be those that limit "currency exposure of domestic operators to developing countries" and "capital flows. There is no need to scare markets or bar free investment flows. I would just introduce duties on incoming short-term capitals to limit and not stop their arrival, as Chile did in the past. To these three priorities I would add a proposal: there's need of more transparency for financial systems in developing markets, better accounting standards, real development of financial supervision institutions, ability to follow investment methods, and evolution in the private sector. In many developing countries private finance liberalization grew up quicker than countries' supervision capacity (Padula, 1999, p. 20).
   Volatility is the product of a genie escaped from a bottle; those free capital flows are traveling around countries. We must learn to live with this genie, but we still have time to reduce the imbalances of the last years. How? Three measures can reduce volatility. First of all it is important to leave the fixed currency-rate system in those countries where currencies are linked to the dollar. Brazil has been the last victim of this illusion. All the crises observed in these last years (Asia and Russia included) would have been less destructive if floating exchange rates would have existed. There could have been a gradual exchange adjustment and strong depreciations could have been avoided" (Padula, 1999, p. 19). "Basil Borssos, with American origins, doesn't have any doubts: 'The South American crisis can be solved.' On the contrary, Alan Blinder, who is one of the economists close to Bill Clinton's Democratic administration and involved in a new global financial architecture project," supports stronger planning (p. 18). The Argentine Model is a obliged way to keep a link with the dollar (Borssos is theory). He managed the GM investment ($350 million) building up the most technological factory of the GM group ("*And we go to the Middle East*," 1999, p. 78).

21. See, on the contrary, Carbone (this volume).

22. Compare, in this sense, Cons. Stato, Sez. IV, April 9, 1999, n. 601, in Cons. Stato, 1999, n. 4, 584 ss.

23. Merli (1999, p. 3) continues: " 'Banks are worried,' said Sir John Bond (president of Hsbc and Iif), 'and the Monetary Fund and other authorities want the private sector to get involved. It is important that the privates get involved to solve crises,' Bond said, 'but we do reckon that a voluntary approach is necessary, as the Brazil and Korea successes have showed. The vice president of Citygroup, Bill Rhodes, said that assertions coming from the G-7 and the Monetary Found about a possible imposition of reconstruction to the private sector, create 'markets uncertainties' and instead, we should concentrate on preventing financial crises."

24. Merli (1999, p. 3) continues: "Fisher reminded the audience that voluntary reconstruction with Korea, Brazil, and others worked well because there were banks as opposition. Related to Ecuador, Romania, Pakistan, and Ukraine, bond holders are the opposition. The introduction of clauses allow them voting reconstruction, and Fisher said that this can increase the developing countries spread and wouldn't be bad if it would take them to more balanced levels than the

1996 to 1997 ones. Dallara reminded the audience that emerging countries opposed to these clauses if developed countries don't introduce them as well."

References

Abi Saab, G. (1998) Preface. In C. Holmgren, *La renégociation multilatérale des dettes: le Club de Paris au regard du droit international.* Brussels: Bruylant.

Aliber, R.Z. (2000) "Capital Flows, Exchange Rates, and the New International Financial Architecture: Six Financial Crises in Search of a Generic Explanation." *Open Economies Review* 11 (Supplement).

Braudel, F. (1985) *La dynamique du capitalism.* Paris: Flammarion.

Brennan, G. and J.M. Buchanan (1985) *The Reason of Rules: Constitutional Political Economy.* Cambridge: Cambridge University Press. Italian translation: *La ragione delle regole. Economia politica costituzionale,* edited by A. Villani. Milan: Franco Angeli, 1991.

Brüggemeier, G. (1977) *Entwicklung des Rechts im organisierten Kâpitalismus* (vol. 1). Frankfurt am Main: Syndikat Autoren V. Verlag.

Brunel, L.S. and J.L. Bodin (1998) *Géopolitique de la faim. Quand la faim est une arme.* Paris: Presses Universitaires de France.

Calderoni, M. (1998) "Senza nuovi fondi l'Fmi non regge. Colloquio tra Camdessus e Fazio." *Il Sole 24 Ore,* 5 July, p. 3.

Caputo Nassetti, F. (1997): *Profili civilisti dei contratti 'derivati' finanziari.* Milano: Giuffrè.

Carbone, S.M. (1998) "The Enforcement of the European Regime for Investment Services in the Member States and Its Impact on National Conflict of Laws: A General Perspective." *Scritti in onore di Giuseppe Federico Mancini* (vol. 2). Milano: Giuffrè, 1998.

Carbone, S.M. (2000) "Financial Derivatives and Private International Law: Some Remarks." In *Open Economies Review* 11 (Supplement).

Cassese, S. (1998) *La nuova costituzione economica.* Rome: Laterza.

Cattaneo, C. (1983/1860) *Memorie di economia pubblica dal 1833 al 1860.* Milan. Reprinted by Banca del Monte di Milano.

Cawson, A., K. Morgan, D. Werber, P. Holmes, and A. Stevens (1990) *Hostile Brothers: Competition and Closure in the European Electronics Industry.* Oxford: Oxford University Press.

Colcker, R. (1998) *American Law in the Age of Hypercapitalism: The Worker, the Family, and the State.* New York: New York University Press.

Conforti, B. (1987) *Raccomandazioni internazionali.* In *Enciclopedia del diritto,* vol. XXXVIII, Milano: Guiffrè, pp. 187–191.

Corradini, M. (1994) *Genova e il Barocco. Studi su Angelo Grillo, Ansaldo Cebù, Anton Giulio Brignole Sale.* Milan: Vita e Pensiero.

Daniels, P.W. (1993) *Service Industries in the World Economy.* Oxford: Oxford University Press.

Dardi, M. (1990) "Il mercato nell'analisi economica contemporanea." In G. Becattini (ed.), *Il Pensiero economico.* Torino: Utet.

Eschilo. *Le Supplici* verse 604.

Fazio, A. (1998) "Il sistema monetario internazionale." In *Conference Proceedings on Idee per il futuro del sistema monetario internazionale, Florence, 19 giugno 1998.*

Fratianni, M. (2000) "Comment on Aliber's 'Capital Flows, Exchange Rates, and the New International Financial Architecture: Six Financial Crises in Search of a Generic Explanation." In Savona (ed.) *Open Economies Review* 11 (supplement):63–67. Kluwer Academic Publishers.

Friedman, L.M. (1975) *The Legal System: A Social Science Perspective.* New York: Russell Sage Foundation. Italian translation: *Il sistema giuridico nella prospettiva delle scienze sociali.* Bologna, 1978.

Gardet, L. (1976) *La Cité Musulmane, vie sociale et politique.* Paris: Vrin.

Gilpin, R. (1987) *The Political Economy of International Relations.* Princeton: Princeton University Press. Italian translation: *Politica ed economia delle relazioni internazionali.* Bologna, 1990.

Guastini, R. (1995) "Norma giuridica (tipi e classificazioni)." *Digesto discipline privatistiche sezione civile* 12. Turin: Utet.

Hamada, K. (1999) "The Choice of International Monetary Regimes in a Context of Repeated Games." *Open Economics Review* 9(supplement 1):417–445.

Henin, P. (1986) *Macrodynamics: Fluctuations and Growth.* London: Routledge. Quoted from A. Heertje, Introduction. In J.E. Stiglitz, *Il ruolo economico dello stato.* Bologna, 1992.

Hicks, J.R. (1954) *Valore e capitale.* Turino: Utet.

Hill, T.P. (1997) "On Goods and Services." *Review of Income and Wealth* 23(3):315.

Hodgson, G. (1991) *Economia e istituzioni.* Ancona: Otium.

Holmgren, C. (1998) *La renégociation multilaterale des dettes: le Club de Paris au regard du droit international.* Brussels: Bruylant.

Hume, D. (1995) *Writings on Economics.* Madison: University of Wisconsin Press.

Institute for International Economics (1999) *Safeguarding Prosperity in a Global Financial System: The Future International Architecture.* Washington, DC: Institute for International Economics.

Kant, I. (1798) *Der Streit der Fakultäten in drei Abschnitten.* Konigsberg: Nicolovius. Italian translation: *Il conflitto delle facoltà in tre sezioni,* in N. Merker (ed.), *Stato di diritto e società civile.* Rome: Êditori Riuniti, 1995.

Kassab, D. (1992) *Income and Equality.* New York.

Keynes, J.M. (1923) *A Tract on Monetary Reform.* London: McMillan. Italian translation: *La riforma monetaria.* Milan: Feltrinelli, 1975.

Kuttner, R. (1997) *Everything for Sale: The Virtues and Limits of Markets.* New York.

Llewellyn, D.T. (2000) "Some Lessons for Regulation from Recent Bank Crises." *Open Economies Review* 11 (Supplement).

Luttwak, E.N. (1998) *Turbo-Capitalism.* Italian translation: *La dittatura del capitalismo. Dove ci porteranno il liberalismo selvaggio e gli eccessi della globalizzazione.* Milan: Mondadori.

Malaguti, M.C. (2000) "Private Law Instruments for Reduction of Risks on International Financial Markets: Results and Limits of Self-Regulation." *Open Economies* 11 (Supplement).

Malintoppi, A. (1958) *Le raccomandazioni internazionali.* Milan: Giuffrè.

Marshall, J.N. (1988) *Services and Uneven Development.* Oxford: Oxford University Press.

Mengozzi, P. (1999). "The World Trade Organization Law: An Analysis of Its First Practice." In P. Mengozzi (ed.), *International Trade Law on the Fiftieth Anniversary of the Multilateral Trade System.* Milan: Giuffrè.

Merli, A. (1999) *Respinta ogni ipotesi di ristruturazione forzata.* Nel 2000 modesto aumento degli investimenti. Pvs, le banche sempre rigide sui debiti, in Il Sole 24 Ore, 26 Settembre 1999, 3.

Ochel, W. and M. Wegner (1987) *Service Economies in Europe.* London.

Padoa Schioppa, T. (1996) "I prodotti derivati: proili di pubblico interesse. Lezione tenuta all'Università Cattolica del Sacro Cuore—Centro studi finanziari, 3° ciclo di Leziofii Emilio Moar." In *Bollettino economico della Banca d'Italia* 26:59–63.

Padula, G. (1999) "Stop the the Fixed Rates: Interview with Alan Blinder." *Il Mondo* 12:19–20.

Pagels, H. R. (1989) *The Dreams of Reason: The Computer and the Rise of the Sciences of Complexity.* New York: Bantham.

Piergigli, V. (1987) "La prassi degli interventi e del potere di esternazione del Capo dello Stato nei primi due anni della Presidenza Cossiga." In *Diritto delle societa* 493.

Pollio Salimbeni (1999) *Il grande mercato. Realta e miti della globalizzazione.* Milan: Mondaro.

Predieri, A. (1964) *Contraddittorio e testimonianza del cittadino nei procedimenti legislativi.* Milan: Giuffrè.

Predieri, A. (1992) *Il nuovo assetto dei mercati finanziari e creditizi nel quadro della concorrenza comunitaria.* Milan: Giuffrè.

Predieri, A. (1996a) "Erosione e trasferimento di sovranita con norme tecniche." In *Studi in onore di Feliciano Benvenuti.* Modena: Mucchi.

Predieri, A. (1996b) "Le norme tecniche nello stato pluralista e prefederativo." *Il Diritto dell'economia* 2:251.

Predieri, A. (1999) "Schedule 36, La Lex Mercatoria come diritto attuale e il diritto transnazionale."

In A. Predieri, *Carl Schmitt, un nazista senza coraggio* (2 vols.). Florence: La Nuova Italia.

Ramonet, I. (1998a) *Géopolitique de chaos.* Paris: Galilée.

Ramonet, I. (1998b) "Strategies de la faim." *Le monde diplomatique* 536:1.

Regoli, D. (1993) "Mercati finanziari in diritto comparato." *Digesto discipline privatistiche sezione commerciale* 9:407–431. Turin: Utet.

Rescigno, G.U. (1980) "La responsabilita politica del Presidente della Repubblica. La prassi recente." In *Studi parlamentari e di politca costituzionale* 9.

Saccomanni, F. (2000). "Introduction: A New Architecture or New System? A Survey of International Monetary Reform in the 1990s." *Open Economies* 11 (Supplement).

Salvatore, D. (1992) *Economia internazionale.* Rome: La Nuova Italia Scientifica.

Sarcinelli, M. (1999) "Cinque sfide per l'Fmi." *Il Sole 24 Ore,* September 30, p. .

Savona, P. and A. Maccario (1998) "On the Relation Between Money and Derivatives and Its Application to the International Monetary Market: Acts of the Conference on Ideas for the Future of the International Monetary System, Florence, 19 June 1998." *Open Economies Review* 9 (Special Issue):637.

Savona, P., A. Maccario, and C. Oldani (2000) "On Monetary Analysis of Derivatives." *Open Economies Review* 11 (Supplement).

Smith, A. (1776) *An Inquiry into the Nature and Causes of the Wealth of Nations.* Italian translation: A. Smith, *La ricchezza delle nazioni*, edited by Anna and Tullio Bagiotti. Turin: Utet, 1987, book 5, ch. 1.

Sylos Labini, P. (1992) *Elementi di dinamica economica.* Rome: Laterza.

Tizzano, A. (1997) "Qualche considerazione sull'Unione economica e monetaria." *Il Diritto dell' Unione Europea* 3:455–459.

Triffin, R. (1997/1986) "Correcting the World Monetary Scandal: Acts of the Bradley-Kemp Congressional Summit on Exchange Rates and the Dollar, Washington, 11–13 November." *Challenge* 28(6) (1986): 4. Italian translation: "Lo scandalo monetario mondiale: Origini ... e soluzioni?," in R. Triffin, *Dollaro, euro e moneta mondiale.* Bologna, 1997.

Von Hagen, J. and I. Fender (1998) "Central Bank Policy in More Perfect Financial System: Acts of the Conference on Ideas for the Future of the International Monetary System, Florence, 19 June 1998." *Open Economies Review* 9 (Special Issue):493.

Watson, M. (2000) "International Financial Architecture and the Economic Renaissance in Europe." *Open Economies Review* 11 (Supplement).

"And We Go to the Middle East." (1999) *Il Mondo,* February 12, p. 78.

Wittfogel, K.A. (1957) *Oriental Despotism.* New York: Yale University Press. Italian translation: *Il dispotismo orientale* (2 vols.). Florence: Vallecchi, 1968.

Open economies review 11:S1 235–245 (2000)

Financial Derivatives and Private International Law: Some Remarks

SERGIO M. CARBONE
University of Genoa, Genoa

Keywords: derivatives, financial innovation, private international law

JEL Classification Number: K33

Abstract

Financial derivatives are a product of financial innovation that is not possible to define by means of Italian legal definitions; the primary source of regulation for financial derivatives is the international trade law. Private autonomy plays a central role in derivatives transaction, and such party autonomy must be recognized by the sovereign state to be legally effective and enforceable. Standard derivatives contracts, although sophisticated, cannot eliminate totally the legal risk. This lacking, together with the problem of unclear identification of the jurisdiction applicable, makes the juridical aspects of derivatives more complex.

1. The term "financial derivatives" and Italian legal definitions

During a recent hearing before the Chamber of Deputies, the Italian Minister of the Treasury, Giuliano Amato, stated that it is impossible to define, by means of Italian legal definitions, certain financial transactions normally conducted on international markets. Ten years ago Natalino Irti expressed himself similarly when he observed that the "particular vocabulary" or the "simple jargon" relative to the regulation of international financial markets forces those who need to interpret those regulations to use terms that do not appear in classical legal science. This in itself reveals, in a significant way, how difficult it is to create and execute economic transactions in the legal system of a particular state. Even more difficult are the securities and financial products relating to them—which, for their features and their regulations, rely on norms and legal values that are foreign to a specific state legal system. Therefore, it is first necessary to acknowledge that the regulation of the so-called financial derivatives has its primary source in the rules of international trade law, codified in specific contractual forms normally adopted in everyday practice, whose main characteristic is that they do not belong to any specific state legal system.

The legitimacy of employing that primary source—that is, the rules of international trade law—has long and authoritatively been recognized. Therefore, given the present state of progress of the legislation, it seems beyond dispute that the parties are entitled to submit "with legal effectiveness" their contractual relationship relative to financial derivatives to rules, principles, and provisions and also through the use of definitions that do not coincide with those employed in a particular state legal system.

To be legally effective and therefore enforceable, however, the exercise of such party autonomy must be recognized by the sovereign states. As matter of fact, the states are the only entities to be exclusively empowered with the means to enforce the economic operations underpinning financial derivatives. In this respect, the experience of the last 10 years shows a positive attitude of the states in awarding legal effect to these transactions. It is noteworthy that such practice is supported by specific international law rules that require, however, that principles of public order of the interested individual states are not affected and that relevant national preemptory rules are given full application.

2. Techniques employed with financial derivatives

Regarding financial derivatives it is interesting to observe the results of practice when, in compliance with the above-mentioned limits and restrictions, techniques and solutions of private international law use (1) widespread party autonomy, (2) reference to contract parameters that are not necessarily ascribable to any specific state legal order, (3) methods and forum-selection clauses for the settlement of litigation consistent with the expectations of the subjects that have drawn up the contractual framework of the economic transaction, and (4) acceptance of legal systems chosen more for their compliance with the solutions adopted in the contract provisions of the relationship than for their connecting links with it.

The use and legitimacy of such techniques are corroborated by the development of case law and by the most recent domestic rules and regulations and uniform legislation. This fosters the widest freedom of the parties to choose the law applicable to the contract and in particular to indicate more than one law according to the various aspects of the contract (for example, see Article 3 of the 1980 Rome Convention on the Law Applicable to Contractual Obligations). On the other hand, it states the legitimacy to use techniques that, stressing to the utmost the practical goal pursued by the parties, allow the shaping of a regulation expressly devised and not necessarily coincident with the one belonging to one or the other state legal order (for example, the Vienna Convention on the sale of goods and French case law).

The effects of the above-mentioned techniques can be obtained, provided they comply, as mentioned before, with the minimum mandatory legal values of the state (basically coinciding with the principles of public policy or with the regulations provided by peremptory norms) within which those effects must be concretely obtained. Regarding those values, if the effects foreseen in the contract conflict with them, not even the possible acknowledgment of such effects in a foreign judicial decision (or in an arbitration award) will allow them to be implemented in the jurisdiction in which they should be carried out. This circumstance therefore deprives the above-mentioned effects of the legal enforceability necessary for the attainment of the practical goal on which the transaction is based.

Moreover, any domestic legal system protects these values in some way and with differing strength, through specific mandatory provisions that impose at least their observance in each domestic operative scope of the legal system they belong to. There is no doubt that it happens when these values are protected by "the rules of the law of the forum in a situation where they are mandatory irrespective of the law otherwise applicable to the contract" (for example, Article 7.2 of the 1980 Rome Convention on the Law Applicable to Contract Obligations). But it is true that many legal systems extend such protection also to the mandatory rules of the law of a foreign country with which the situation has a close connection (as is the case of a country on whose territory the effects of the transaction are to take place) when those rules must be applied whatever the law applicable to the contract (Article 7.1 of the above-cited Rome Convention, even if the application of that provision can be excluded by the contracting states by virtue of specific reservation to this effect, as has happened in the United Kingdom).

3. Coordinating jurisdiction

Besides the cited rules and techniques of private international law, there are also provisions regarding the exercise of jurisdiction. These are used in the field of financial derivatives to optimize the intention of the parties regarding the choice of the competent court to hear the disputes arising from or connected to the contract. The Italian legal system is a significant example of such a trend. Influenced by the progressive development of the 1968 Brussels Convention as amended, it has radically changed its approach with respect to it. Therefore, the exercise of the jurisdiction has no longer been considered as an institution relative only to the implementation of law in an objective way with an operational scope substantially universal and not limited, except in very incidental and exceptional cases, by the will of the parties involved in a particular litigation.

In this respect, Article 4 of Law 218/95, drafted on the basis of solutions provided for by the 1968 Brussels Convention, attributes a great relevance to forum-selection clauses in all the cases where disputes concern waivable rights and where the will of the parties to override the Italian courts is proved in writing, provided that the forum selection is confirmed by effective exercise of jurisdiction by the court chosen by the parties.

The will of the parties is therefore legitimated to achieve the objective, at present also shared by the Italian legal order, of avoiding the concurrence of various proceedings relative to the same dispute in different jurisdictions—and the possible formation of conflicting final judgments. It may, in fact, rule out the competence of judges other than the one agreed on and, on the other hand, give legitimacy to the exercise of jurisdiction of the court chosen by the parties, by virtue of such an appointment.

4. Self-sufficient definitions regarding "financial derivatives" and the choice of applicable law

Standard contracts, relative to the so-called financial derivatives, employ the above-described techniques of private international law in a very advanced and sophisticated way that does not, however, eliminate the legal risk of the transaction and guarantee anywhere an identical treatment of the various contractual aspects involved in it. The use of such techniques by standard contracts elaborated by different associations in accordance to similar criteria (particularly relevant though is the International Swap and Derivatives Association (ISDA) Master Agreement) helps nonetheless to reduce such risks. In this respect, such models turn out to be extremely useful when they supply (1) a definition of the expressions adopted on the basis of autonomous criteria irrespective of their belonging to any specific legal system and (2) interpretative criteria of the discipline that is applicable to the contracts (and of the discipline applicable to swap contracts to be concluded, each time, between the interested parties to render it directly effective). In so doing, it is more likely to ensure the intrinsic consistency to the contracts, their prospective completeness with respect to the underlying economic transaction, and the uniform application that would be undermined by the multiplicity of legal sources otherwise applicable by the various competent jurisdictions.

Equally valid, but from a different and very important point of view, seems to be what is provided for in the various general framework agreements or model contracts relative to swaps and currency options to avoid (even in cases where the transactions take place on nonregulated markets) such contracts being exposed to the risk of being void or nonactionable (as some critics say happens in the Italian legal order due to the fact that Article 1993 of the Civil Code is considered applicable to contracts where they provide for a "liquidation of difference of the derivative contracts").

The choice of a single legal system competent to govern the Master Agreement, the single collateral, and the derivative contracts between which the liquidation by difference intervenes (once checked that such operation complies with the law chosen by the parties) is particularly suitable to exclude any interference of other laws that may undermine the validity of the transaction.

It is worth noticing that some legal systems, like the Italian, may assimilate such economic operation to gamble and, as a consequence, prevent the filing of any claim that may arise out of the relationship (see Article 1933 mentioned earlier). Such domestic provisions, however, do not seem as strong as to affect, according to the principles described in the previous paragraphs, the application of the law chosen by the parties to govern the relation as to liquidation by difference. This is particularly true if such choice is made in good faith and the law chosen by the parties is considered appropriate, either because of the completeness and accuracy of the discipline provided or because of the relevance of the financial market of the state to which it belongs to govern the type of transaction at hand in a way that is consistent with the legitimate expectations of the operators.

5. Collateral contracts and transactions with derivatives

A more complex and difficult control is required by the legal risks relative to collateral contracts linked to derivative transactions—that is, risks relative to the nonaccomplished and regular execution of the contracts on which the transactions with financial derivatives depend.

It is first of all a question of verifying if, each time, the collateral contract is valid and effective under the law (or the laws) applicable to it by the court (or the courts) having jurisdiction. Special attention also must be paid to whether its legal regime is adequate to play the role that the various systems of "netting" assign to it, thus verifying its adequacy according to the specific rules applicable to them. Therefore, regarding this aspect, only the law governing that aspect of the relations under discussion and its concrete execution (in case *lex executionis* is not the law of its constitution) can provide precise information regarding the effectiveness of the collateral obligation or of the collateral asset to guarantee the economic value on which the regulation of the transaction on derivatives relies, according to its applicable law.

According to such criteria it is necessary to verify, for example, which effects are caused by the possible insolvency of the title holders of the collateral obligation or of the collateral asset with respect to their employment for the derivatives transaction. This ascertains if it is possible to use and in particular to offset their asset in the derivative transaction with priority with respect to all other creditors also if the holder is subject to insolvency proceedings.

Many master agreements of financial derivatives include specific provisions that guarantee that effect, (1) through the choice of the law applicable to the underlying transaction of the financial derivatives, (2) through contractual clauses that aim at automatically netting effects such credits or assets with the corresponding indebtedness immediately before the presentation of the bankruptcy petition, or (3) through comparable proceedings that aim at ascertaining the insolvency of the subject that is the title holder thereof. Such contractual clauses are valid, for example, in English law and in that of the State of New York, which are usually indicated as laws applicable to the transactions relating to financial derivatives in conformity with the contractual models drafted to that purpose.

But the automatic and anticipated effect of the compensation, as permitted by the law chosen by the parties, will be fully and concretely achieved without "legal risks" only if it is also acknowledged within both the domestic jurisdiction in which the insolvency proceedings has been initiated and the country whose law governs. The collateral asset in principle can be identified with the law of the place where it can be located (even if such location can raise doubts, especially in case of dematerialized financial products). The recognition of such effect, however, should not be taken for granted. As a matter of fact, contrary to English and New York laws, many legal systems do not attach effects to the anticipated compensation against other creditors and the bankrupt.

The situation outlined above therefore shows how objectively difficult, time consuming, and expensive are all the necessary investigations regarding the different legal relations underlying trading in financial derivatives according to the logic agreed on by the parties and in particular their use in compensation transactions.

6. Practical solutions for objective autonomy and subjective novation

These difficulties have compelled financial operators to adopt alternative practical solutions to provide with independent value and effectiveness the contractual positions material to and underlying transactions with derivatives when they are to be used to fully realize the relative compensations. In this way they tend to cause a breaking off of the objective identity of the credit regarding the contractual relation that represents its source (and justifies its existence) and of the subjective reference to the original title holder at the time when it is assigned to subjects who employ it in transactions on compensation and derivatives. Therefore, they try to obtain an asset aid and a credit detached from its original statute suitable to represent and guarantee a specific and definite economic value.

Such transformation of the credit (which causes an objective novation thereof linked with the subjective one) during its assignment and its employment in transactions on compensation and derivatives to guarantee an otherwise impossible legal certainty must obtain the debtor's consent because it implies a worsening of his legal position. However, should it not happen or should the original debtor not be entitled to dispose, the consequences of the so-called objective novation of the credit affects the position of the assignee when he uses it for the derivative transaction for the relevant compensations.

This solution cannot disregard delicate aspects of private international law, such as laws relative to the effects of the novation of the assignment of credit and of its further transferability with respect to the assignee debtor. In the Italian legal system, attention must be drawn to the 1980 Rome Convention on the Law Applicable to Contractual Obligations, which as a general rule provides that such relations are governed by the legal system applicable to the assigned credit. However, the above-mentioned effect of novation shall be verified, as far as its use for compensating purposes is concerned, in compliance with the law applicable to the transaction of netting, which, as noted before, can fully perform the economic function assigned to it, only if it can guarantee an autonomous configuration (and therefore an autonomous evaluation) of the legal situations used. So much so that, as already noted by many scholars, only the combination of the so-called netting by novation and of the so-called close-out netting allows such a function to perform with adequate certainty and reduction in the various forms of risk (delivery, systemic, sovereign, market, credit risks, etc.) material to that respect. Such evaluation is to be carried out according to the independent choice of the law applicable to the transaction of netting, which will have to take into account the ordinary rules and principles to determine the law applicable to contractual obligations and any special provisions adopted with specific regard to this. Among the latter, for example, Article 9 of the proposal for a Regulation on the insolvency proceedings presented at the European Council on May 26, 1999, provides for an applicable law specifically intended for payments, for the so-called liquidation by settlements, and for the compensations relevant to a financial market irrespective of the proper law regulating the relations from which such transactions derive.

7. Jurisdiction and party consent

Certainty and uniformity of law, as far as contracts on derivatives are concerned, are very much influenced not only by the applicable substantive law to them but also by the methods and criteria relative to the exercise of the jurisdiction on possible ensuing disputes. And in this connection (according to what has been stated in Section 3), the development of the law in the various domestic legal orders is definitely in the direction of allowing the will of the parties, through specific clauses relative to the exercise of the jurisdiction, to coordinate the exercise of the various domestic jurisdictions, each interested in the solution of such disputes for different motives.

Therefore, from this point of view, there can be no doubt as to the utility and the general legal effectiveness of the clauses inserted in the so-called master agreements and in the relative operational contracts, aiming at guaranteeing (when the circumstances allow the exercise of alternative jurisdictions in different countries) that only one judge belonging to a specific domestic jurisdiction has the exclusive authority to settle all disputes arising from the various relations concerning the derivatives transaction. Only this clause makes it possible to avoid resorting to concurrent proceedings relative to the same dispute, thus realizing obvious legal savings and above all ruling out the possibility of conflicting judgments.

To obtain this effect, according to the perspective adopted by any legal system, it is necessary that the genuineness of consent with respect to the clause oustering jurisdiction be verified. And in this connection, as it is well known, there are legal fields (for example, the one effective in the so-called European Judicial Space) where such genuineness of consent can be acknowledged also by virtue of the existence of usages alone, which allow to verify such consent: that is, when there are "usages known to the parties or usages widely known and observed by the parties to contracts of the same type in the commercial field under examination." In other cases, on the contrary, the requirements to be met are more severe.

The situations presenting more uncertainties, and yet very frequent in the practice relating to derivative transactions, are the ones where the clause of choice of the court of exclusive jurisdiction is included in an annex to the document signed by the parties to a certain relation. In such situations it is then essential to secure that at least a precise link exists between the two documents, if not a specific reference (*relatio perfecta*) to the clause oustering jurisdiction, because it is from such link that it is possible to actually attribute to the parties (and thus reconstruct) their unequivocal will to choose that particular court for the settlement of their disputes.

It is therefore obvious that, when the framework agreements or master agreements include the forum selection clause and are undersigned by the same parties that enter into the individual contracts on derivatives (for example, swaps or financial futures), there is no doubt as to their full effectiveness.

More perplexities arise in the other cases in which the actual will of the parties has, from time to time, to be considered by means of considering both the methods by which the reference to the master agreement is made and, above all, taking into consideration some substantive requirements of the case. It will then be necessary, in particular, to verify the real awareness of the parties to the various contractual relations of their being necessarily assigned to a broader and more coherent transaction, for which the master agreement including the forum-selection clause, provides the general legal framework.

Such assessment, even if expressed according to different laws, is uniformly required by all domestic jurisdictions and often implies a complex assessment of the merits of the objective and subjective circumstances on the occasion of which the individual contracts have been entered into. In certain cases it is easier to perform such assessment, and the discretionary parameters are clearly oriented. For example, when it is proved the presence and the awareness of the existence of a precise etiological link of the contract (for instance an interest swap) entered into by the parties together with another contract (and/or master agreement) that includes the forum-selection clause, it seems there are no doubts as to the adequacy of the expression of the will of the parties to accept the submission of the settlement of their disputes to a precise foreign court or arbitration tribunal.

8. Forum-selection clauses adopted in financial-derivative disputes

The above-mentioned (and increasingly stressed) role of the will of the parties in coordinating the functioning of the exercise of the various jurisdictions linked to the possible disputes related to the contractual relation allows the various modes relative to its exercise to be usually provided with "legal effectiveness." No doubt arises as to the effectiveness, in the majority of legal systems, of clauses indicating two or more courts alternatively competent according to the law applicable to the contractual relation (as stated in Article 13(i) of the ISDA Master Agreement) or the choice of a court with freedom of the parties to alternatively submit their disputes to any other court having adequate jurisdictional connecting links (see, for example, Article 9.2 of IFEMA Master Agreement).

On the contrary, great uncertainties on their possible legal effectiveness or even serious doubts of legitimacy arise with regard to those jurisdiction clauses, or parts of jurisdiction clauses, that aim at avoiding the forclosing effect of the so-called international *lis alibi pendens*. They are provisions by virtue of which the beginning of a proceedings before one or more judges does not preclude the beginning of the same proceedings or of other proceedings linked to that before another judge (as stated, for example, in Article 13(b)(ii) last section of the ISDA Master Agreement and in Article 9.2 last sentence of IFEMA).

In this connection, clauses that contradict precise procedural rules of the legal systems in which they should be enforced (for example, Italian Article 7 of Law 218/95, which acknowledges the foreclosure effects of international *lis alibi pendens*) do not seem to be appropriate to obtain legal effectiveness. All the more so as, in that way, the will of the parties does not seem to be used in its legitimate sense—that is, to realize judicial efficiency and avoid conflicts of judgments.

9. The role of home state law and of host state law when financial derivatives are considered as securities

Besides the issues mentioned above and their respective solutions in private international law, other issues add to them when the relations under discussion are also considered as securities or linked to securities—that is, when securities are issued representing derivative products relative to such relations. All the more so since rules of international law apply, and, above all, rules of EC law that guarantee the freedom of movement of such securities according to criteria and to a uniform legal regime applicable in all the geographic area to which the relevant law refers. The most common and significant norm of such legal system is the one requiring the mutual recognition of securities by applying to them the same regime according to which they have been issued in their home country, with the only limitation of the necessary consistency with principles protecting the general good in force in the jurisdiction of the country on the market of which they are offered.

Such a principle has truly established itself and essentially concerns aspects of public law relating to issuers, brokers, and general aspects of financial activity. But it is just as true that such a recognized predominance of the jurisdiction of the home state compared to that of the host state seems to have to be necessarily reflected also in the private law applicable to securities and to the transactions of which they are representative to achieve a real freedom of movement and mutual recognition of such securities and services linked to them.

Therefore, to that purpose the existence of a specific "special rule" of private international law does not seem to be necessary, as I already explained elsewhere. The general rules applied to the conflict of laws are in themselves fit to guarantee the application of home law in all cases where it is the most suitable to guarantee full and complete implementation of the principles relative to freedom of movement and mutual recognition of securities in compliance with their home law. Such law does not seem to have to be imposed, departing from the otherwise applicable rules of private international law, as the law necessarily applicable to the securities representative of derivative products and to the material part of them when or due to specific circumstances or the parties' will, it results that another law is applicable to them just because it is more consistent with the features of the underlying transaction or because it appears to be more suitable to guarantee the practical purposes or the expressed (or implicit) choice of the parties interested in it.

On the other hand, the general rules on conflict of laws seem just as suitable to provide techniques to employ in cases where the law of the host state has to be safeguarded to guarantee its legitimate and primary interests, beyond what provided for by *lex causae* (both if it is the home state law or another law relevant to that respect), without contradicting the principle of mutual recognition and freedom of movement of securities. On the contrary, it is precisely according to this principle and the limitations to its application when the general good of the country is involved (on whose market the securities are traded) that it is possible to indicate the circumstances and the limits within which international public policy and peremptory norms of the host state can be appealed to in order to limit or bar the application of *lex causae*. This happens in cases where such an effect appears to be proportional to the goal pursued by the host state, nondiscriminatory, necessary, and nonrepetitive of comparable provisions already implemented by *lex causae*.

From the above it appears clear that the provisions of the 1980 Rome Convention on the Law Applicable to contractual obligations extend their scope of execution also to the obligations relative to transactions on derivatives, or to the part of them, where securities are issued. Such a regime, as a matter of fact, is to be referred to all "obligations which have their title in an act of private autonomy." On the other hand, a regime of private international law that emphasizes, within the scope of contractual obligations, the contents of the underlying economic transaction and of the private autonomy in which it is grounded (rather than the different procedures of formation of the binding obligation) is by far the most suitable to designate the law applicable to the underpinning elements, and in particular to the contractual scheme, of which the financial derivatives are representative instruments.

Obviously, the above-outlined means that the other aspects of the regulations of derivatives tightly linked with their nature of securities (as those relative to their assignability and to the ensuing modes or to the safeguard of the legitimate reliance caused by them) must be governed by the specific rule in force in the relevant system of private international law. In Italy such a rule is provided for by

Article 59 of Law 218/1995, which assigns the regulation thereof to the domestic jurisdiction of the country of issue of the securities. In this way and within these limits, the home state law seems to find, once again, adequate acknowledgment in the regulation of derivatives, according to their features and to the rules and general principles of private international law, without it being necessary to pass a specific rule that legitimates its effectiveness as regards derivatives.

Open economies review 11:S1 247–257 (2000)
© 2000 Kluwer Academic Publishers. Printed in The Netherlands.

Private-Law Instruments for Reduction of Risks on International Financial Markets: Results and Limits of Self-Regulation

MARIA CHIARA MALAGUTI
Court of First Instance of European Communities, Luxembourg

Keywords: financial markets, risk, self-regulation, private law, public law, international law, European Union Community Law

JEL Classification Number: K33

Abstract

International financial markets are characterized by self-regulation among private parties and international action in the regulation of such behavior. The Group of Seven plan, the World Trade Organization Agreements, the General Agreement on Trade in Services principles, and European Union Community Law provide a minimum standard of derivative transactions with the aim of reducing the risks related to those products. Codes of best practice are a source of regulation at an international level, but their effectiveness depends on their acceptance by the business firms operating in the markets. The role of self-regulation is very important; it can prevent and manage risk in an optimal way, under the condition of a harmonized international law. Public law has to manage the externalities that arise from private transactions, and private regulation has to make the rest.

1. Self-regulation among private parties in the international financial market

For a jurist, one of the most interesting aspects, and surely one of high complexity, in the analysis of the international financial system[1] lies in the interaction between *public-law* and *private-law* instruments of regulation. Central banks increasingly use, for their monetary interventions, market instruments that are subject to regulations and whose source is either the law of the state or the law of the contract, developed on the basis of civil law as typical of relationships between private parties.

On the other hand, the speed of currency circulation and of disinvestment of securities makes the traditional activities of supervision of financial dealers and of market control in an international context increasingly difficult and often inadequate. Private parties have tried to replace or integrate the solvency guarantee—normally provided by the control of the supervising organizations of their counterparts—with types of self-regulation or risk insurance protecting them (by means of private law rules) against insolvency risk, thus obtaining the indirect result of reducing systemic risk.

The Group of Seven (G-7) (Canada, France, Germany, Italy, Japan, the United Kingdom, and the United States), in its October 30, 1998, plan,[2] requests that the private sector take a more active role in the prevention of market crises and in the management of their consequences in an attempt to institutionalize this role within the framework of the international financial system.

Besides the invitation for a more active use of loan guarantees to encourage greater private-sector involvement in the financing of emerging countries (item 3), the plan points out the need to adopt reforms aimed at increasing the transparency and openness of the international financial system, adopting international standards and codes of practice, and guaranteeing the stability of the system (item 4). Each of these measures is urged also in connection with the private sector, thus each country should commit itself to issuing regulations on transparency standards, principles of corporate governance and accounting standards (items 7 and 8), as well as risk-management systems (item 13).

It also suggests that private parties, through self-regulation, draw up guidelines that enable them to better respond to market setbacks, including resorting to *collective-action clauses* and applying innovative techniques for financing that strengthen flexibility in payments and guarantee greater safety to creditors (item 14).

2.   State measures of intervention on the behavior of private parties

The G-7 plan deals first with regulating the intervention of the state on the behavior of private parties. In this connection we should clarify a few points briefly, such as the binding effects of recommendations by organizations like the G-7.

2.1.   The legal nature of declarations of states in meetings such as the G-7

The contents of the plan of October 30, 1998, do not have any legally binding effect. However, it is necessary to give an account of the issue of the binding effect of the recommendations of international bodies.[3]

It can be said that recommendations of international organizations do not bind the states to which they are addressed to follow the recommended conduct. Nevertheless a so-called *validation effect* (Conforti, 1997) can be presumed, whereby a country does not commit an offense when, complying with a recommendation of an international organization, it behaves in a manner contrary to obligations undertaken under previous agreements or arising from customary international law. However, such an effect is normally acknowledged only when the recommendation is legal (that is, when it does not go beyond the statutory tasks of the organizations that issue them) and only with respect to the member states of that organization.

Moreover, any principle of this kind is based on the obligation to collaborate with the organization that should be implicit in any treaty establishing an international organization and in the power, also recognized as typical of any international organization, to pursue, even through nonbinding acts, goals that go beyond the interests of individual member states.

It appears clear that all these elements are lacking in cases such as the G-7 meeting, which has not been established by any specific treaty or organized according to a structure of organs endowed with specific powers and tasks (on the basis of which it is possible to evaluate the legality of its recommendations). Since the theory of the validation effect of recommendations lends itself to a particularly strict application within institutionalized international organizations, it is, in my opinion, risky to try to affirm its applicability to the results of what are almost exclusively political meetings involving variable structures.

However, if we credit the existence of a validation effect, we have to wonder why there should not be a corollary of compliance with the recommendations that an institution helped to draw up (or agreed to, in any case). If the implementation of a recommendation justifies the nonobservance of a previously undertaken obligation, a certain value of compulsoriness has to be acknowledged for the recommendation itself, a value that goes beyond the moral suasion that undoubtedly characterizes this kind of measure. In light of an implied principle of international cooperation to pursue goals that go beyond the interest of individual member states, it can be wondered whether one could say that the states should at least comply, in good faith, with the principles underlying the specific recommendations and not have openly conflicting behaviors with what has been gradually acquired as common fertile ground.

Therefore, starting from the assumption of the nonbinding legal effect of the recommendations or guidelines under discussion, we must then ask whether principles are at the basis of such measures in the financial and monetary fields or more generally in the economics field.

The issue is once again linked to one of the most controversial problems in public international law—whether a set of principles of international economic law exists to the extent of providing a subsystem of general international law and, if so, whether such principles can rise to the status of customs (therefore becoming binding). [4]

It is normally thought that a recommendation becomes binding only when it is converted into international custom (that is, when it is confirmed by *diuturnitas* and by *opinio iuris*) or when it is included in an international treaty. Regarding economics, if we wish to talk of customs, it would have to be clear that we are talking about a so-called particular custom (one that is binding for only very few countries). This is because in the economics field one talks of customs only when practices modify treaty rules. Therefore, such customs could bind only the countries that have adhered to the modified treaty rules.

Homogeneous principles that enable us to speak of an integrated system of economic norms can be found, however, in the system of the World Trade Organization (WTO). The WTO is based on a series of agreements necessarily underwritten in their totality and interpreted as a whole by a body for the settlement of disputes that, as an appellate body, decides only questions of law. Since its establishment, it is possible to speak with more certainty of a core group of principles on the subject of economics, which at least lay the foundation for the Marrakesh agreements and by which the signing countries have agreed to be ruled.

Therefore, the WTO agreements can be said to represent an integrated system governed by a set of homogeneous principles whose force is somehow guaranteed by the practice of the bodies in charge of dispute settlement (see Mengozzi, 1999). It is in the light of this that we shall very carefully look at the results achieved in the matter of the openness of financial services market within that organization.

2.2.   Provisions regarding financial services and prudential rules within the General Agreement on Trade in Services

When in 1994 the Uruguay Round negotiations were concluded,[5] a political consensus was reached to the effect that the basic agreement would have been followed by subsequent negotiations, both for further reducing barriers to the service performances and for expanding the scope of their application. The General Agreement on Trade in Services (GATS) Annex on Financial Services affirms the legitimacy of the adoption of prudential measures and of measures to safeguard the stability of financial markets by the governments that strongly limit the applicability of GATS principles to the sector (article 2). However, the Decision on Financial Services made at the conclusion of the Uruguay Round provided for opening negotiations for the gradual extension of nondiscrimination and most-favored-nation principles to that sector as well.

An Interim Agreement was reached in 1995 that extended liberalization of the sector in part. Other negotiations followed (concluded in December 1997) that instead extended, in a much more comprehensive manner, the openness of financial services, thus increasing for each country the amount of specific commitments undertaken and reducing the range of many exceptions to the most-favored-nation principle. In particular, many exceptions based on the reciprocity principle have been removed. A more extensive presence of foreign dealers has been allowed through the reduction of the barriers to foreign controlling interests in local financial companies, and the elimination of the compulsoriness of specific forms of companies for the establishment. In many cases the range of products that can be offered and financial activities that can be exercised has been expanded.

The commitments of each country have been specifically undertaken and listed in schedules that are signed from time to time and that are subject to the general exception by which national governments maintain full right to limit access under prudential and surveillance regulations to guarantee the stability and safety of the finance system. Activities linked to the management of the monetary policy of each country are left out of the agreement, as are those of central banks (Article 1, GATS Annex on Financial Services).

The purpose of the Marrakesh agreements was to deregulate international trade and not to standardize domestic laws. Furthermore, regulations on prudential standards are conceived as exceptions to free-market access and therefore left to the full discretionary powers of individual countries. Nevertheless, the inclusion of the sector of financial markets in the integrated system of the WTO agreements makes the interpretation parameters worked out within the WTO applicable to that sector as well. In particular, the exceptions contained in the GATS should also be read restrictively, and therefore their application is acknowledged only as strictly necessary for the purposes they have been devised for.

It must be concluded that the principle governing a government's regulatory activity for prudential purposes in compliance with WTO agreements is as follows: regulations must be *functional* to reduce market risk and ensure stability, *necessary* in the sense of being proportionate to its purposes, and *nondiscriminatory* and nonhindering (or not making market access to foreign dealers effectively more difficult). Therefore, the supervision of private parties' behavior for prudential purposes must be subject to these principles, and in case of failed observance, the interested country shall be deemed responsible for breach of the GATS.[6]

Moreover, Article 2a of the Annex on Financial Services sets out that when prudential measures and measures to guarantee the integrity and stability of the financial system do not comply with the provisions of the Agreement, they shall not be used as a means to evade the commitments or obligations that the agreement attributes to the member states. Such wording follows that of the nullification or impairment clause of the GATS (Article 23).

The acknowledgment of the restrictive nature of the construction of the exception for prudential purposes greatly influences the choices of legislative policy of the countries. Since the principle is the liberalization of markets, and the supervision of dealers is the exception, any evaluation of supervision instruments must take into account the level of pervasiveness of the measure itself. Once the supervision intervention of the state has been reduced to the minimum required, the guarantee of market stability and solvency is largely left to the private system, through instruments (obviously, private-law instruments) of risk insurance or securitization. In such a context, the borderline zone between public and private intervention must somehow be found in the externality of the system: should there be risks that cannot be managed by the private interest or that the private interest would transform in an unbearable cost for the community, the instrument of public control has to intervene, as a backup.

2.3. Harmonization in the European Community experience

Community law—which is based on the principle of the liberalization of the markets according to principles that affect the legislative power of member states much more than WTO agreements—provides a minimum action of harmonization, by virtue of which, at the European Union (EU) level, there exist common minimum prudential standards that member states have to comply with.

Omitting the examination of the directives on financial matters that regulate the markets, I would like to draw attention only to some particularly important aspects thereof: the principle of freedom of services is based on the acknowledgment of the prudential supervision by the country of origin. Once the control on solvency, or in any case the control on compliance with the prudential standards, is made by the country where the dealer is established, the country where the service is rendered has no control power, except in cases where such control is needed for reasons of general interest. The rule of the exception imposed by EU case law is in principle subject to the same restrictive application as the above-mentioned Marrakesh agreements, but on the basis of assessment parameters that are much stricter and at a much more advanced level of liberalization.

However, in financial matters an interesting problem is posed regarding the relationship between the control of the dealer and the control of the market where that dealer operates: even if the control of the subjects is the task of the *home country*, that of the activity is the task of the *host country*, on the basis of the fact that anyone dealing on a certain market must be subject to the same rules of the game.

This is the starting point of an interesting issue on the relationship between control over dealers and control over activities. In particular, if the activities are carried out through centralized counterparts (clearinghouses), the control over the centralized counterpart is necessarily delegated to the *host country*. In this game of roles it has to be made clear to what extent the control over activities by the host country may be extended, especially when that control leads to the prohibition of certain activities. To mention only one of the emerging issues, it is necessary to determine to what extent the host country should grant *remote access* to its organized markets or the opportunity to participate in its system without any kind of presence on its territory.

Furthermore, here all the delicate problems of private international law come into play—problems that no longer have anything to do with Community law but that leave the question of the definition of the case in point unresolved as to determining what pertains to the instrument used (contract), what to the exercise of financial activities (behavior), and eventually what to the qualification of the dealer (personality) (see Carbone, 1998).

Even if a certain degree of harmonization of the regulation on prudential controls exists, extreme attention must be paid to assess to what extent public law controls are legitimate and to whom they pertain. The problem of coordination among control bodies plays an important role, even in view of the role that the private sector is likely to be given as to prevention and management of risks.

3. Codes of best practice

Once the limits to the countries' action in the regulation of private parties' behavior have been examined, the role of self-regulation remains to be analyzed. First of all, it is necessary to say a few words about the codes of best practice mentioned in the G-7 plan itself. The instrument of the code of best practice is widely known in international economic law. It essentially responds to the problem of imposing specific behaviors on private transnational bodies that, by being established or active in various different jurisdictions, can allow themselves to benefit by the legislative differences—to the advantage of lower standards of behavior.

In the face of the impossibility or lack of will to achieve harmonization of laws, or even of the incapacity to tackle the problem posed by the forms of inevitable avoidance or *forum shopping*, the code of best practice is based on the voluntariness of the behavior by the private party: on the commitment to take on itself, although a private body without international personality, behaviors that may be considered beneficial to the international community.

But the instrument of the code of best practice has never become widespread, especially because in reality it does not represent an instrument of self-regulation. The code is in fact drawn up by the countries for the purpose of meeting the needs they have identified, with the consequence that it does not differ greatly from the above-mentioned recommendations of international organizations, except for the obvious aspect that it addresses the private sector, while recommendations address countries.

Whereas a certain legally binding effect of the recommendations addressed to countries can be surmised, nothing similar can be conjectured in case of codes of practice because only the voluntary acceptance of the code's rule by the business firm will make it applicable.[7]

4. The results of self-regulation

In financial markets, the role played by self-regulation is very significant, especially on so-called regulated markets that operate precisely on the basis of standardized contract texts. In this case, self-regulation of private parties reaches such a level of structurisation as to take over, in effect, from government regulation. At least from a sociological, if not from a juridical point of view, regulated markets are actually real orders.

Beyond the organization of the market itself, there is a heavy standardization of contract texts regarding financial instruments. As Professor Carbone brought out clearly in his article, the standardization of contracts does not resolve certain extremely serious, basic problems about their validity in all the legal systems in which they are executed. However, it is just in these texts that we find the most concrete and perhaps the most effective efforts to reduce the risks connected with markets. These remedies cannot counteract the failure of the other party to the contract to respect the prudential standards required by its organs of control, but they can greatly reduce credit exposure or create forms of allocation of risk that will reduce their effect on each of the parties.

It is not our place here to provide an in-depth analysis of the various standardized contract clauses. We need only point to the use of compensation of credits (on both a bilateral basis and a multilateral basis) to reduce exposure to its sole net result; to the use of advance termination clauses and automatic contract termination in the case of the insolvency of one of the parties; to the methods of recalculation of the results of daily compensation in the case of the insolvency of one of the parties to the system, without taking into account the debtor positions of the latter, so that the risk is largely supported by the entire system (by each participant regardless of its individual exposure toward the insolvent participant); or to the many examples of securitization of exposure.

All the clauses or standardized contract texts mentioned do entail a certain number of legal risks, due primarily to the juridical qualification of the various schemes used in the legal system under which they are executed. By way of example, I would just mention the difficulty of qualifying both bilateral and multilateral systems of compensation or the high uncertainty of opposition of the clauses of early termination in case of declaration of bankruptcy by the other party.

The parties to a contract can react to these difficulties by attempting to adopt the most sophisticated formulas possible, as well as by choosing as applicable laws those that offer the greatest assurance of effectiveness. Professor Carbone, however, has warned strongly of the inevitable limits that arise in the application of the mandatory rules of the legal systems involved, so that the legal risk can never be entirely eliminated without legislative intervention (or at least consolidation of a favorable position of judicial courts as regards the validity of these clauses and schemes).

5. The limits of self-regulation

The well-known cases of Baukhaus Herstatt, BCCI, and Barings—just to mention a few—have highlighted the limits of self-regulation. In addition to the many problems already described by Professor Carbone, the bankruptcy of these institutions revealed a number of problems that cannot be resolved through contracts, such as problems relating to the effectiveness of compensation clauses or early or automatic termination of the contract in case of bankruptcy. International financial operations pose, for example, the problem of the lack of simultaneity of compensation of the two arms of the operation. Particularly when we are dealing with operations that involve different currencies, compensation of each occurs in the country of each currency. Orders of execution of operations in Japanese yen in counterexecution to operations in U.S. dollars or German marks receive execution before the markets of the other currencies involved have opened, so that the possible insolvency of the other party cannot be discovered until after payment has been made.

The negotiable instrument is unable to provide an answer to this problem or to the problem relative to *zero hour* (setting back the time of bankruptcy of a subject to the hour zero of the same day on which bankruptcy was declared), except possibly some form of risk insurance or securitization. Harmonization of laws thus appears to be the only possible solution (e.g., this is a legal term, en law EC Directive).

In this context, then, there is a different relationship between public-law and private-law instruments. Public intervention is no longer aimed at control of the operators on the market but at harmonization of laws so that all private operators can act on the market under the same conditions and using the most appropriate private instruments for their needs. Public intervention is not meant to limit private power but rather to provide the premises for the free exercise of that power.

6. Conclusions

There has always been a lively debate on the subject of relations between self-regulation on the part of private parties and state action in international trade. The contrast lies, traditionally, between those who recognize two levels of autonomous regulation—one that is among countries and thus of a public nature (international economic law) and one that is private and transnational, that deals with regulation of relations among private parties, and that has a more autonomous position with respect to state laws—and those who prefer, instead, to emphasize the common origins of the two types of regulation, based on state laws. For the most part, self-regulation seems to find its reason for being in the spontaneous withdrawal of the state that decides not to regulate a specific question, leaving it to the autonomy of private parties. International economic law is largely composed of rules for the self-limitation of countries with respect to other countries. In this context, it also foresees areas in which state laws should withdraw in favor of self-regulation (see also Picone, Sacerdoti, et al., 1982).

The structure of international financial markets, their intrinsically global nature, and the inevitable influence on the international monetary system force us to reflect certainly not on possible changes to the conceptual bases that justify the relations between domestic legal systems and self-regulation but definitely on the new role that is delineating itself for private instruments in regulation of markets and in the prevention and management of risks. In place of the self-limitation of national laws in favor of self-regulation, we find that delegation of traditionally public functions to private bodies is practically inevitable.

The derivative products, developed as instruments for safeguarding against risks, have intrinsically facilitated the loss of significance of the classical instruments for control by the monetary authorities and have introduced a new element of systemic risk. While the former of these two aspects can be resolved by using new monetary instruments, the risk of insolvency that generates the market systemic risk can be reduced only through a combined intervention of both private law and public law instruments, where those of a public nature should (in the light of the principles illustrated above) be considered residual and limited to the management of externalities. I think that in a similar context it is, in any case, essential that public authorities intervene to achieve uniformity of laws so that self-regulation can operate effectively for the prevention and management of risks.

Notes

1. I deliberately use the expression *international financial system* (with a nonlegal value because we cannot really speak of a system in law) with the intention of including in it both (1) the aspects relating to currency control and regulation typical of the monetary policy of the states and (2) the aspects of control and regulation of financial markets. Otherwise, it is not possible to understand the real meaning of the analysis of the legal issues related to the so-called legal risk of derivatives and of the private law instruments devised to reduce it, unless we understand how the monetary activities of the states and the financial activities of the private agents interact in the framework of today's international monetary system. The separation of tasks traditionally entrusted to central banks, with participation in the management of monetary policy, on the one hand, and of control of financial institutions and their activities, on the other, loses today much of its importance since classical monetary instruments have no doubt become inadequate for currency control, and private parties play a decisive role in the movement of wealth and therefore in the stability of the markets.
2. The complete text of the statement can be found in Predieri (1998, annex).
3. This is not a merely theoretical issue. The greater the number of countries taking part in such meetings (and it has recently come out in the press that the G-7 will be enlarged to become G-20 precisely for the purpose of making emerging countries participate in decisions regarding the international financial system), the more complicated it becomes to obtain any guarantee of the observance of the principles agreed on by the adhering countries in the first draft. If one of the problems inherent in market recessions lies, on the one hand, in the inadequacy of the standards of conduct and control applied in countries with less up-to-date financial structures or in the offshore markets, on the other hand, it is easy to understand that the above issue is a rather important one.
4. See again the outline of the issue and solutions in legal science in Conforti (1997, p. 242).
5. The 1994 Uruguay Round negotiations also led to the stipulation of a multilateral agreement on services (the GATS) based on the principles of most-favored-nation status, nondiscrimination and market access.
6. See GATS, Article XIV (General Exceptions) and Article XX. In the two articles the synthesis of the construction principles of the general exceptions arises from an analysis of the various panels adopted in the subject matter.
7. Since private parties do not have international personality, they are not entitled to be the addressees of international rules.

References

Carbone, S.M. (1998) "The Enforcement of the European Regime for Investment Services in the Member States and Its Impact on National Conflict of Laws: A General Perspective." *Scritti in onore di Giuseppe Federico Mancini* vol. II, Giuffrè ed, Milano, 1998, p. 75.

Conforti, B. (1997) *Diritto Internazionale*. Ed. Scientifica, 197, Napoli.

Mengozzi, P. (1999) "The World Trade Organization Law: An Analysis of Its First Practice." *International Trade Law on the Fiftieth Anniversary of the Multilateral Trade System*. Milan: Giuffrè, 3.

Picone, P., G. Sacerdoti, et al. (1982) *Diritto Internazionale dell'Economia*. Milan: Angeli, 83.

Predieri, A. (1998) *Euro, poliarchie democratiche e mercati monetari*. Giappichelli, Torino.